The
Empty Nest

The
Empty Nest

31 Parents Tell the Truth
About Relationships,
Love, and Freedom
After the Kids
Fly the Coop

Edited by Karen Stabiner

VOICE
V
Hyperion • New York

"Flown Away, Left Behind," by Anna Quindlen, was originally
published in *Newsweek*, January 12, 2004.

Part of "Regime Change," by Charles McGrath, was originally published in
The New Yorker, c. 1995. Courtesy of Condé-Nast Publications.

Part of "Without a Net," by Jon Carroll, was originally published in
The San Francisco Chronicle on August 1, 2000.

"Good-bye to the Sunset Man," by Lee Smith, was originally published in
The Independent Weekly, October 2004.

Excerpt from "The Crack-Up," by F. Scott Fitzgerald, copyright 1945 by
New Directions Publishing Corp. Reprinted by permission of
New Directions Publishing Corp. and David Higham Associates Ltd.

Excerpt from *The Prophet*, by Kahlil Gibran. Copyright 1923 by
Kahlil Gibran and renewed 1951 by the Administrators CTA of
the Kahlil Gibran Estate and Mary C. Gibran. Reprinted with
the permission of Alfred A. Knopf, a division of Random House, Inc.

Library of Congress Cataloging-in-Publication Data
The empty nest : 31 parents tell the truth about relationships, love, and freedom
after the kids fly the coop / edited by Karen Stabiner.
p. cm.
ISBN-13: 978-1-4013-0257-3
ISBN-10: 1-4013-0257-2
1. Empty nesters.   2. Parent and child.   I. Stabiner, Karen.
HQ1059.4.E47 2007
306.874—dc22   2006049789

Hyperion books are available for special promotions and premiums. For
details contact Michael Rentas, Assistant Director, Inventory Operations,
Hyperion, 77 West 66th Street, 12th floor, New York, New York 10023,
or call 212-456-0133.

Design by Chris Welch

FIRST EDITION

10 9 8 7 6 5 4 3 2 1

"... the thing about children is, they push away any other world."

—*There Will Never Be Another You,*
by Carolyn See

For Sarah Ivria

Contents

The
Empty Nest

Proof of Love

Karen Stabiner

An old hard-shell suitcase is like a book. It sits open on the bed, symmetrical, cracked along its spine, waiting to see what story it gets to tell this time. A family vacation means shorts and sandals and a big floppy hat that rolls up; a business trip means good wool in a monochromatic palette. Either way, an old suitcase demands planning, and rewards economy of scale. There is no room for extraneous detail; the frame won't yield. My husband has one that belonged to his father, stiff cream leather with trim two shades darker and brass fittings. We never use it.

A new suitcase is more of a receptacle, with its soft sides, its wheels, and zippers that open to reveal another six inches of space. It allows for indecision and spontaneity—an extra pair of shoes even though red goes with nothing else you brought, the goofy souvenir that will go onto the back shelf with all the other souvenirs. A mother might say that a new suitcase lacks discipline, having spent her share of trips lugging a bulging case that a little girl can no longer manage. A daughter sees it differently. A pouchy case on wheels is all about potential. It's ready for adventure.

We don't yet own a suitcase big enough for our next major trip, which will be to take Sarah to college in the fall. I doubt that such a case even exists; how can you pack an entire life into a finite space? I expect that we will have to use more than one: We will stride onto campus together, Sarah in the middle, Larry and me at either flank, pulling her future behind us in thirds, as we walk up to the first room she will live in that is not down the hallway from ours.

She was four when the Northridge earthquake hit, and I was down that hallway and at her bedside before I was fully awake. She giggled as I reached down to grab her and get her away from the windows. "Mommy, I tried to sit up, but the house made my legs fly up in the air!" she said. This is the thing about an impending departure: My mind scrolls back and forth through history, as though I could lock onto a memory and slow things down.

Not a chance. Like any child, Sarah has been leaving in increments since she got here, and she has stayed, briefly, in rooms that were not hers—summer programs and school trips to here and there. But we handled those with easy denial and a single suitcase. Sarah is the granddaughter of one man who sold restaurant equipment and another who sold liquor, so she has the DNA to pack light. One underfed red duffel? She couldn't be gone long. Besides, there were brackets at either end of those trips, which always took place during spring break, or right before school started. The obligations of young life waited for her. We knew she'd be right back.

WHEN SARAH WAS a little girl, I was the one who traveled, just once or twice a year, and I had a simple and inviolate rule: I could pack anything as long as the suitcase fit as a carry-on. Homebound delays upset me. Sitting on the plane while we waited for an open gate, standing behind another passenger who wanted to complete her makeup before she walked down the aisle, walking behind what might have been an angelic child if not for the *Beauty and the Beast* wheelie she kept bumping into the seats, slowing us down—things that wouldn't have bothered me if I were with Sarah drove me crazy when I wasn't. I could not spend a half hour watching everyone else's suitcases revolve around the luggage carousel. I had to be able to get off the plane fast, to trot down the moving sidewalk and head directly for a taxi.

I embraced minimalism. There was always a bulky sweater left behind, always a tough decision in favor of navy or black but never both. My suitcase was light, its top as concave as a starlet's pelvis. I was coming home from the moment I walked out the door.

Sarah sat on our bed to watch me pack, the first time, silently considering the unfriendly way that time and space conspired to create separation. She tallied every sock and belt, and then she got up and disappeared down the hallway to her own room. Moments later she returned and held out a small stuffed bear to me. She always has a ramrod spine when important matters are on the line, and I could tell from the way she stood that we had entered a realm that had nothing to do with whether I'd packed enough underwear.

"Here," she said. "You can take her with you."

In a spasm of responsible parenting, we had bought three identical oatmeal-colored bears with lavender ribbons around their necks, all because someone with credentials had mentioned that it was very bad for little children to lose a favorite stuffed animal. Sarah was fairly tidy about her favorites, though, so we had a surplus of this particular model, which turned out to have an unexpected advantage. We might be separated by an entire country, but we each had an identical bear, and that link was as strong as a steel span between us.

I took the bear. While a more rational mom might have left it in the suitcase, I believed as devoutly as Sarah did in the magical ability of bears to erase distance, if properly displayed. It sat on my pillow for the duration of the trip.

As she got bigger, the tokens changed: I traveled to New York with a good-sized one-eyed patchwork horse, with a crib blanket that Sarah was proud no longer to need now that she had a big-girl's bed, with a shredded baby blanket that we had to fold inside a plastic bag lest it shed flannel lint all over my dark suit. On one trip, I took the largest doll Sarah owned, a by now rather blowsy platinum blonde with one sagging eyelid, dressed in a shiny white polyester wedding gown.

In return, I made a book out of colored construction paper each time I went away: "Sarah's Book about Mommy's Trip,"

"The Story of Sarah and the Magic Heart," titles like that, illustrated with plump airplanes that smiled, talking horses, and floating hearts. If it seems slightly frantic in retrospect, it seemed as essential as air at the time. We had been a family for such a short time; the way it felt was so new, and as fragile as it was overwhelming. We had to keep love right in front of our eyes at all times. Evidence reassured us.

THE INSIDIOUS THING about Sarah leaving is how subtly the balance tipped—how we endorsed the inevitable without realizing it. We taught her to flee, didn't we: Her first piece of luggage, the diaper bag, got her not just to the park but to the train station, to the airport, to places no self-respecting baby would ever go unless her parents packed her supplies and took her there. We encouraged her to take a look around, and once she's gone I will have lots of time to wonder why we didn't stick to the neighborhood, where we might have successfully raised a kid who never wanted to be more than a zip code away.

By the time she started first grade she had a passport and her own little flowered knapsack, into which she packed the things that mattered to her when we went on a vacation: eight or nine stuffed animals and a pad and colored pencils for drawing. On one trip she listened to *Charlotte's Web* while the grown-ups talked, our separation from her punctuated by the occasional random chuckle or sigh from the backseat of the rented car. She might not have had any idea of what to pack to survive on her own, but she had learned that going places was fun, and that she could find ways to entertain herself while the adults droned on about whether we should've taken that last left turn and the likelihood that we were lost.

Once she got to middle school, she acquired a series of backpacks of increasing and worrisome heft. A tiny friend who hoisted her pack onto her shoulders but forgot to lean forward to compensate fell right back on top of it, and lay there for a minute, helpless, her arms and legs wriggling like a beetle flipped onto its carapace. The other girls had to grab her arms and help her up—and yet we could not persuade Sarah to leave the history book in her locker until she needed it at the end of the day, or to leave the math book home if she didn't have math class. Those literally weighty tomes were the keys to the kingdom, though we didn't comprehend it at the time: Learn all this stuff, fill out a bunch of forms, graduate, and presto, you get to go to college.

In a scramble to manage the growing distance between us, I worked her magic in reverse and gave her things to carry with her that would remind her of home, even though she was no farther away than school. I tucked notes into her flowered bag, I gave her my wallet, I made sure she had a little elastic-bound notebook like mine. I presented one memento after another, as she did when I left town, to make sure that we were together even when we weren't. I did so with the increasingly bleak awareness that Sarah's departures were different. For me, the best part of leaving was coming back. We had no guarantee that Sarah's trajectory would bank into a similar return curve.

———

ONE DAY, ON the way home from elementary school, we ran out of conversation before the traffic cleared, so I raised a question that had bedeviled generations of philosophy 101 students, including myself: If a tree falls in the forest, I asked Sarah, does it make a sound?

She looked at me as if I were mad.

Of course it does, she said.

I presented a counter-argument. What if sound requires a witness? If I said I'd bought a blue sweater, it undoubtedly wouldn't be the same color as if Grandma said she'd bought a blue sweater, so maybe some part of color and sound, some part of what our senses perceived, resided inside us, not in the thing itself.

Now she knew I was nuts. She went on at some length in defense of her position; having mastered all of her senses far more recently than I had, she wasn't about to abandon her hard-won notion of a universal order.

I'd mentioned the falling tree because Sarah liked puzzles, and I thought we'd dispatch it before we got home—but the conversation continued for years, off and on, with increasingly sophisticated references to sound waves and audio nerves, to tape recorders and surveillance equipment. No matter what the level of discourse, Sarah remained as firm as she had been in the car, that first day: Noise and the elements of the color wheel and lots of other things existed even if nobody was there to see or hear or touch or smell or taste them. Some things, she insisted, just *are.*

———

THAT WAS A while ago, when the simple fact that I had a driver's license and she didn't guaranteed that we would have plenty of time to chat. Now, at the start of her senior year in high school, a disproportionate number of those conversations have as their subject the coming shift in our family landscape. I struggle not to compile a list of what a friend with an older daughter calls "the lasts"—the last time we are guaranteed all holidays together at home, the last year we definitely will celebrate all of our birthdays in person, the last time I will take a first-day-of-school photograph of Sarah posed in the same place she's stood every year for the past twelve. How will I persuade her to let me take a first-day photograph next year, and where will the new wall be?

I see that the fulcrum of her life was the college tour she went on over spring break in her sophomore year. It was the academic equivalent of speed-dating—a college every three hours!—and in truth, we sent her not so much to find a campus as to let her have ten days of fun with her pals. It worked. Before the ink on the check was dry, we were getting calls like this: "I'm on the corner of Sixth Avenue and Forty-fifth Street. Where's the restaurant with that cheese and tomato thing?"

The pace picked up dramatically after that. The girl who had never evinced the slightest interest in sleepaway camp—or in spending more than the very rare night at a friend's, for that matter—came home one afternoon with a brochure for a three-week summer program and didn't call home as often as any of us had anticipated once she got there. The summer before her senior year, she found a four-week program in a city where she could see friends she'd made the previous year. Temptation was everywhere; suddenly colleges in cities neither Larry nor I had ever visited were sending seductive brochures addressed not to us but directly to our daughter—and she looked at them and started to construct a hierarchy of desire.

And we, the reluctant but dutiful coconspirators, bought her a file cabinet in which she could keep all the brochures and letters and applications, so that she would have an alphabetized plan for her escape at her very fingertips. As much as I didn't like the idea of losing her for four weeks, I began to look forward to the summer program—as I might look forward to root canal, which would hurt temporarily but would protect me, down the line, from a world of pain. For I had come to understand the subtext of all these small departures: Whatever a program like this offered our children, it offered parents an honorable experiment in being alone. This was a chance to build up calluses so that the real thing wouldn't hurt so much.

Sarah packed for her month away without any assistance from me; in fact, she preferred that I not offer any opinions unless she asked. But Sarah is not unkind about growing up, so she did allow me to sit on her bed, as she had sat on mine, back in the day. I made a conscious effort not to give her something to put in her suitcase, to rise above magical thinking—and in the end I failed, sort of. I gave her a little leather horse on a key chain, a little horse emblematic of a couple of favorite family trips, but I dignified it by pointing out that she needed a key chain for her room key and the main key to the dorm. This was no mere totem. This was something a young woman could use.

If she saw right through me, she let it go. We got all the way to our destination before she suddenly realized that the one thing she absolutely needed and did not have was a summer-weight cardigan exactly like the one I had happened to pack for myself. I transferred it from my suitcase to hers without complaint. I like to think she took it not just because she was afraid her shoulders might be cold.

A few days before Sarah was supposed to come home, she called to say that her throat hurt, so she was going to sleep for the afternoon, because the next day was full of wonderful events she could not possibly miss. It was a half-and-half call: the little girl who wanted her mom to make the sore throat go away, and the busy young woman who had to get over it fast so that she could get back to her life. We went through the regimen—liquids, rest, compulsive hand-washing—and then we got to the truth.

"I really want to see you and Daddy, and you know I miss you," she began, "but I wish this could go on for another month."

There it was: If she had the choice, she would have stayed away a while longer, which did not mean that she no longer cared about us. It took me a moment to find my breath.

"Somebody asked me if you were having a good time," I said, "and I told her that if you could find a way to stay in the dorm room and start your freshman year in the fall, you'd do it. And that would be okay with Daddy and me."

I could not believe that I had said such a thing. I could not believe that I meant it, but in fact, I did. This was startling to me. Faced with a truly happy child, my complaints vanished. Faced with a truly happy child, I could not mention such pinched and irremediable concerns as missing her, as wishing that time would stand still, as wanting just for a moment to have a toddler in my arms.

I can't hang on to it; *blithe* will not be a word anyone uses to describe me once Sarah goes to college. I will tuck a memento into her freshman suitcase, knowing that it will not bring her back the way we used to count on. I'm sure I'll call too often, I'll send an e-mail for no good reason, I will find compellingly irrelevant excuses to visit, and sometimes I will be hurt if she's too busy to talk. I will feel all the things I felt in miniature this past summer: lost, lonely, old, irrelevant; and, yes, capable, rested, focused, and occasionally even well groomed. It was, and it will be, intolerable and appropriate. Painful and a vicarious thrill. Heartbreaking and elating. F. Scott Fitzgerald wrote, "The test of a first-rate intelligence is the ability to hold two opposed ideas in the mind at the same time, and still retain the ability to function," in which case I am in the midst of a very smart season.

People don't usually quote the next sentence: "One should, for example, be able to see that things are hopeless and yet be determined to make them otherwise." We cannot hold Sarah back, and who would want to? Sarah leaving is a work in progress—and leaving really is the wrong word, since it implies an absolute state, either here or gone, and she is not that. She will never be gone, no matter where she is, because feelings, because family, survive circumstance. The tree in the forest resounds without witness—and Sarah is our girl, always. That is our "otherwise": If I pay attention to it, I might be able to put the sad moments in their place, and to be glad that my happy child wants to stay at the party, whatever that party is, for just a little while longer.

Love like this requires faith. I will have to work hard to remember what Sarah insists is true: Some things, she says, just are.

Flown Away, Left Behind

Anna Quindlen

I was something of an accidental mother. I don't mean that in the old traditional whoops! way; it's just that while I barreled through my twenties convinced that having a baby would be like carrying a really large and inconvenient tote bag that I could never put down, I awoke one day at thirty and, in what now seems an astonishingly glib leap of faith, decided I wanted that tote bag in the very worst way. It was as though my ovaries had taken possession of my brain. Less than a year later an infant had taken possession of everything else. My brain no longer worked terribly well, especially when I added to that baby another less than two years later, and a third fairly soon after that.

That was twenty years ago. You do the math. The first one went to China to polish his Mandarin. The second left for college in the fall. I still have a chick in the nest, and what a chick she is, but increasingly it feels like an aerie too large for its occupants. Recently I told her we were going to be doing something we had always done as a family. "We don't have that family anymore," she said. (Here I pause to remove the shiv from between my ribs, breathe deeply, and smile.)

Tell me at your peril that the flight of my kids into successful adulthood is hugely liberating, that I will not believe how many hours are in the day, that my husband and I can see the world, that I can throw myself into my job. My world is in this house, and I already had a great job into which I'd thrown myself for two decades. No, not the writing job—the motherhood job. I was good at it, if I do say so myself, and because I was, I've now been demoted to part-time work. Soon I will attain emerita status. This stinks.

I wonder if this has a particular edge for the women of my generation, who found themselves pursuing mothering in a new sort of way. We professionalized it, and in doing so made ourselves a tiny bit ridiculous and more than a little crazy. Women who left their children in the care of others to work for pay often wound up, by necessity and habit, scheduling their mother life as they did their working one. (See us logging teacher conferences into our PDAs in the parking lot of the preschool.) Women who eschewed the job market despite the gains of women within it sometimes wound up making motherhood into a surrogate work world, full of school meetings and endless athletic teams. (See us chairing bake sales even though it would be cheaper to write a check than to make brownies.) For both groups, the unexamined child was not worth having:

from late crawling to bad handwriting to mediocre SATs, all was grist for the worry mill. Motherhood changed from a role into a calling. Our poor kids.

The end result is that the empty nest is emptier than ever before; after all, at its center was a role, a vocation, a nameless something so enormous that a good deal had to be sacrificed for it, whether sleep or self or money or ambition or peace of mind. Those sacrifices—or accommodations, for those of us waxing poetic about their end—became the warp and woof of our lives; first we got used to them and then before we knew it they had become obsolete. Those of you waiting for your babies to sleep through the night will be amazed how quickly they come to sleep through the afternoon after a night out.

For years I wrote only between the hours of nine and three, when the children were at school. (God forbid they should actually see me work.) Now that two of the children live at school and one has play rehearsal, basketball games, and random hanging-out when school is done, I still write only between the hours of nine and three. It has become my routine; I did not choose to change it. In the kitchen is a magnet that says MOM IS NOT MY REAL NAME. See our heads snap up in the supermarket when someone yells the word, as surely as our milk once let down when we heard a baby, any baby, cry.

Much has been written about the pernicious nature of having it all, the perfection syndrome required of women who must play so many roles in the lives of others, jamming loving obligations into days that feel too short, discussing endlessly how to balance work and home. But many of us eventually ratcheted up our metabolisms accordingly. First overfull was a cross, then a challenge, eventually a commonplace. Anything less is empty.

It's not simply the loss of these particular people, living here day in, day out, the bickering, the inside jokes, the cereal bowls in the sink, and the towels in the hamper—all right, on the floor. It was who I was with them: the general to their battalion, the president to their cabinet. The Harpo to their Groucho, Zeppo, and Chico. Sometimes I go into their rooms and just stand, touching their books, looking out their windows. "The shrine," the youngest says derisively, although she misses the other two as much as I do. But she has her own plans, has one eye now on the glitter past the window glass. At the end of the month she heads Down Under on a six-week school exchange, leaving the bulletin board, the photograph albums, and the wallpaper with butterflies on it behind. And me, of course. Three rooms empty, full of the ghosts of my very best self. Mom is my real name. It is, it is.

Regime Change

Charles McGrath

We delivered our youngest child to college the other day. This was a moment my wife and I had been both dreading and anticipating for weeks, and it happened so swiftly, so unceremoniously, that the actual instant of separation took place almost before we could register it. We unloaded the station wagon: computer, trombone, popcorn maker, and, wrapped in the original plastic bag, a Brooks Brothers time capsule—a navy blazer and gray flannels that can be dug up, mold covered, from the closet four years from now. We met the roommates, shook hands, and stood around awkwardly for a while. We inspected the bunk beds—testing those gridlike springs that with only the slightest squeaks of protest have borne aloft the bodies of so many sleeping freshmen (excuse me, freshpersons)—and toured the unisex bathrooms. (They were, well, unisex.) We waited in lines for a while, and we wrote a bunch of checks. Then we went out and wandered around town for a bit, and while we were waiting at a corner for the light to change the nest suddenly emptied. A quick hug, a wave, a promise to call, and, in an instant, he was gone.

It's too late for us now—we will have to work through our grief in other ways—but I kept wishing that the college had arranged some ceremony to mark the occasion. A circling of the wagons, perhaps—with those Conestogas of the suburbs, the parental Volvos, Cherokees, and Caravans, lined up according to age and mileage while the dean affixes a brand-new college decal to the rear window of each. Or maybe an interfaith blessing of the first-year stereos, with suitable prayers offered up by the chaplain for hours of distortion-free bass and superior graphic equalization.

As it happens, my son is attending the same institution of higher learning where my parents dropped me off some thirty years ago. My father, who had never been to college, wore his best suit and tie and was so nervous he couldn't speak. My mother, equally nervous, couldn't stop talking. They've both been dead for years now, but I found myself wondering what they would have made of parents like the couple I saw, in matching T-shirts, sunglasses, and Tevas, lugging an Oriental rug between them while their daughter trailed behind, bearing a cocktail shaker. Or what they would have made of the safe-sex display in my son's dorm, featuring not only free condoms but free dental dams and instructions in dental dam etiquette. (Actually, in my mother's case, I think I know. Sex, she always said, was too beautiful to talk about.)

What would they have made of me, for that matter, concerned less with my son than with whether or not I was going to blub. (I didn't, thank goodness.) All over the campus I saw, or thought I saw, dozens and dozens of parents in a similar state, trying not to do or say anything that would embarrass their offspring or themselves. I've never witnessed such a concentration of good behavior.

In private a couple of us parents remarked that college was wasted on the young, and volunteered to become freshpersons again, now that we know all that we know. In truth, though, we probably don't know the first thing. Who would install our computer software? Who would tell us what music to listen to and which side to get our ears pierced on? I had a momentary and depressing vision of myself and my roommates of thirty years ago reunited now in the old suite. There we are, four middle-aged guys without a clue. We pop a few brewskies, maybe spark a jay or two—just the way we did in the old days. Somehow, though, it isn't the same. As night falls, we make a big effort. We turn the radio up full blast, put on the bedsheets, and do the toga dance across the quad. It isn't as much fun as we'd hoped. We're tired and out of breath, and our feet hurt. Most of all, we're lonely. We miss the kids.

I WROTE THAT more than ten years ago, though it hardly seems that long. The college dean—who had actually been a classmate, of the studious variety and not one of the toga dancers—sent me a decal in the mail. I got a very nice note from the literary critic George Steiner, of all people—not someone I imagined to be preoccupied by empty-nest issues—and one of my son's high school friends began eyeing me with new respect. He said he especially liked the part about "sparking jays."

I also heard from someone who wrote: "It's interesting, and typical, that people who love their children very much approach this important moment in their children's lives with almost total self-absorption. I'm a parent. I don't feel that way. Frankly, I just don't understand it. Must be part of this 'me' thing."

Guilty as charged, and why not? I wasn't worried about my son, who went on to enjoy himself immensely in college, just as I suspected he would. I was worried about me, and about how my wife and I would cope with a house that for a while seemed to echo with emptiness. The refrigerator no longer needed to be replenished daily. We needed to run the dishwasher no more than once or twice a week. My son's room no longer needed to be tidied, or to have the door shut so that we needn't look upon the mess within. It was like a museum of boyhood—the sports trophies gathering dust, the baseball cards under the bed, the paper crown from the senior prom dangling from a lampshade.

There were a couple of evenings early on when my wife and I were at a loss for words. What was there to talk about, if not the kids? Plenty, it turned out, as gradually, like a change in government, a new era of liberation set in. Dinner on TV trays! Wine! Living room nudity! We slept soundly at night, no longer waking up in those early, white-knuckle hours, waiting for the blessed sound of a car pulling into the driveway and the back door softly shutting. On weekends, we stayed in bed late if we felt like it or else, on the spur of the moment, we hopped in the car and went somewhere without a thought as to when we might return. In a way, we became kids ourselves.

Eventually, in classic American fashion, we enlarged the nest. This was in part an attempt to create a grandchild trap— a place to attract the offspring of our offspring—because by now our daughter, the first to fly the coop, had a husband and a daughter of her own. But in a way I suppose we added on to the nest simply because we could—because there were no children to get in the way of the construction. So now we have state-of-the-art bathrooms that are always clean, and where we can conceal the various geezer pills we have lately become obliged to take. We have an upstairs sitting room where we can unself-consciously play any kind of music we feel like. We have fewer disagreements than at any other time in our marriage. This must be the condition that real estate agents call "tranquility."

We're fortunate in that both of the kids live nearby, and visit fairly often. They come in like whirlwinds, with all their stuff—the duffels, the iPods, the laptops, and, lately, the toys, the portable crib, the bales of disposable diapers. Who are these people? I sometimes think. They lead such busy lives and have such funny and interesting things to say. It barely seems possible that they're related to us.

And then, after a day or so in which the whole house seems to vibrate with energy, they're on their way again, as suddenly as they turned up. We hug them, thank them, promise to be in touch by phone and e-mail, and then we start to clean the counters, dump the towels in the washer, rearrange the silverware drawer, stack the magazines, put the CDs back on the shelves. We love it when they come. We also love it when they leave.

Careful What You Wish For

Susan Crandell

As my daughter Brook checked items off the packing list and filled boxes with sheets and towels and computer components, getting ready for her freshman year in college, I found myself worrying more about me than about her. I imagined that my husband and I would rattle around the empty nest like the last two crullers in a big Dunkin' Donuts dozen box. Brook was lifting off into an exciting future, opening a new chapter in her life while we were slamming one shut. Without the manic sideshow of a joyful, emotional, hyperscheduled teenager, I feared our days would be thin, pale, anemic. I brooded extra-much because Brook is our one and only. In the days preceding her early-September departure, I ricocheted between emotions—sad for us, happy for her. I only hoped that together Steve and I could withstand the wave of sorrow that was sure to wash over us when we returned to an unnaturally quiet house.

There is something worse than an empty heart, though; it is a homesick child. On a soggy September morning, the day after we'd settled Brook into her new college digs, we walked from the little guesthouse near campus to her dorm. Brook was standing out in the rain waiting for us, tears streaming down her face. Did she hate her roommates? No, all four young women were lovely, and everyone had been gracious about deciding who'd get the desk by the window and the larger of the two sleeping rooms. Was she terrorized that she'd gained entry to one of the top schools in the country by some hideous clerical mistake and would soon be found out as an intellectual imposter? Nope, that was my paranoia at her age, not hers. Brook knew she'd worked hard for her grades and accolades in high school; she could do the same here.

She was just plain homesick. Right now, her future was a question mark. She didn't know another soul on campus. Raised in a little time-forgotten Hudson River town, she would be living in a bustling city two hundred miles from home. When I went away to college, I couldn't wait to be independent. A wallflower in high school, I saw it as an opportunity to reinvent myself—to be the popular girl, not the nerd, to have more friends and to study subjects that weren't even on the radar screen at my humble secondary school. Brook, on the other hand, was quite fond of the life she would hereafter refer to as her past. She had a great circle of friends, a happy enough family life to outshine the bumps and scrapes of adolescence, and a boy she would be leaving behind. Al was a year and a half younger, a handsome high school junior with a brilliant smile. He was the quarterback and the school's best pole-vaulter. More important, he was Brook's first love. In her mind, at college she had everything to lose, and who-knows-what to gain.

Steve and I did our best that sad September day to cheer her up before we hugged all around and climbed in the car. On the drive home, I fought back tears of my own, worrying about my little girl in the big bad world. My friend Ellen and I used to laugh about her mother-in-law's comment when Ellen was facing a breast biopsy: "This is so much harder on Alex than on you." There was my friend, lying on a hospital bed facing surgery and an unknown prognosis, and who's enduring the greater pain—her husband! Suddenly I understood what Alex's mother meant: In the calculus of parenting, all pain is raised to the tenth power if it's happening to your child.

Brook's unhappiness didn't come out of nowhere. She had a history of battling the blues; for her, homesickness was a chronic condition. When she was twelve and crazy for ballet, she'd signed up for a two-week dance camp at a college campus forty-five minutes from our house. A few days after she got there, she called in tears. She was miserable, would we please, please, please bring her home. Steve was unreachable, out of the country on business, so I had to figure out what to do. There was no decision, really; I was a mother lion protecting her cub. I canceled the day's meetings, hopped a commuter train, and went to fetch her.

That fall, Brook threw over her passion for dancing to join the tennis team, and the next summer, she begged to go to tennis camp. "Okay," Steve and I bargained, "we'll send you, but this time there's no early dismissal option. If you decide to go, you have to stay." Absolutely, Brook promised. Her best friend Randi was going too, they'd room together, it would be wonderful. Well, Randi made new friends at camp while Brook sank into homesickness. Two days in, my office phone rang. When I reminded my distraught daughter of our deal (and contemplated the crafty planning of my husband, who was out of the country again), she played her ace: "If you loved me, you'd pick me up." I didn't have a snappy response; in my heart of hearts, I agreed. But with the tough-love encouragement of an Aussie friend who'd trotted off to boarding school at age eight and—Brook's bad luck—happened to be in my office when she called, I managed to hold the line. She would have to stay. Shaken, I hung up the phone.

Brook survived that week at tennis camp. Her next foray into independent travel came her junior year of high school, when one very brave French teacher took two dozen hormone-drenched adolescents on a fourteen-day exchange program to Provence. Sobbing phone calls ensued.

Given that Brook had once again stuck it out, and remembering my own unbounded joy at being on my own, I figured she'd be okay for college. Call it denial, but I truly believed that she had scaled the barrier of homesickness. Now here we were in the September from hell. Brook was melting down in Boston, and I was doing a good impersonation back home. I worried that she'd drop out of college, move home, and marry Al. They'd have babies right away and go to work flipping burgers. That was the night terror that had me snapping awake in a chilling sweat at 3 A.M. The bright future I had imagined for my daughter seemed in danger of vaporizing at any minute.

All that fall, my stomach churned every morning as I booted up my computer and scanned my e-mail. I jumped every time the phone rang. Steve had been the on-duty parent who worked from home and raised Brook while I commuted a hundred miles a day to New York City. I was the touchy-feely one; my shift started when the emotional chips were down, yet I felt inadequate to the task of helping her find her way.

Alongside empathy for Brook's pain, I was serving myself a heaping helping of guilt. No matter what theory I embraced to explain her unhappiness, it all boiled down to one inescapable truth: It was all my fault. Had my "let's be pals" relationship with her created fertile ground for homesickness to flourish? Had I cuddled her too much, breast-fed her too long, urged her to spend time with me instead of her friends, made her too dependent on me? Then again, homesickness could be my responsibility in a completely different way—maybe it was genetic.

I remembered my own failed experiment at childhood independence. When I was eleven, I headed off to a girls' camp on a little lake with a school friend who'd been attending happily for years. It was two weeks of pure misery. I had no idea I could be so unhappy, but I never let my parents know. Phone calls home were forbidden except in an emergency (hard as that is to imagine in this day, when kids don't go anywhere without a battery of personal communication devices), and the camp director encouraged us to write upbeat letters to our folks. As I recall, in my series of chirpy, chatty notes, I only let my game face slip once, asking my parents to please come early on the day they'd pick me up. I never went to camp again, but I always figured that being forced to deal with the difficulties had been beneficial in that medicinal "has to taste bad to be good" way.

Struggling to make it through the fall from hell, I printed out and kept all of our e-mails, hoping that rereading them would somehow suggest a solution. Recently, I found them stuck in a file folder at the back of a drawer. As I page through them now, almost ten years later, I am struck by how lame my advice to her was. "Set goals for yourself," I suggested. "Make sure you talk to three or four new people every day. Once you have a good friend, it will color your whole attitude. And remember, you may have to do a little interviewing before you find your soul mate." Gag! Okay, I was a women's magazine editor, well versed in platitudes and simplistic advice, but did I really write this stuff?

In my own inept way, I also managed to imply that she was letting the entire family down—no, make that the entire family tree. "You come from tough stock," I lectured. "Your grandfather went off to war when he was your age. Your grandmother left high school to take over her parents' business when they died." What was I thinking?

Like the boomer mom I am, when I wasn't writing treacly or belligerent e-mails, I was trying to micromanage Brook's "independent" experience. As soon as we got home that rainy September day, I called her resident adviser, a first-year law student who lived across the hall. When I told her about Brook's difficulties, Amy was cordial but brief. "I can't even talk to you about this without Brook's permission. She is an adult, and those are the rules." I was momentarily dismayed, but somehow the message got through. A few weeks later, when Steve and I thought Brook should have a talk with the dean, we were smart enough to suggest that she set up a meeting rather than ringing him up and getting her on his calendar ourselves. This powwow would prove to be a turning point, though for a reason we didn't imagine. I had figured the dean would put Brook on the couch, probing the roots of her homesickness, but he took a more pragmatic approach. If she was that unhappy, he told her, perhaps she'd like to take a semester off. The school understood and would welcome her back. Far from an opportunity Brook was craving, the offer came as a shock. "I worked so hard to get here," she told us. "There's no way I'm going to leave." This didn't make Brook's day-to-day any easier, but it helped keep her eye on her goal.

Meanwhile, back at home, I was developing a serious case of maternal envy. In early October, I rounded up the mothers of four of Brook's friends for a chatty dinner where we'd swap stories and help one another deal with the adjustment of sending our kids off. I brought us together with an ulterior motive in mind: to learn some smart strategies for handling homesickness. The first meeting of the Lonely Moms Club was a wakeup call of quite another kind. These other mothers weren't moaning about how unhappy their kids were; they were complaining about how little their kids missed them. I wanted to shake them, saying, "Don't you know you're the lucky ones. Your kids are thriving. Mine is counting the days until she can be released from this emotional torture chamber they call college life."

Brook made it through her first, rough year with determination, gumption, and lots of trips home. That summer, she and Al broke up. When September rolled around, I was stunned to deliver a very different young woman to her new dorm room. She embraced her roommate with a big grin, a smile that never faded even after the last carton had been unloaded and I was back in the car waving good-bye. This time, it was me who was crying, tears of happiness and pride that my daughter had found her place in the world. Could it be that she hadn't been homesick at all—that this time, the sorrow had been garden-variety boy trouble?

That seemed to be the case. For the next three years, she came home only for the between-semesters vacation—plus spring break if she didn't have a more delicious destination, like Cape Cod or Barcelona, at her disposal. Otherwise, if we wanted to see Brook, we drove up to Cambridge. I realized that this was just fine with me. She was making the proper transfer: As Steve reminded me, "home" was not her bright fuchsia bedroom under the big catalpa tree; it was room 507 in Pforzheimer House. Because I'd spent her freshman year in a cold sweat, worrying about her future, I'd accommodated to the empty nest without noticing. Her misery had trumped the letdown I would have felt otherwise. By the time I was able to focus on the hollow spaces in my own life, they had magically filled.

Brook surprised me again a few years later, with her graduation gift request: an around-the-world air ticket. Five days after receiving her degree, she set off for Asia with an enormous backpack and plans to spend nine months seeing the world on twenty dollars a day. Maybe all those traumatic trips as an adolescent and preteen had been character building, after all. Meanwhile, I was left to reflect on how quickly we can swap seats on the good mom/bad mom teeter-totter of life. Now, other parents were congratulating me on what a resourceful, independent child I'd raised, saying their kids could never travel to far-flung foreign lands alone. I'd smile and say, "Be careful what you wish for." Now, Brook was off on a grand adventure, and I was homesick for her.

Always Close

Annette Duffy

Everything I know about mothering I learned from my father. This is an accident of history, and maybe also of biology. My mother almost died when I was born, and for the first few months of my life my father had to feed me and clean me and dress me and put me to sleep while she recuperated. When my mother was finally well enough to care for me herself, she learned that her own mother was dying, and she turned all her energies to nursing my grandmother through her illness. I was two years old when my grandmother died and my mother at last became free to mother me. But by then, the bond between me and my father was absolute, and his eccentric way of mothering was the only kind that could interest me.

For me, mothering was when, at one, you stood in your crib while your dad fed you, and you rattled the crib's bars and roared, and he loved it and he laughed and fed you some more. Mothering at two was when you plunged into the huge breakers of the Atlantic Ocean on your dad's shoulders, and you weren't too afraid because he'd mimed for you the way to hold your breath when the breakers hit. Mothering at three was when you rode ponies in Van Cortlandt Park, in the Bronx where you lived, and your dad wouldn't let the stable boy lead you because he knew you could control the pony yourself. Mothering at four and five and six was when you walked with your dad for hours every weekend along the eastern bank of the Hudson River, and he showed you how to avoid the third rail of the Hudson Line's tracks, which ran that way, a trick that it was obvious every little girl should know. Mothering was when you learned how to tell what direction you were headed in—New Jersey being to the west across the Hudson, you could easily figure out the other three directions. Mothering was when, walking on the bank of the Hudson, you heard brilliant stories from your father about a little girl who just happened to have your same name, and who led her male cousins across the Hudson to Animal Land (sorry, New Jersey) in astonishing adventures in which she figured as the only one with any brains. She knew how to build a raft to cross the River, she knew how to talk to the unpredictable Lion King of Animal Land and save her cousins' skins, and she knew how to get them all home safe before any of their parents even missed them.

Because, you see, mothering assumed that children had secret lives and their own adventures that their parents didn't have a clue about. Mothering understood that separation is the destiny of mother and child, and it is the mother's job to remember this—for the child's sake. Mothering knew that you have to raise your children to go away, or else you've failed utterly.

My father didn't always like it when the lesson was learned. When I grew up and fell in love—*really* in love, and not just pleasantly amused, as I'd been with previous boyfriends—my father appeared unannounced one day at my lover David's apartment on the Lower East Side. My dad, who'd been in the construction business in New York all his life, said he'd get some of his steelworkers to come break David's arms and legs unless David agreed never to see me again. I found this exasperating and histrionic when David told me about it, but even now I'm amazed at how *not* surprised I was. It never dawned on me that this behavior could scare David away, and it didn't. David is a screenwriter, and I suspect he admired my father's gesture as just the right touch for a first act turning point.

The next act was hard for my audience to take: I married David and moved to the West, to the real Animal Land, which was Hollywood. My ancestors on both sides have lived in New York, pretty much on the banks of the Hudson River, ever since they got off the boat from Ireland. My parents' picture of the continent was exactly like the Saul Steinberg cover of *The New Yorker*, in which the three blocks between Ninth Avenue and the Hudson River take up four times as much space as the small oblong containing New Jersey, Kansas City, Chicago, and distant Los Angeles. My move to the West meant I was dropping off the end of the earth.

My dad promptly expanded his imagination to include the end of the earth. Over the next twenty years, he showed me that if you wanted your children to be close, you had to treat them as if living at the end of the earth was a mere trifle in the matter of love. Filial love, in fact, was much more alive when never poked with the fork of guilt. That actually works both ways. Once my dad realized David couldn't be intimidated, he accepted and admired him, and neither David nor I ever mentioned to him those pesky steelworkers with the primitive intentions.

David and I have two sons now, Benjamin and, seven years younger, Thomas. They are a fine matched pair of young men, both six foot three, both handsome as the day (I'm allowed to say that), and, Thomas being Ben's middle name, both named after my father.

When Ben was five days old, my parents flew to California to see him, their first grandchild. My father drove my mother up the Malibu coast and escorted her into our little cottage. Then he rushed past me and David, and into the baby's room, where he peered at the enormous newborn (Ben had been eleven pounds, six ounces at birth), took note of his shoulders, and declared, "He's a swimmer."

This turned out to be quite right. By the time Ben was in high school he was a nationally ranked freestyler and backstroker. Throughout Ben's childhood and college swimming career, my father and I kept up a lively telephone communication about Ben's races and times. We had a lot to say because we spoke the same language—my dad had been captain of his college swimming team, and he'd coached me to become a long-distance champion in Westchester County. But my dad never by word or deed hinted how unfair it felt that we lived in California, where he couldn't see Ben's races. When he got the chance, though, he took it. Ben wound up going back east to college, and my dad became the one who saw Ben's races and called *me* to report. He was particularly triumphant when Ben's team beat West Point, which had destroyed my father's college team in what my dad considered an ungentlemanly manner at a meet fifty years before.

Ben did me a favor the day he graduated from high school by telling me that he absolutely did not want me and David flying east with him in September to move him into his college dorm. I was shocked. I had assumed that every right-minded family carried its offspring to college on a sea of love, and in person. I started to argue, but Ben had brought reinforcements: David and my dad. In a sunny courtyard of Ben's high school, right after the graduation ceremony, they hemmed me in, a solid three-generation wall of males, and they forced me to agree to Ben's request. And then Ben pressed his advantage: "If you cry at the airport," he said, "I'll kill you." He was cutting me off at every pass. I hadn't planned to cry at the airport—I hadn't even planned to *leave* him at the airport, dropping him off like a package to be shipped east. Long after this, Ben explained that it was for his own sake that he warned me not to cry. "You represent the most tender part of myself," he said. "I needed to be strong when I left. I couldn't afford to see you cry."

I've always had to struggle to reach the high standard of mothering set by my father. If Ben didn't want me to cry at the airport, I'd have to learn not to. So that summer I took the crying cure. Whenever I felt tears coming on, I'd walk calmly upstairs and away from the family, I'd play music at a volume that drowned me out, and I'd just sob, making sure Ben never knew. In fact, I practically induced crying, like farmers practicing controlled flooding of their fields. I drove around Los Angeles, listening to Irish folk songs that to me were clearly about Ben, and I watched a lot of traffic through sheets of tears. To bolster my resolve I sometimes recalled the monsters' lament in Maurice Sendak's *Where the Wild Things Are*: They beg the boy not to leave them—in fact, they love him so much they'll eat him up if he stays. Only monsters, I reminded myself, would rather consume the darling boy than let him go.

By the time Ben left in September, I had mourned, and I had adjusted. David, eleven-year-old Thomas, and I took him to the airport and said good-bye to him at the gate. When he'd disappeared down the ramp into the plane, I turned and walked away, till I realized I was walking alone. I looked back and saw David and Tom with their noses pressed to the glass, counting the windows of Ben's plane, trying to figure out where his seat was, hoping to catch one last glimpse of him. In fact, thanks to the crying cure, I was in better shape than they were. This became even clearer over the next few weeks as David took to reading me menus from the Web site of Ben's freshman dining hall, worrying over his food choices.

These days, David's computer is set to show the weather report in Cairo. It turns out that sending off our firstborn to the East Coast was child's play compared to what lay before us. Last year Thomas graduated from college on June 9, and on June 10 he flew to Egypt to continue studying Arabic, his college major, at the American University in Cairo.

Like war and rumors of war, I'd heard this coming for all of

Tom's senior year, and I hadn't liked the sound of it even a tiny bit. In the time since he'd taken up the study of Arabic on September 12, 2001, Americans had gone from being objects of sympathy around the world to being objects of hatred, particularly in the Middle East. No amount of belief in raising a child to go away was enough to make the fierce mother in me step aside to send my astonishingly American-looking, auburn-haired, green-eyed, white-as-paper boy to Egypt. Or so I thought.

I don't know if it was a clever ruse of Tom's, or if it was truly the madness of being only twenty-one, but he made it clear that if he wasn't accepted into the program in Cairo, he'd hitchhike around the Middle East, sort of freelancing his own Arabic immersion program. At this point David started talking fondly of Egypt's "nice repressive regime," by which he meant it was a country where good order was imposed and people weren't routinely kidnapped and beheaded. I, reeling from the horror of the phrase *hitchhike around the Middle East*, began to think fondly of Egypt, too. When Tom called to tell us he'd been accepted into the Cairo program, we were actually relieved. The day after Tom's college graduation, David, Ben, and I saw him off with love and good wishes, and a certain measure of peaceful acceptance.

For years now, the four of us have followed my dad's method for erasing distance. The method is not just to call, write, and e-mail each other frequently, but to do so with the tone of colleagues touching base about a shared enterprise. The enterprise is adventure: We are out to have what my dad used to call "good fun."

Tom is not above using this method to tease us about what he regards as our hopelessly ignorant, unjustifiably fearful attitude about the Middle East. In August 2005, Tom had a month off from school, and he used the time to travel through Lebanon and Syria, where we feared the regimes weren't quite as nice and repressive as Egypt's. His first e-mail to us from Syria read as follows: "Against all odds, I am not yet dead . . . Just joking, I am dead . . . No, but seriously, it wasn't really against the odds, though it's true that I am not yet dead."

But he is kind, too. The first snail mail I had from him in Cairo was a postcard showing an ancient painting of the Holy Family escaping into Egypt. This is Catholic speak for: A precious son can be safe in Egypt, can even be safe *only* in Egypt, and he can grow there so as to be prepared to fulfill the destiny of his adult life.

The truth is that as far as family relationships go, Tom has it easy in far-off Egypt compared to his brother, Ben. Ben lives in far-off-sounding Venice, but it is Venice, California, a beach town of hip young adults, pensioners, urban poor, and the artsy rich, three miles from where David and I live today. It has been obvious for most of Ben's life that he is a writer like his mom and dad. In the last few years he's settled into professional writing. He writes screenplays, novels, manga, videogames, animation, and things I don't even know about. On a few of his projects he collaborates with me and David. This means that Ben has to put up with comments at work that his other colleagues wouldn't dream of making. His choices of girlfriends, food, haircuts, clothing, sleep habits—everything personal, private, intimate, and nobody else's business—seem like natural subjects to Ben's coworkers when they're his parents. Ben has had to labor long and hard to train us, and we've been slow to learn, despite our good intentions. During a recent story conference in our living room, I said to Ben, "Daddy is saying the necklace should not be from the museum but be picked up at the murder site..." I stopped because I knew from Ben's pained expression that something was wrong. "Please," he said. "Don't call him Daddy." It is on such matters of tact that our working relationship with Ben depends. I get it; I just slip sometimes.

My own dad died while Thomas was still in college. He'd been fighting cancer for sixteen years; he did terrifically well until the last seven months. I don't think I understood the sense of mortality that cancer gives its victims until after he'd died, but looking back on it now I realize he began to say good-bye in a new way that perfectly reflected our whole life together, but which carried added poignancy for someone looking at death. It was always hard for me to leave him, no matter how joyous the life I was returning to. In the last years of his life, when I'd hug him good-bye at the airport, he took to saying, "Always close." To me it meant I might move to the end of the earth, but there was a place inside, the true inner self, and there we were always close.

I flew back to New York to nurse my dad through his last months, as my mom did with her mother when I was an infant. When he died my mother actually said to me, "He was really your mother. Your mother has just died."

But in my mind, the words I heard were, "Always close."

The Rules of the Road

Vicky Mann

I t was okay for me to move away from my parents. At the time, they seemed so old to me—fifty-two and fifty-three—and they lived with one foot firmly in the Lebanese ghetto where they were raised in Scranton, Pennsylvania. My mother never graduated from high school and my father never finished college. My mother was a housewife and my father worked for the post office. They were not people I wanted to grow up to be. As far as I could see, anyone in their right mind would want to vacate that nest, and I did so without giving much thought to how my parents felt about it.

A generation later, as my older daughter, Sarah, got ready to leave for college, I had changed my mind rather completely about who deserved to be left behind. I was almost fifty, very close to the age my seemingly elderly mother had been when I left home, but I was a different kind of fifty. My husband,

Hummie, and I were cool and hip. He is a composer and a musician, and I teach middle school; I have my finger on the pulse of today's teen. Why on earth would anyone want to leave our nest?

Because that's what children are supposed to do, I guess. But if we couldn't keep Sarah at home indefinitely, at least we could try to preserve our cool and hip reputation. We've dropped her off twice, now—three times, if you count the semester abroad—and along the way I've developed a useful set of rules to smooth out the good-byes.

Rule Number One: *Never rent a hotel room with more beds than you need.*

I didn't figure this out until Sarah's sophomore year. Freshman year is kind to parents because it gives us so much to occupy our time. I felt like we spent hours each day commuting to the local Target, multiple trips for plastic storage bins, canvas storage bags, stainless-steel storage baskets—in fact, anything that came from the aisle labeled ORGANIZERS, because our only hope of fitting all her things into her dorm room was containers. There was the trip to buy toilet paper, Windex, and laundry detergent—which she would have to learn to use without me telling her to change the toilet paper roll, clean her bathroom mirror, or wash the multicolored anthill of cotton and spandex that was her dirty laundry. College was like a giant game of playing house, without the mortgage payments or the clogged gutters.

My primary emotion was longing—couldn't she seem even a little bit sad that she was leaving us?—but envy ran a close second, and it distracted me from how much I was going to miss her. Sarah's was the age to be: feeling independent and moving away from her parents, but still living within the safety and comfort of their bank account. The world of university classes—The History of Protest Songs 101?—awaited her.

Sophomore year required much less effort; we were so casual that Hummie planned a business trip for the week Sarah needed to move in. I hadn't intended to go with her, because we'd put everything she needed into a storage unit, and she had arranged to borrow a car to move her things into her new room. She knew the way to Target, and if I didn't go, I could save the money I would have spent on a plane ticket and a hotel room, for another trip later in the semester. But the borrowed car fell through, so I got to be the helpful, rental-car mom for another year. "Sarah needs me to help her move into her dorm room," was my late-summer mantra as I apologized to my friends for canceling our plans. Secretly, I relished the chance. Sarah was no longer the sulking, self-centered high school teenager who would rather spend time with her friends than with her family. She willingly went to the movies with me and offered to help me make dinner. She did the laundry so I wouldn't have to. I had spent the summer getting to know this new and improved daughter of mine, and I was going to miss her terribly. I was glad to have an extra few days with her when she moved in.

Or so I thought. We flew down from Seattle to Los Angeles late in the day, had a nice night together, and the next morning we shifted everything from the storage unit to her room and set up her combination microwave and refrigerator with enough food to last her for a couple of days. Finally, there was nothing left to do but put the pictures up on the walls. I was too exhausted to think of any reason to stick around, so I gave her a long hug and kiss and went back to the hotel room I had rented for the weekend.

I lay on my bed and looked around. The double bed that Sarah had slept in the night before was now smooth and snug, unused. The longer I stared at it, the bigger and emptier the room seemed to be, and the smaller and emptier I felt. We might have been crowded sharing one double bed, but at least I would have had less evidence that she was missing. So take two rooms, or endure one big bed, or change rooms if you have to. That first night's a killer in a room with an empty bed.

Rule Number Two: Get someone to take good photos of you and your spouse for your child to hang in her college dorm room.

Not the one your husband took of you posing with the mariachis and wearing a sombrero in Puerto Vallarta, and not the one of him pretending to balance the Eiffel Tower in the palm of his hand. Sarah hung dozens of photographs on her wall to remind her of happy times at home, and to show off her life to her new friends—and among all those favorite pictures, of parties, graduations, her younger sister, there was only one of Hummie and me. The rest were too goofy for words. If I had it to do over again, I would ask someone to take a good photograph, a posed one that made us seem like the kind of couple anyone would rush home to visit.

Don't panic at the start of sophomore year, when the photos share wall space with a poster that says something like, "The

Ten Reasons Why Dancers Do It Better," as well as other wall adornments I've worked hard to forget. This is your child's home. I was simply grateful still to be part of the collection. Sarah was moving further and further away, but she wasn't aggressively trying to forget us.

And never forget that a college dorm room is a transition space, a metaphor for an in-between stage of life. Sarah had color-coordinated sheets and a comforter, right out of a Martha Stewart catalog, a very grown-up look—with her aging stuffed-animal collection arrayed on top of the bed, a nod to the childhood she was not quite prepared to abandon. I don't know if boys feel a similar need to bring a piece of the past to college with them—an old Darth Vader action figure with a broken light saber? A favorite catcher's mitt from that twelve-inning Little League game back in '98? Whatever memento they choose, let them, and take it as a compliment. No matter how many arguments you had when they were growing up, all in all, they want to take something with them to remind them of life as your child.

Rule Number Three: Learn to use your communications equipment.

I'm a perfectly conflicted member of my generation when it comes to technology. I've come kicking and screaming into the twenty-first century: I do own and use a Palm Pilot, but if there's something I really have to remember, I resort to sticky notes which I plaster on the screen of my PDA. If it were up to me, I might choose to ignore some of the latest technology, but the umbilical cord to our children's generation is an Ethernet cable, and if I want my relationship with Sarah to continue in a satisfying way, I have to be available online or on my cell phone.

I figured this one out when the first thing Sarah had to set up in her dorm room was her laptop—not so that she could get the book lists for her classes or set up her school e-mail, but so that she could have access to her iTunes, and could set up her Facebook account. She had to see which one of her Seattle friends had already e-mailed about coming to visit her on the first available weekend. Connections are a primal need for college freshmen, and if you want to be included, you'd better be available on your child's terms.

I liked the calls, that first year, which began, "So here's what happened," or "Can you help me edit this paper?," because they meant we were still connected. I liked finding an e-mail during my lunch period at school. The only disadvantage to all this easy contact? The phone might ring in the middle of the night, when it's not going to be good, and you're jolted from a sound sleep because your child is sick, or has broken out into a mysterious rash after sleeping in a friend's bed, or has blown a tire on the freeway, coming home from a dance practice at eleven at night. In that last case, we told her we loved her, we helped her find the phone number for the Automobile Club—and we offered to track down the nearest all-night pharmacy or emergency room, if she needed them. She didn't, but she felt much better when we were done talking. Hummie and me? We had the rest of the night to work on calming ourselves down—trying to focus not on the crisis but on how much worse it would have been in the days before cell phones.

Rule Number Four: *It's not the end. It's just different.*

Closing the door on Sarah's dorm room, after the last container had been wedged neatly under the bed, was one of the hardest things I've ever done: She was always going to be my daughter, but at that moment it didn't feel that way. I couldn't help but think of earlier times when I felt that my relationship to Sarah was about to change. The first time was when I was pregnant with my second child, and I had to think about how to create a family of four while making sure that each girl got the individual attention she needed. The second time was when Sarah started preschool, and suddenly there were other adults and other children who would have as much influence on her as her father and I had for the first four years of her life. Leaving her at college, her freshman year, felt too much like the end of the story, and I remember feeling angry. It was as though I had just realized that I only got to have her for eighteen years, at which point I had to hand her over to the outside world. Damn it. Why hadn't anyone mentioned that to me on the day she was born?

As she finishes up her junior year—and we get ready to send Jessi off—I know that the story continues. We heard all about her wonderful semester abroad, in Spain; we got calls and e-mails as she traveled to Morocco, Rome, and Brussels. It was one great vicarious travelogue—okay, except the part where an immigration official suggested that Sarah and her traveling companion lacked the proper paperwork, and they were left to figure out whether they were really in trouble or whether it might be appropriate to offer a small cash incentive to let them go. We got that phone call as well as the fun ones, and in both cases, we were reassured. She liked us and still occasionally needed us, even if she was an ocean away. Life was the same as it always had been, except that it wasn't.

Rule Number Five: Never forget where you came from.

One thing about having a semi-empty nest, with Sarah gone and Jessi on the brink, is that I have had time to think more about my own parents, and about my departure a lifetime ago.

My mother didn't drive, and my father's fear of big-city driving made maps about as useful to him as the Rosetta Stone. They never came to visit me at college, even though I was living a mere ninety minutes from where I grew up. As for calling, that was in the days of long-distance rates that got cheaper at night, so the only time I could call home, if I called home at all, was late at night when I preferred to be out with my friends. When I left home, I could have been living in Siberia, as far as my parents' ability to communicate with me was concerned. The only conversation I can remember is the time I called my mom to inquire about her medical history, because I was about to start taking the Pill.

I was so indifferent to what they went through; I put all my energy into separating myself as far as possible, both physically and emotionally. After all, I'd been working since I was sixteen, I'd paid for my own education, and I'd never asked them for any help—in part because I knew they couldn't afford it. The awful truth is that I was embarrassed by them, by their lack of money and their unsophisticated lives, by the fact that they had few friends and little social life.

It wasn't until I became a parent myself that my roots began to matter to me—and my parents' struggles to fit into an alien world became a source of pride, not shame. The traditions, foods, and family stories of my childhood took on a new importance, as something to celebrate and share with my own daughters.

Having a Lebanese mother and a Jewish father is at the core of who Sarah is, and she wears her United Nations heritage like a good piece of vintage clothing. She feels an instant kinship with other Lebanese kids, and she calls me to ask how to make a particular Lebanese dish to contribute at her campus Thanksgiving. I'm beginning to think that her Lebanese heritage may have made a genetic contribution to her affinity for belly dancing—but in any case, her leaving, in a strange way, has helped to tie the family together.

I am luckier than my parents ever were. Sarah lives two and a half hours away by plane, but Hummie and I can fly down to Southern California for parents' weekend, or to help Sarah celebrate her birthday. We have more and cheaper ways to stay in touch than I ever could have imagined when I was in college. I would like to think I've learned something from my good fortune. I can't change the way I left the nest, but I have tried to be a better member of the sandwich generation. My parents moved across the country to be closer to us; my mother lives nearby now, and my dad was here for five years before he died. I did my best to give them a chance to be doting grandparents, to attend dance recitals and birthday dinners and holidays with our family, to bring all of us back together even as Sarah and

Jessi prepare for whatever their futures hold. I am my mother's caretaker now, just as the girls no longer need as much of that kind of help from Hummie and me. The roads branch out in all kinds of unexpected directions, and at the same time they all lead back to home.

The Last Summer

Hilary Mills

I watched him in the surf as I had for so many summers past. His body moved easily now with the slow, strong undulations of the waves, as if he was in his own element. Graceful, fearless. I felt a quiet triumph that he had mastered the vicissitudes of the sea; yet buried in that triumph was the devastating awareness that he no longer needed me to be there watching.

Miles was leaving for college in the fall. The whole previous year I tried to prepare for the moment, inadvertently stepping outside of daily life to silently embrace his presence, like a small prayer of thanks, knowing that soon he would be gone, his room would be dark, and some fullness or happiness would go with him. On Saturday nights when the fire and candles were lit, a good dinner cooking on the big Garland stove, music and wine flowing, our little family cozy and warm together,

I would imagine him absent, feel a sudden hollowness, and hold on harder to that transient moment of happiness. Since he is an only child, we had been very close—but as his departure loomed, that final summer, I began to sense more than just the normal sadness of a parent over losing a child. He would be only seven hours away, at Bates College, in Maine. Still, there was some darker apprehension about his leaving that I could not then name, something deep and slightly panic-inducing. I felt like I was teetering on the precipice of an abyss. And perhaps it was my son's uncanny awareness of this sudden fear in me which caused his unexpected coldness that last summer.

The summer began with a new Labrador puppy, picked up just after high school graduation and brought to our summer home in Sag Harbor, Long Island. My husband, Bob, thought I should have something to nurture once our son left, but the timing was wrong. Coping with a needy new baby as Miles's childhood was ending did a disservice to the puppy, my son, and me. My husband's imagined plan of son and puppy bonding and playing together all summer, perhaps cementing his emotional link to home, never materialized. Miles had loved our first dog, which we got when he was eleven, but that affection was now replaced by a cool, bemused detachment as he watched me clean up one more puddle of pee by myself before he headed out the door. The only bonding that went on was between me and the puppy, on the barricaded front porch where we sat imprisoned for most of the summer, Miles off somewhere, and Bob in the city all week, at work.

My husband was sad, certainly, about Miles's imminent departure, but he felt none of my darker anxiety, and Miles's estrangement rarely extended to him that summer—perhaps because their bond had always been more reserved, less emotionally charged than Miles's and mine. When he arrived on weekends to find son and wife at odds, his alliances necessarily shifted from one to the other as he tried to forge some peace, and I felt deserted when he abandoned my side. Add to this emotional familial stew my dying eighty-five-year-old father and a needy, deteriorating stepmother who lived in the next town. Miles often remarked how stressed out I was that summer, that I wasn't a "chill" person, and noted sardonically how often my second glass of wine led to the third.

I don't think any parent is ever ready for a child's criticism when it comes, when that tender bond of unconditional love suddenly grows barbed. Intellectually I knew it had to come for him to be able to separate, but the emotional pain was more piercing that summer than I expected. Maybe it was more hurtful because it was so late in coming. Miles had gone through four years of high school with none of the fabled delinquency, no attitude, just a loving, charming, engaging boy who actually liked to be with his parents, even on weekends in the country. Now, suddenly, here was attitude in spades. I began to see myself through his judgmental eyes until I, too, became critical of that stressed-out woman who was not chill about being left alone with her peeing, barking puppy; was not chill about her son suddenly staying out till three or four in the morning without calling; was not chill about eating alone at the last minute after having bought and prepared dinner for two; was not chill about making movie plans together only to have them canceled just before we were to go. The affectionate togetherness of our lives was jettisoned so abruptly that I felt constantly off balance, and his mocking disdain left me emotionally gutted. So much for the wise, all-seeing mother who tried to help the separation along.

A friend of mine says she does not believe in nostalgia when it comes to her children because she does not like to look back with longing, or to romanticize the past. But that last summer was full of memories of all the previous summers, when Miles and I filled our days together before his father joined us on the weekends. The sweetness of those moments now seemed like salt on my heart, but as his childhood fled I could not stop playing them back. So much of our time was in nature, walking myriad trails and beaches with our previous dog. When Miles was around ten or eleven he liked to hold my hand as we walked, and worried he was too smitten, I would urge him to walk independently, swinging his arms for exercise. Now I wished I had held his hand for as long as he wanted.

On many nights we raced back from a movie or dinner to watch the sun set at exactly 8:00 P.M. at Long Beach in Sag Harbor, cuddled together as the crimson ball dropped off the edge of the world, a fiery benediction to another day. There was no other religion in his life, and I could not help but smile when I heard the daughter of a friend remark she had never met any boy so ardent about the beauty of a sunset.

It was on one of these outings, when he was about seven or eight, that he turned to me and asked, "Why do you take such good care of me when you know I am going to leave you someday?" I don't know how he managed to juxtapose the future against the present at that age, or if even then he felt some anxiety about the intensity of my mothering, but I was startled by his prescience. I answered something about getting him ready for life, about building a loving base that would give him the confidence to weather whatever he might have to face in life later on.

IT IS NOW many years after that question and four years after that last summer, enough time for me to see more clearly why I took such good care of my son, and why I felt such a deep dread at the thought of his absence. My close mothering of Miles allowed me to give to him—and also to give back to myself—what I had severely missed as a child: a warm, feeding, hugging, kissing, tactile, and enveloping sense of nurturing mother love. My mother was a good, intelligent woman and loved me in her own distant way, but she suffered from severe postpartum depression (she later told me), as well as depression over a philandering husband, my father, who left her by the time I was ten. She was an anomaly in the pre–Betty Friedan 1950s, a woman who preferred an engaging job to domesticity, first as a *Life* researcher, then as a founding editor of *American Heritage* magazine. Her remoteness, I know now, had less to do with her work than with some emotional reticence she could not overcome, and it would have been the same if she had stayed at home—but all I knew as a child was that my mother was not around like other girls' mothers, and that I was missing her, somehow.

When Miles was born, I was surprised at the almost primitive ferocity of my instinct to nurture him, as though I could repair my own childhood in the way that I mothered him. This involved not just physical and emotional affection, but the entire feathering of the nest: fires in the hearth, candles on the table, cozy pillows and down comforters, warm lighting, comfort foods like beef stew and chicken with dumplings. No wonder I had unconsciously dreaded his absence that last summer: It was not just sadness over losing my beloved young companion; I feared I was losing his warm insulation against an existential chill I had long kept at bay.

AS MILES HEADED out for parties that last summer, or on dates, or to movies with friends—or as he stayed up all night reading a new author, or talked endlessly about philosophy or politics—I saw that he was so ready to go, was so primed for life, was so interested in and intellectually excited by everything beyond the boundaries of home. I envied his confident exuberance, the passion he had for ideas and the world, but I now sensed, in stark contrast, a sudden absence of it in myself. It was as if all the life in the room were suddenly sucked out with him as he went out the door. He had been the focus of my maternal and creative energies for so long that his leaving left a vacuum in me that I was not wholly prepared for.

I felt my husband's weekday absence more acutely, as well. When Bob finally arrived on the weekends, I would fall into his proverbial arms, desperate for engaging conversation, any comforting, distracting buffer from the alarm I was beginning to feel over my creative wasteland.

For if mothering had in some way helped to repair my childhood, it had also been the source of a creativity far deeper and more compelling than what I was doing in my work life. I had written a literary biography before my son was born, and was under contract for another when he was born—but for me, the visceral needs of being a mother were more powerful than I had anticipated and were in stark conflict with the cerebral demands of a literary biography. (I still remember trying to interview Ring Lardner Jr. for my Lillian Hellman biography when copious amounts of breast milk began to express through my beige silk blouse; not good for concentration.) After a year of trying to manage the book and the baby, I paid back the advance. I kept my hand in by writing an unsuccessful novel and some magazine profiles, but nothing seemed as deeply meaningful then as mothering, and somehow my own ambition morphed into ambition for my son. Now that Miles was leaving, I had to find another way to sustain myself, and I had no idea what it might be. As much as I like to think I was being stalwart in letting my child go, I sense now that his cruelty must have been in direct proportion to my neediness.

On a morning in late August, a week before college officially began, Miles left for a freshman class camping trip. We were not even driving him to school to help set up his room; there would be no gradual detox for his father and for me. Instead, we hurriedly gathered before dawn in the kitchen to feed him a quick breakfast and help pack the final gear in his Jeep. Out in the dark driveway his father embraced him, and then I, in my bathrobe, gave him a tight hug, smiling bravely at his cool, bemused expression. I held on fast to his father as Miles pulled out of the driveway; and in that eerie morning twilight, the tears finally came as I felt my motherhood and his childhood ending their long run together.

Back in the kitchen, Bob and I sat in a state of shock, our son's warm coffee mug evidence that he had just been there—as he had been most mornings for the past eighteen years—and now he was not. His father wiped away his own tears, and I loved him more, then, for I knew his loss was as huge as mine, and I knew we would have each other to carry us through this transition in our lives. Perhaps it was that sense of connection to each other on our bleakest day that makes me think of the moment as a beginning rather than an end.

I still do not know how I made it through that day, especially since I had accepted a lunch date with a group of prominent political and literary women. This might have been a good distraction if our hostess had not insisted that we go around the table and talk about our most recent accomplishments. Barely able to speak, my eyes still stinging with tears—and no recent accomplishments other than losing my son—I managed to blurt out something about the pain of him leaving, and that I might write a book about the end of motherhood.

An older writer, a woman I did not know, leaned across the table.

"Motherhood never ends," she said.

THAT FIRST THANKSGIVING vacation, Miles was home again. I anticipated his arrival with a muddle of emotions: giddy joy that he would be part of us again, wariness that he would not want to be, that I should not expect it, that I should quell my hopes. Still, I had butterflies in my stomach as his father and I drove to Islip airport on Long Island to pick him up from his flight down from Maine. As he walked through the gate, there was a surreal moment after these months apart: I saw what had been (in my mind's eye) my little blond boy transformed into a tall, dark, handsome young man—not exactly a stranger, but a young man with his own secrets, his own life. His shock of tangled brown hair reached his shoulders. He was wearing sandals with no socks in November, his guitar was slung over his shoulder, and he held a rolled cigarette in his hand. He made me think back to my own radical college days in the 1960s, and with that recognition came a surprising new empathy for his independence.

His hug, his smile was again the old warm, engaging Miles. The cold disdain was gone, and his evident happiness at being with us felt like he had draped a warm blanket over my shoulders. On the drive home, he talked nonstop about his four roommates and their respective personalities (as well as their varying levels of cleanliness), the courses he was taking, which teachers he liked or did not. Once home his empty room was again filled with light and music. Dirty clothes filled the hamper and lay like discarded skins across his floor. His instant, casual reversion to old habits startled me after three long months, and I slowly began to see that this would be a new dance for the three of us. He might bolt one day, and revert to his old self the next. Bob and I would have to follow his lead if we wanted to help guide him across the dance floor toward his future.

———

MILES IS A senior now. Each time he leaves home, the hollow ache returns, but in briefer increments. That first year, the stress of his absence made me literally sick: Though I am rarely ill, I came down with an upper respiratory infection that refused to quit, as if my body were physically mourning his loss in deep bronchial bays. In the spring my psyche struck back. I no longer wanted to walk by his empty room in New York as though it were a black hole. In a marathon burst of energy and optimism (and, admittedly, opportunism, given the size of New York City apartments), I turned his room into my "office," moving my computer from the bedroom to his old homework desk and reestablishing my writing space—just as, eighteen years before, I had done exactly the reverse to set up his nursery. His pictures are still on the bulletin board, his books are still on the bookshelves, but while he is gone the room is my own. It has become the wellspring of a new creative life, one intent on writing from as deep a place as mothering once was (except for when Miles is home and I cannot get access to my computer, only to him). For now that creative life involves writing memoir instead of biography or profiles, haltingly finding my own voice as I chisel my own experience. The long dog walks in the country are solitary now, or with friends, and instead of communing with my son I commune with all of nature, which brings a different, if no less expansive, kind of happiness. And of course there are always the fires in the hearth, the stews or roast chickens in the oven, the talks with my husband—with perhaps a few more dinner parties, movies, and good restaurants thrown in.

TALKING TO A friend recently, I said "postpartum" when I meant "empty nest." At first I thought I must have unconsciously meant I had to push my son into the world, but in fact I meant that his leaving had been a double birth, or rebirth, for both of us. In four years he has evolved from a biologist to a historian to an anthropologist fascinated by the inner lives of our cities. He is haltingly finding the mysteries of a new adulthood independent of his mother—and I am haltingly finding the mysteries of a new selfhood independent of my son.

My Cart

Harvey Molotch

I began my regular push down the aisle, once again gathering up thoughts and strategies for how I would do the grocery run. But this time was different—after about fifteen years of shopping for a family, I was for the first time in it alone. My son had just gone off for a life of Colorado snowboarding and maybe (fingers crossed) some college. My daughter married early and preceded him out the door. The departures took place in a flux of small anxieties, arrangements, and detail. My nest may have been about to empty, but my mind—in part because of it—had been full of specifics.

And then somewhere in that brightly lit aisle, like the proverbial flash-bam alakazam of the 1950s love song, it hit. I was heading toward some long enshrined staple (Heinz ketchup perhaps) when I realized that there was no reason for it. I didn't use ketchup. Not only were the kids not living under my roof, they were no longer the center of my moves. They would not be dictating my choice of flavor and brand, or setting off my search for a new surprise, a personal best for me to deliver as their delight. The grocery-shopping cart was where my rubber hit the road, the place where I realized that life had changed.

I stood for a moment, stymied with mild wonder: Which aisles do I now walk? What jars do I check out? Into which freezers do I dip my hand? Other than for my mild-mannered and undemanding domestic partner—who was out of town most of the year on business anyway—I could buy anything I wanted. More important, I could buy nothing at all. I didn't even have to be there. I felt the luxury of ennui.

A lot had been riding on those wheels. The market aisle was not just where I got groceries, but where I lived life—sometimes, like on weekends, with the kids right with me, especially when they were little. We negotiated on-the-spot agreements. Okay on chocolate milk, but no on Tootsie Pops. We endured conflict. Coke will not happen, I announced, "because I said so." We engaged in joint operations. The younger one scouted for the graham crackers, sighted the berry juice, and made other suggestions from his rear-facing seat above the basket. I allowed the elder to drift farther afield, lifting up the Aunt Jemima pancake mix that had only recently come within her reach.

Math happened. It was from his chrome-wire perch that my four-year-old advised which container, by his calculation, provided the most detergent for the dollar. I did not notice this firsthand. I was too preoccupied to really take note, but my friend Betty, shopping nearby, told me she had witnessed his counsel from just behind us and it was "adorable."

But shopping was serious business. As a single father—my wife had died when the children were ages two and five—I was the market player, and from the moment my body weight tripped off the entry doors, I rolled out the mental maps and kinetic strategies. In addition to our weekend family outing, I shopped on my way home from work; I can still feel the fatigue. I used to tell people that if my life were a soap opera, it would be *Search for a Nap.* There were other places I would rather have been at cocktail hour than under the supermarket fluorescents. My Vons, a standard issue edition of the California chain, burnished the light headache that often came my way at sundown.

Not only was there no lay-down ahead, I would be facing a lot of hubbub as I unloaded the grocery bags—the kids' reports on what went right and wrong, and some possible wrangling between them. I had to get dinner on the table. Depending on who was taking what class, I might help with homework. Or with the science fair project, an event that demanded its own items from Vons, in one case cellophane wrap that was a base material for the project: Do Insects See Color?

Buying food means making lives, and of course I wanted to do the moral and nutritional right thing. But there was also the imperative of what they wanted—the right stuff, exactly the right stuff. Each era generated its own specifics. During the elementary years, peanut butter ruled. But not just any peanut butter. It had to be Skippy crunchy. No, the second child protested, make it smooth like Peter Pan. For a while, they favored smooth peanut butter already mixed in with the jelly—as provided by Smucker's. I eventually ruled in favor of Laura Scudder's (no preservatives) with the oil right on top that you mixed back in with a stiff knife. I did not want them to get cancer.

Breakfast cereal started with Cheerios, an early choice of my own, and then moved on to Honey-Nut Cheerios that would carry us through junior high. Cheese was to be Monterey Jack and certainly never Swiss; granola bars (flavor unknown) were the ones that come in green packets. Fruit roll-ups were grape or cherry, strawberry was out. Fish was never an option, because my daughter ate no fish, never and no way. I knew exactly where the paper plates with daisies were, for her special occasions, and just how high they shelved the orange juice with pulp.

The illusion of an orderly universe was of importance to me, putting me at risk when things went off course. My supermarket would from time to time make a change, and I did not always handle it well. What is this? What the *fuck* is this? The favored Chocodiles, which are chocolate-covered Twinkies shaped like crocodiles, are NOT HERE. Who moved my Chocodiles? Where's the guy? Do I take my cart in search of the guy? He could be on the wrong side of a clog of box openings that I won't be able to roll through. Maybe I'll make better time by leaving the cart. But if I leave the cart, I may have trouble finding it again.

THE DISORIENTATION PROBLEM can start lower down the food chain. The potpie company changed its labels, and so what was once a frozen field of icy blue became all tan. A landmark vanished and I had to cope. All hell broke lose when Vons took over the beauty spa next door to enlarge the bakery goods and deli, setting off a domino effect that left only the perimeter refrigeration sections standing as they were. Still, one adjusts, even while processing orders from a ten-year-old for whom wheat tortillas have become inedible, so make them corn.

Sometimes I would plan to get out quick by using the express lane—twelve items or less. But having a full nest makes it hard to stay within limits, and there I am with thirteen. Do my "twin packs" count as one item or two? If I have to, what do I sacrifice? I must return home with key elements for the s'mores I promised: graham crackers, marshmallows, and chocolate. We are out of white milk. I think it's nature's perfect food, so it has to be in the basket. The chicken breasts with skin as requested; they are tonight's dinner base. I really need the cantaloupe to make a nourishing dessert that will be karma balance for the Chocodiles. Then what about the ak-mak crackers and cream cheese that I enjoy. Give them up? What am I—chopped liver? They stay and, whaddaya know, the checker lets me through. Sweet victory.

TIME PASSES, AND the hormones of teenage years leave marks on the grocery list. After embracing dietary principles somehow linked to what he learned about the Navajo in his progressive middle school, my son went vegan, which eliminated chicken, Hebrew National salamis, presliced Hormel turkey, and the franks and baked beans I would mix together in the pot to much appreciation. I had to scout the tofu region—aisle spaces I once happily sped past like the pet food and white bread zones.

Eighteen months later, nutritional whiplash: My son reappraised the indigenous wisdom of the school headmaster, deciding he was full of shit. He came out as a severe dude, taking up red meat with a vengeance. He wanted it thick and he wanted it rare. This coincided with the purchase of his first vehicle, a secondhand pickup truck with a windshield NRA sticker, something he was careful to retain.

My daughter, at fifteen, took up with a homeless boy I shall call Carlos. There were major grocery implications to this relationship. It turned out she was provisioning not only Carlos but also Carlos's extended kin group from our kitchen cabinets. Cans of tuna came in and cans of tuna went out. Lots of other stuff, too. I knew I was in the market more frequently but didn't consider shrinkage as a factor.

Eventually, I got wind of it when my daughter and I had a high-noon about different Carlos-related events. Like the fact that he had been, it turned out, living in one of our closets. Or that he caused her to miss the bus for a school camping trip that was to initiate her enrollment at a private school I could barely afford. She nailed me with my hypocrisy: I talked the talk of support for the poor, and for civil rights, but I didn't walk the walk and feed Carlos and his family. All I could think of during the accusations was that I didn't even know what they liked. All those grocery trips for people I hadn't met. I was buying Crinkle Crisps for people who, for all I know, wanted something different.

A FRIEND ONCE gave me a T-shirt that said THIS IS NO ORDINARY HOUSEWIFE YOU'RE DEALING WITH. I don't recall ever actually wearing it, but it might have served me well at the checkout. It was unusual, back when my kids were growing up, for a man to present so large a payload at the cash register. I often filled the top basket completely and had to stuff bulky things like toilet paper rolls and paper napkins on the bottom shelf. At holiday time, I'd be a two-carter, awkwardly rolling both into the cashier lane.

And the content was off. People expected men to check out with beer and some TV dinners, maybe also dog food and briquettes. I had stuff for kids (chewy this and chewy that). When my daughter began to menstruate, I had Tampax.

The checkers at Vons, mostly women, thought I was great. "I wish my husband would do that for me," they might say and comment appreciatively on my wise choices: the low-fats and the extra virgin olive oil. They saw I had mastery of cart management. As I shopped, I rearranged to build my base with cheese bricks, maple syrup, and canned goods, then midlevels of apples, half-and-half, and celery. When I appeared at the checkout, it was with eggs, tomatoes, and bananas on top. If a checker squinted to find the code on the lettuce, I'd say, "That's Romaine." On occasion they said, "Your wife is sure lucky."

I dreaded these interchanges. It was not just the gay coming-out problem, not just that my partner is a man and that, yes, there are kids even so. There is more. My life has been touched by tragedy—our car crash in Greece in which my wife died, my hospitalization and surgeries. How do you get over that, and how do you help your small children get over that? I didn't have a recovery scenario, but Glenn came along about a year later, and his presence got me through my post-traumatic syndrome. The mournful widower or the disco fantasist; I made my peace with both and got on with my life. Hardly where a checker wants to go when making chat with a regular.

I had choices. I could nod pleasantly. I could strike out for gay liberation and make a pronouncement with pride. I could push the reality envelope by telling of my wife's death but let them know, almost friend to almost friend, that things are really okay now. Or I could just express my sentiment for paper over plastic and let it go at that. What should I reveal, just how much, in just which way, and how often? Once per checker? Once per month? I kept quiet or, once or twice, tried to mutter—not tragically but not happily either, "I don't have a wife."

There are old comedy routines, Woody Allen's comes to mind, about the guy trying to buy porn or condoms with minimal notice in the store. But shopping is always a series of on-the-spot revelations. We've all seen stories in line—the alone people buying single portions, poor folks pulling out food stamps, an obese person with whipped cream and a stash of Oreos. When the nest empties, the exhibit—whatever it was before—changes. In the case of my goods, it meant having less to declare.

BUT FULLER DISCLOSURE: More was coming. Just after my kids left home, my partner gained two children of his own.

They are twins, now twelve years old, who live in Vancouver with his sister and her partner, for whom he was the sperm donor (explain that one at the checkout). And my two have grown the group as well: My daughter has two children of her own, and my son—the doctorate in snow hydrology (!)—married a young woman in the movie business.

When they all come to visit, I'm the supermarket basket champion. And as grandparents often report, it's much more relaxed than the first time around. They like what I buy, maybe just because it's me who buys it. History has also changed things: The checkers are more ready for my story. They don't think it's so odd or so noble; there's less reason for them to ask or for me to tell.

Mostly it's just the two of us at home, though, and I get in and out of the market with less work, but no hope of delivering cheap thrills with good condiments either. Now pushing through my sixties, I'm looking for high fiber, not the makings of s'mores. I reach the scanner with a cart only half-empty. Or is it half-full? Usually, I just grab a basket at the door; I don't need a cart at all.

Time Traveler

Marian Sandmaier

When our daughter, Darrah, left for college three years ago, I knew only that I would miss her. I imagined a certain hollowness and stillness coming over our house, a low-grade pall that I would fight with more activity—writing more articles, seeing more friends, enlarging our perennial garden, traveling. I've done those things and a few others, but I've come to understand that they're only the cover story for a much stranger, and totally unanticipated, change. After Darrah left, a particular engine of self began to rumble and move—the one that travels through time. I find that I feel both much younger and distinctly older than I did before, and in ways I never could have predicted.

AT FIRST, NOT much seemed to happen at all. Our only child was gone, and my husband, Dan, and I found ourselves alone together in our comfy old house and overgrown yard. I missed my daughter, keenly, but other than that, I went about business as usual.

Looking back, I think that this abrupt entry into a new life stage was like a cage door swinging open for a zoo animal: I didn't immediately realize that I was free. Lest that seem too strong a statement, let me explain. I love being Darrah's mother. She is an exuberant presence, full of warmth and wackiness and sudden, stunning insights about people and life. Nonetheless, a few weeks after Darrah left, I began to experience an odd sense of lightness. It was as though springtime had entered my brain and body. I felt myself taking bigger, looser strides and standing a little taller, like a plant reaching up toward the sun. This sense of sprouting felt familiar, but it took me a little while to place it. It was the bodily experience of youth.

When I say "youth," I'm not talking about the hormone-buzzed, bouncing-off-walls state of adolescence. I'm referring to feeling young in the specific way I did as an adult in my twenties and early thirties, before becoming a mother. Back then, I was far from blissful, but I had the relative luxury of obsessing about just one person—me. By the time I'd hugged Darrah good-bye in the parking lot of her freshman dorm, my brain had spent some 18.5 years reeling with worries, plans, second guesses, and unanswerable questions about the growth and development of another human being. I loved Darrah desperately, yet I did not have the power to guarantee her happiness or well-being.

During those child-raising years, my running internal monologue ranged from health concerns (how upset should I be about the headaches she's been complaining about, even though her pediatrician said they were "probably nothing"; should I take her to a neurologist anyway just to be sure, or am I being totally neurotic?) to matters of character (what does it mean that she refuses to clean her room, and should I make her so she'll grow up responsible, or should I let it go because it's really all about me, a certifiable neat freak?). Then there were the run-of-the-mill terrors about life and death: How will she learn to drive without smashing herself to bits, and how much booze might she drink at that party tonight? Should I talk to her about it (again) or shut up and trust her good judgment— and by the way, where is Darrah right now?

Within weeks of her departure, all of this internal hand-wringing simply fell away. I was perfectly willing to continue worrying about my daughter, but since I no longer knew, or could even guess, what she was doing on an hour-to-hour basis, I had no focus for my fretting. So I gave it up. I think that's what the lightness was about: I'd begun to recover a space in my being that was essentially empty. Not empty as in lacking, but as in free.

With this new sense of buoyancy came another, even more delicious experience—I began to feel sexy again. It had been a long time. In the months following Darrah's birth, I'd begun to wear a bleak assortment of baggy T-shirts and sweatpants, somehow convinced that my life as an attractive, sensual woman had ended. I was Mother, and a squishy bodied, exhausted one at that. Desperate to reclaim some shred of allure,

I got my hair permed. The results were scary: I looked as though I'd been electrocuted. In my most abject act of self-negation that first year, I went to the lingerie section of the local department store to buy a stack of "sensible" panties—the white cotton variety that come all the way up to the waist. I remember standing in line to buy them and actually having this thought: "It's over."

As Darrah grew into toddlerhood, I lost weight and discovered an activity I loved—jazz dancing—so the sense of matronliness began to fade. Then, when she hit high school, it returned in force. In the presence of Darrah and her girlfriends, dressed in their navel-baring micro-tees and lit up with the incandescent energy of early adolescence, I felt older and more faded than ever. The sense of "good-bye to all that" was attended by a kind of muted, shrouded grief. I didn't talk to anyone about these feelings because I believed that they were somehow shameful. Instead, I tried tough love on myself. You're middle-aged! I'd rail inwardly. Get over it!

Then, in the midst of Darrah's freshman year of college, something started to shift. I began to look in the mirror and see the woman who was actually reflected there. She was middle-aged, for sure. But still quite slim—maybe even shapely. One evening, at a friend's urging, I borrowed her slinky black skirt, topped it with a deep-necked new tank top, and walked into a dinner party. Heads turned; I heard a couple of whistles and "whoas!" I was honestly shocked. Then delighted. I hadn't realized how much I'd been hiding.

I began to buy clothes in brighter colors, corals and plums and aquas, instead of the basic black that I'd convinced myself was sophisticated but was actually another way to make myself invisible. I weeded out my flowing shirts and pleated slacks and replaced them with more youthful styles—no tiny tees or low-rider jeans, but clothing that at least suggested that I had a body underneath. I reclaimed sexy underwear. I began to flirt with my husband again. Let's just say he liked it.

Dan is a major player in this tale of recovered youthfulness. He and I have been together practically forever—thirty-five-plus years—which meant we had a lot of time together before Darrah entered the picture. We started out in a tiny third-floor studio apartment in West Philadelphia, close enough to the University of Pennsylvania campus to sample its endless roster of delights—foreign films, folk music concerts, and fringy art shows, along with the neighborhood's all-night diners, dance bars, and vast array of ethnic restaurants. We took the train to New York on weekends (five dollars round-trip); we traveled to Europe on the cheap in the summer. The nature of the careers we ultimately chose—freelance writing and college teaching—allowed us to continue this semi-spontaneous lifestyle for an absurdly long period of time, so long that it began to seem normal.

Once Darrah was born, of course, everything changed. But then she grew up, started leafing through college catalogs, and one day was gone. After a brief period of stasis, when Dan and I acted out our familiar, homebound routines like a couple of slightly battered windup toys, a day came when we more or less stared at each other and said: Damn, we can do whatever we want! It was a kind of rubber-band moment, where we simply let go and snapped back to our former shape.

Okay, so maybe it wasn't quite that easy. There was the matter of making regular tuition payments, keeping up a century-old house, and other distinctly un-youthful tasks. But there has been a palpable loosening up of unspoken rules. When Darrah lived at home, for example, we regularly ate dinner by 6 P.M. so she'd have sufficient time afterward to do her homework and get ready for bed. Now we eat dinner whenever we feel like it, or not at all, and we're less conscientious about making meals that represent all the major food groups. We've been known to have milk shakes for dinner, or Doritos topped with melted cheese and jalapeño peppers. Period. No side salad, no redemptive plate of carrot sticks. We don't usually eat so foolishly, but I find it wonderful to know that we can.

We were somewhat slower to realize that while Darrah was safely tucked away at college, we could travel again. Not just a cautious overnight to Washington, D.C., or New York, which we'd done several times during her high school years, but big-time, faraway travel. Last spring, toward the end of Darrah's sophomore year, we took off for Amsterdam. There was a point in our planning process when I almost backed out—it was the moment I realized that the travel week that worked best for us collided with the date of Darrah's return home for the summer. "How can we let her return to an empty house?" I fumed. Dan reminded me that Darrah was now twenty years old, a highly responsible sort, and would be within shouting distance of several full-fledged adults whom she could call on for help or a hot meal. It was okay for us to go out and play.

So we did. For seven glorious days, we wandered the streets, canals, cafés, and museums of Amsterdam with absolutely nothing to do but drink in the moment—the slant of sun on a seventeenth-century church spire, or the sight of houseboats festooned with masses of flowers, bobbing in the canals like floating gardens. We ate Dutch potato pancakes with strong coffee for lunch and listened to gypsy music by night. We clambered up a windmill and cruised a huge, rambunctious street market, stopping at a stall to sample warm, homemade crepes drenched in *stroop* (Dutch caramelized sugar syrup). Each morning, we woke up with just one thing on our minds: How shall we please ourselves today?

Of course, the whole point of a vacation is to "vacate" oneself from the rigors of daily life. Holidays have to end, and soon enough we were back in our house that needed work and a yard that needed trimming (with a machete, by now), bills that needed paying, and prescriptions that needed refilling. This might be a good moment to bring up the other side of my post-child-rearing experience—the side that feels older than ever before. I suppose it's fortunate that the youthful feelings arrived first—I don't know that I could have survived our only child's leave-taking and a slide into geezerhood at the same time. It's been harrowing enough as it is.

Take the prescriptions. We have lots of them. In fact, both Dan and I now have enough health issues that we've gone the route of weekly pill organizers. Dan's is red, mine is blue. They are positioned prominently on the kitchen counter, side by side, so we'll remember to take our meds on schedule. When Darrah comes home on breaks, we squirrel away the boxes in a corner so we can spare her what we call the "nursing home look." But when she's away at school they stand squarely, irrefutably, in the middle of the counter. I can dress up in a fabulous, shimmery outfit, go out to a dance party, and come home brimming with cool. But I come home to his-and-her pill organizers.

Darrah's absence has brought something else into bold relief—our attachment to certain routines. Without her youthful energy buzzing through the house, some of our longtime habits have deepened—calcified?—into codgerlike rituals. The one that most amazes and amuses Dan and me takes place after dinner, when we boil water for tea (herbal ginger for me, Earl Grey for Dan), amble into the living room with our steaming cups, put on a CD, and pick up our respective books (these days, usually from the library). We then commence what we call "parallel reading."

We talk some, but mostly we just sit together and read. It turns out to be a very satisfying and comforting way to spend an evening, and unless we have other plans, we enact this domestic ritual virtually every evening of the workweek. When Darrah comes home, we make some effort to appear busier and more spontaneous—but, truth to tell, we don't try very hard. Her absence has outed us to ourselves: We're parallel-reading freaks. Once in a while, one of us will notice the rutlike quality of this activity and say something to the effect of, "What have we come to?" Then we'll chuckle, sip some tea, and go back to our books.

The power of my child's absence, or presence, to shape my sense of self continues to catch me by surprise. As I write this, Darrah has just come home from college for the summer. Dan was out of town when she first arrived, so for several days she and I were a cozy twosome. One evening, she stayed out late with friends, returning home long after I'd gone to bed. The following morning, I sleepily entered the bathroom and stopped short. There, on the counter, stood an enormous bottle of hydrogen peroxide, two boxes of sterile pads, and a roll of adhesive tape.

My heart thudding, I rummaged through the wastebasket, where I found a blood-soaked bandage. "Oh my God," I whispered. I imagined my daughter's face slamming against a windshield. I ran to Darrah's closed bedroom door, about to fling it open and see for myself how serious the damage was, when some sliver of my rational brain kicked in and informed me that if my daughter had been seriously hurt, she would have awakened me.

That thought didn't stop me, however, from dashing out the front door to thoroughly inspect the car she'd driven the night before. There was no apparent damage. Coming back into the house, I heard a drowsy voice call out from the second floor: "Morning, Mom." Clumping heavily down the stairs, Darrah appeared in front of me, her right big toe swaddled in bandages and tape. She explained that she'd been walking outside in bare feet the evening before and had tripped and scraped up her toe. There was a little swelling, and it hurt some. "But I'm totally okay," she said.

I nodded. But my heart kept knocking for a while. Later, I would recognize the feeling that had seized me at the moment I'd seen that impromptu first aid kit. I'd experienced versions of it several times before—a few times, very late at night, when Darrah didn't call in as promised, when she was suffering some kind of medical problem that nobody could diagnose, or on the afternoon a plane had crashed right next to her elementary school and I'd heard the sound of the explosion at home, four blocks away.

There is no sense of "young" or "old" connected to those kinds of moments, no sense, even, of inhabiting a distinct personality. Boundaries collapse, the conscious mind shuts down. There remain only love, terror, and the raw rage to protect, a primal stew of self that, I believe, withstands all of the seismic shifts and smaller twists of life's evolving stages. We can't outgrow it, transform it, or transcend it. We're parents.

The Science of Ghost Hunting

Fabiola Santiago

Legend has it that a ghost haunts the Herlong Mansion bed-and-breakfast in the tiny town of Micanopy, near the University of Florida campus in Gainesville, and I could swear I felt her presence when my daughter and I were there. I imagined the ghost hovering near the white lace curtains, tugging at my covers, and then, like a sneaky child playing a prank, sliding under the door to roam the creaky halls and bother the other guests. It kept me up all night.

I had booked a room at the bed-and-breakfast for a couple of days of mother-daughter fun in my old college town before Erica, the last of my three daughters, began her freshman year at my alma mater. Instead, I got a sleepless night.

I reported this the next morning to Erica as we drove through the steamy, midsummer heat toward campus for her freshman orientation. "You slept right through it all," I said to her. "But I would check on you, wrap the covers tightly around you, and try to go back to sleep. I did this all night."

I was trying to justify my cranky mood. No reply. I glanced over to the passenger side—and saw that look of impatience I know so well.

"Mom, you never do mornings well," she finally said. "Just like me."

So I wasn't fooling her. I never could. We read each other like what we are—mirrors of one another. Erica is the uncanny reflection of my best and my worst. Our mother-daughter bond is as mushy as it gets, and our disagreements as high pitched and hurtful as a betrayal between lovers.

If I had done what I wanted to do that morning, I would have cried, long and hard. As much as I had expected it, our upcoming separation was turning out to be more difficult than I was willing to admit. My attempts to dress it up as a fun and adventurous transition weren't making it any smoother. One minute I was excited for her, proud of her admission to the top university in our state, but the next I wanted to turn the clock back, way back, so I could have another lifetime with Erica.

The flip-flop of emotions caught me off guard, for I had already done this twice, with Erica's two older sisters. Nature has a way of turning those once-adorable children into odious, messy teenagers, a nifty trick to make the letting go easier for those of us who bring them into the world and love them fiercely. But letting go of Erica—the daughter who once proudly wore a tiny T-shirt proclaiming in big, bold letters BRAT; the one nicknamed "The Diva" for all that attitude—was turning out to be the toughest of all transitions.

I should have been dancing my heart out: I had been waiting for this moment for a long, long time. True singlehood, total freedom, here I come. No more Erica putting the brakes on my wanderlust, cutting short my overseas adventures with a curt phone call: "Mom, when are you coming home? I miss you." No more Erica sizing up my dates, treating rudely those who had daughters with even the remotest possibility of becoming my stepdaughters. No more Erica setting curfews for me with her plans. Or threatening my dates, as she once did a colleague with whom I went to Peru: "If my mother comes back with even a broken nail, you will have me to deal with."

Certainly, there would be no more of my yelling "Naked mother in the kitchen!" when she unexpectedly burst into the house with her friends.

Without Erica in the house, with her six hours away from me, I could live out dreams deferred by motherhood: Spur-of-the-moment weekend trips in my convertible; a month in my favorite Latin American city, Buenos Aires, with my favorite party-hearty cousin. I would take French lessons, shutter up the house, buy a ticket to Paris with an open return, and search for the charming Frenchman who once showed me the way to the Great Sphinx of Tanis at the Louvre. I would write about my adventures. I would write the great Cuban-American novel, without interruptions at the height of inspiration. Surely, with Erica living it up at college, my cell phone would stop constantly ringing with requests for permission to do this and that. I could even have a man over without having to explain myself! On and on went my fantasies.

So—now that Liberation Day was here, and my nest was

truly, completely, finally empty—why couldn't I put on my dancing shoes?

Because I am Cuban, and we Cubans don't have empty nests.

Empty nest. *Nido vacio?* The term isn't even in our lexicon. In translation, it rings hollow, false, a too-literal interpretation of a foreign concept. Whoever heard a Cuban talk about a *nido vacio?* We are a tight (euphemism for oppressive), loving (overwhelming), caring (in-your-face), fun (name-the-dysfunction) tribe. Our children may go to college, even get married and have children of their own, but the residency rights remain.

"*Esta siempre es tu casa,*" my parents said after I got married at the end of my third year of college.

Always my house.

I took them up on it. When I finished school, became a journalist, and got a job at the *Miami Herald*, Tanya, our first daughter, was three months old. Her father, however, was a year away from his engineering degree. He stayed in school, and Tanya and I moved in with my mom, dad, and younger brother—into my old room, which hadn't been touched in the four years since I left home. The only new piece of furniture was Tanya's crib. I have never seen my parents happier than the day I moved back home.

After my divorce, in the early 1990s, I moved to Miami Beach, but I only lasted a year that far from my family. I moved back to our suburban neighborhood, and that's where I've remained despite recurring daydreams about moving to one of the trendy artist hubs in town.

So it is that, even though my brother and I have our own

homes, we've never quite left *mami* and *pipo*, or each other, for that matter. Our three houses are within a two-mile radius of each other. My Erica and my nephew, Sean, born only four months apart, went to school together. They started in the same kindergarten class and graduated together from the same high school. Nicole, eight, the youngest of our joint brood, spends all her after-school time at my parents' house. All our children did while they were growing up. They spent more time with the *abuelos* than with us.

And, even now, in my forties, I am still my parents' very own spoiled brat; I never left the nest completely. At seventy-seven, my mother, who quit work to take care of my children, still cooks dinner three nights a week for Erica and me, and she often calls on Saturday or Sunday to tempt me, "Fabi, I made your favorite . . ." At eighty-three, my father pots and plants my garden.

With our large brood—my daughters have added to the group one husband and two boyfriends, and my nephew, his girlfriend—there's always an excuse for a weekend family celebration and the accompanying feast. We mark every holiday, every birthday, and every wedding anniversary together. Notice I don't quantify, with "extended family." That's another foreign concept to us. Who ever heard of *la familia extendida*? Never heard it said in Spanish. To us, there is only one kind of family, and that includes the ex-husband and the best friends from Cuba.

And yet, there I was, driving my daughter to campus like so many other parents around the country, facing that most American of milestones—the empty nest—in spite of myself.

No wonder I was having trouble staying in touch with my own dreams. They were at war with my heritage, and at the moment, tradition was definitely winning.

As Erica joined the freshman class at orientation, I walked around the campus, conjuring memories of my own undergraduate years. I remembered the feeling of euphoria the day my parents left me here, Sweet Freedomland. They hadn't even made it to the south ramp of I-75 when I was on my way to the mall to buy the bikini my father had never let me wear when I lived in his house. Unencumbered by tradition, free to make decisions far from parental restrictions, I bought one with red and white stripes, like the American flag.

I DON'T KNOW why I thought it would be easy this time.

My firstborn, Tanya, my book-gobbling, happy-go-lucky child, declared her independence at eighteen by getting a tattoo. She was so afraid of how I might react that she told me about it in an e-mail. I did want to kill her, but the electronic letter gave me the space to rein myself in. Plus, it was so well written that it became another clue to the wonderful writer she would become. Then Tanya upped the stakes: She went off to live with her boyfriend. I screamed into the phone something about maturity not arriving through the exchange of bodily fluids nor the pain of a tattooing needle.

It got so bad between us that her father had to intervene, like a marriage counselor, to restore the peace. She came back home for too short a time, and then she got married. I had just bought the four-bedroom, two-story house of our dreams, but at least I got to host her wedding there, a Renaissance-style affair on a Halloween night, as unique and fun as the new, grown-up Tanya is. As the clock ticked solidly into her twenties, we found our way back to each other through our dual careers in journalism and our love of writing.

Next to leave was Marissa, the musical, sporty girl and the in-between child, who began college in Miami. The most quiet and private of the three, Marissa wasn't taking any chances sharing her plans to fly the coop. After a year at home, she announced that she was going away to a college in Jacksonville that had the computer program she wanted. Her employer, an electronics giant, was giving her a transfer to a better store there; plus, the North Florida city was home to her dad. I stewed plenty about her leaving Florida International University for a less academically rigorous college. I didn't move the needle one inch. Again, I was forced to accept, to support the chosen path.

That also has turned out well. At twenty-two, Marissa is already a homeowner. When she delivered the news it was a done deal: She'd bought a two-bedroom condo with her boyfriend, a hard worker carving a career in banking with his bilingual skills. They would make Jacksonville their home. All I could do was drive up the five hours, bring housewarming presents, and help her decorate.

On the outside, it looks like I am the perfect incarnation of motherhood, accepting, supportive, and always full of solid, useful advice for my daughters, who have grown into three fabulous women. Privately, I've mourned every step of their lost childhoods.

———

NOW IT WAS Erica's turn. That day in Gainesville, as I prepared to let go of one more daughter, one more time, I reached deep into my reservoir of "whatever is best for you" poses. As I walked through campus, I remembered the promise I made myself when my daughters were born: to walk alongside them, but to let them choose the path.

Then, one hour into her orientation, I got Erica's call.

"Mom, I have made a decision," she said.

There was a definition in her voice I had seldom heard before.

"I am not going to school here. I have nothing to do with these people, with this place. I am not going to live with strangers in these dorms. Coming here was your dream. It is not mine. I love my house, I love my room, I love my dog, my turtles, I love my grandparents, I love you. I don't want to leave home."

No amount of counseling by me to think it over, or by the school staff to simply defer her acceptance another semester if she was not yet ready, made any difference. Erica's mind was made up. She wanted to go to college in Miami. She would live at home.

A funny thing happens when you get your heart's most secret desire, especially when you didn't allow yourself the knowledge that, in fact, it *was* your secret desire: I got angry.

I was mad at Erica for what I thought was a hasty decision based on fear, or on wanting to be near her new boyfriend, or both. I was disappointed at what I thought was romanticizing a bad decision (a concept I know well). She, in turn, was mad at me for not gracefully—and gratefully—accepting her choice. We packed up our things at the old haunted bed-and-breakfast, cut our weekend short, and drove home in the most disconcerting silence of our lives. After we got home and she drove off in her car to celebrate the news with her friends, I finally had my long and hard cry.

As I write this, Erica and I have been living alone in our house, together, for a year.

By American standards, I have two-thirds of an almost-empty nest: She's so busy with school and her manager trainee job at a restaurant nearby that I hardly see her. But by Cuban standards, I am nowhere near being left alone, nor am I at the tail end of raising a family. After all, we all know grandchildren are on the horizon, and the add-ons to the family come with a family of their own. This is simply the middle of building my substantial share of La Familia. It's a useful thing, this living in two cultures: when I examine my life carefully, my reality has always been better than my dreams. Plan B has always been a better idea.

I started out dreaming of being a foreign correspondent, and grounded by family, I ended up reporting and writing, for almost three decades now, about one of the most fascinating cities in America, a world-class city in the making where more than half the population is foreign-born. Last year, I got to spend two unforgettable weeks in Italy with Tanya, and we're looking forward to traveling to Brazil next year. Marissa, the musician, has signed up for a tour of Vienna with Mom. Erica promises to have conquered her fear of flying by the time I am ready to explore Egypt.

I'm not so attached to my hip status anymore, and as I am not getting younger, that's a relief. I like staying home with Erica and her boyfriend, making them dinner and watching a movie. Once touted by Erica as "the best sandwich maker in the world" (euphemism for my mother can't/won't cook), I have now graduated to "the best salad maker in the world." With more time on my hands, I am on my way to greater culinary heights, even if I still can't stop multitasking while cooking and I burn the steaks. It's not a necessity. Truth be told, we both prefer the food at *abuela*'s house.

In October, when Erica was supposed to have been away at college, we lived through the onslaught of Hurricane Wilma, the two of us alone in our house. Actually, Erica slept through it all, as usual. I kept watch, restless as that night in Micanopy. For two days without power, the roads blocked by fallen trees and power lines, no gasoline at the pumps, we cooked our defrosting hamburgers and pizza on the barbecue grill. We played board games by candlelight. I beat her at Life and added to my memory box the pretty paper on which we tallied our scores. After my winning millions, she had written: "This game sucks!" Not a good loser, just like me.

And so goes our joint life, mine with "two-thirds of an empty nest," hers in the embrace of home and family.

"I will never leave you," she often says.

I know she will, and that's okay. I also know my house will always remain full of family, never truly an empty nest.

For the record, it was Erica who that haunting night in the Herlong Mansion was pulling at my covers in her sleep, keeping me awake with her little snores, jolting me into attention with a leg slung over my hip.

But as ghosts go, she's a keeper.

Who Knows Where the Time Goes

Fran Visco

Like so many women of my generation, I waited to
have a child. I was thirty-seven when I became pregnant, in my third marriage, on my second career. I
didn't intend to wait so long to have children; I simply didn't
find myself in the right place in my life, or with the right person, until then. It's just like me to wait until the last minute.
Most things over which I have some control, I do late: finishing
college, finding the right guy, having a child, meeting any dead-
line imposed by somebody else. It's the things that I cannot
control that tend to come early—puberty, and, when my son
was only fourteen months old, breast cancer.

I had my first mammogram when I was thirty-nine, and by
the time I got back to my law office from the radiologist's there
was a phone message for me. They'd found something—and
before I knew it, I was trying to be a great mother, a successful

lawyer, a good wife, a community volunteer, and a cancer survivor. Just like that, the chance for having another child was gone. My maternal life would be totally focused on David.

How much of a chance would I have? As an older mom, I had wondered whether I would live to see David's wedding, to experience him as a dad with his own family. With breast cancer, I had a whole new set of fears: that I would not see his second birthday, would not be there when he left for his first day of school or played in his first baseball game. In those first days, after my diagnosis, I focused on short-term goals. I forgot about his wedding and his children. I couldn't even bring myself to hope for high school graduation. The sorrow of the empty nest was something for other, more fortunate women to endure.

But here I am, nineteen years later, sitting next to my husband, Arthur, both of us in tears, as David walks up onto the stage of the high school auditorium to receive his diploma. I can't help thinking about the appropriateness of our seats: David has to walk away from us, he has to turn his back on us, to pick up that diploma. That's as it should be, I tell myself between pieces of Kleenex. He has to move on, and we have to let him. Except at the far end of the stage he turns, finds us in the crowd, and waves. Gone but not forgotten, I guess.

We are so proud of him. We are so pleased that he is eager to move on, and so pleased that he still looks for us in the crowd. I hear other parents say that they can't wait for their kids to leave home, that they look forward to having their house back, to the freedom. Well, I don't want it. Now that the unimaginably good future is here, I don't want it. And yet, I don't want anything less for David than his freedom. I just keep crying—happy tears, sad tears, sad, and then happy again. The tears are for David, and then the tears are for me, left behind. I want to grab onto him and I want to let him go.

DAVID AND I have always had a close relationship. After I finished my treatment, I traded a career for a mission, really, and for his whole life I have been the president of the National Breast Cancer Coalition. In the early years of his life, he came with me when I traveled—somewhere I have a videotape of David sitting on Arthur's lap in the White House as I stood at President Clinton's side and listened to him announce a new breast cancer research program. I couldn't ignore my breast cancer; that's not my way. I made the issue a central part of my life, even if it meant shuttling back and forth on trains and red-eyes to keep from missing time with David.

Anyone who knew me knew how I felt. Several years ago, a group of researchers came to Philadelphia, where I live, for a breast cancer meeting, and they happened to hail a cab driven by a cabbie I use all the time. He overheard them talking about breast cancer, and so he mentioned that he knew me. They prodded him to reveal something personal about me; what could he tell them?

His answer: She really loves her son. One of them replied that he didn't know me very well at all, but he already knew that. Hardly a secret.

Like so many breast-cancer survivors, I counted every day with David as a gift. The combination of having one child and a premature sense of my own mortality was intense. Each decision about his life consumed me, in part because I felt so fortunate to be there to make it. Elementary school? I grew up poor, living with my grandparents, my mother, and my siblings in an Italian neighborhood in West Philadelphia. I had no choice of schools, and I worked my way through college—so David would have to have a better experience. A private kindergarten with a campus right out of a movie. Visions of Harvard and Yale, followed by incredible success and happiness after that.

Except that David grew extremely unhappy at his first school. We moved him, and when he got to high school, we tried one and moved him again. We learned the beginning of a lesson: A parent's dream may not fit the child in question, and then it has to be revised.

But the closeness never changed. When it was time to think about colleges, I thought of the day, almost twenty years earlier, when Arthur and I toured campuses with his daughter, Jill. I was pregnant then, thinking of the day we would take our child on this same circuit, another lifetime, so far away. And yet for all my early fears that I would never see another college tour, it got here so quickly, long before I was prepared for it. We picked out six schools to visit, the closest only thirty minutes from home, the farthest a bit over an hour's airplane trip.

Off we went. I prayed secretly that no one would ask if I was David's grandmother. I fell in love with the nearby school, the enthusiastic guides, the lovely campus, the large, bright dorm rooms that come with maid service (when does he learn to take care of himself?). Five days later I fell in love with the two more distant campuses for all the same reasons. On the drive home, David announced that he preferred the campus closer to home, and I was surprised at how disappointed I felt. What did I do so wrong that my son is unwilling to take bigger risks? Is he so frightened that he's choosing a school because it's familiar? Will he ever learn responsibility? Become self-reliant?

I smiled and told him I was so happy, and that I supported his choice.

A week later he announced that he had changed his mind and intended to go to one of the schools that were farther away. I was just as upset with this new direction, and even as I told him how pleased I was, I heard "No!" resounding inside my head. Too far away! Too large! He would get lost in the crowd. He should stay closer to home, where I could be a bigger part of his life, where I could better protect him.

In sum, there was no acceptable way for him to leave the nest. I had focused for so long on the threat of me leaving David; I was only now beginning to grasp the fact that he was leaving us. It would take me a while to get used to the idea.

AS THOUGH I had a choice, as though I could slow things down. Over the summer, I started to see something new in him. He was getting ready to go. It was in his eyes when we spoke; we weren't quite finished with a topic, but he was already looking away. He didn't jump the way he used to when I scheduled a trip to New York to see a new show. He had to remind himself to say yes when I asked him to have lunch with me. He already had his other life, away from us.

Without realizing it, maybe I helped him get ready to leave after all. We'd lived in the same house since three weeks before David was born, an 1840s house in a historic neighborhood in center city Philadelphia. David had lived in almost every room of that house, from his toy room on the first floor, to the sitting area with the television in the kitchen, to his bedroom, complete with marble fireplace, on the fourth floor. But when David was a junior, I got it into my head that I was ready for something different—and my husband, Arthur, liked the idea of fewer stairs. I'd always dreamed of living in a loft in New York City, but lofts in Philadelphia were actually in our price range. So we sold our house. The loft would be ready about two weeks before David's high school graduation.

David's reaction was not what I'd hoped for: He refused even to go visit the new space. He would never forgive us for selling the home he'd planned to live in when he had a family of his own. What had I been thinking? I wanted to make certain that David came home from college every chance he had, but would he be less likely to return to such different surroundings? Could I find a way to make it feel like home? I worked very hard to make certain that his room was something a college man would appreciate. I designed the den so that he would feel the way he did in our old kitchen. We might have a new office space, but it was the same old computer. I wanted him to have everything he needed, even though he would not be there full-time any longer.

Finally, when it was time to move in, he had no choice but to come to the new house. I held my breath as he walked through the loft. It was, he said, "very cool," even if he liked our old home better. I could breathe again. And while I can't take any credit for figuring this out in advance, it may be that the new place will make it easier for him to head off to college. We moved into our old house to raise David. It might help him to go—it might help us to let him go—if we moved out when it was time for him to leave.

WHAT DO I worry about now?

That he's going to be living a couple of hours away, which might not seem like much to people whose children live far away, but seems like a lot to me.

That selling the house couldn't have come at a worse time, and David will never again feel comfortable coming back to see us.

That he'll call too often or not call often enough.

That he'll spend too much time with his friends and too little time on his studies. Of course, if he spent every night at his desk and never saw his pals, I'd worry about that, too.

That I can't rewrite history and be a full-time mom—and even if I could, I probably would have made the same decisions.

I have no strategy for dealing with all this, except to say yes more, to book more speeches, to stay as busy as I can be. I don't look forward to the quiet night at home that so many parents talk about; I can't imagine it. I want my son there. When David was younger, we two were the ones who rented movies and talked about them, and now he goes with his friends and tells me what to see. Next thing, I guess, is that he'll be going to movies at college and maybe remembering to make recommendations, and maybe not. The prospect of silence holds no appeal for me at all. I tell myself that I can do more for breast cancer, but that's the only thing I can come up with when I think about having more time. No hobby, no cooking.

The only other thing I might consider is a spa. When David was at home, no matter where I went, I came right back: I flew to Rome, I gave a speech, and I turned around to come home. I flew to the West Coast and never saw the cities I was visiting. Now, I think, I could go to a spa. Maybe the Canyon Ranch in Phoenix for a day, next time I go there. Or if I fly to San Francisco, I can stay overnight; I can stay an extra day. That's something I can do for myself.

But do I look forward to it? No. I'd gladly trade in the spa for time with David.

All these years after that fateful phone call from the radiologist, the apocalyptic fears have subsided; I have come to think that I just might see David's wedding, and I just might spoil those grandchildren. For now, I wallow in the sadness of knowing that I'm not going to have him around. My worries, I realize, are the kinds of worries that other women have when they send their children out into the world, the mundane, everyday worries of women who adore their children and never stop trying to get it right. That doesn't make me feel any better—it's not like I'm going to stop worrying anytime soon—but it does put my worries into perspective. What a luxury, in a way, to be as brokenhearted as anyone else.

Migrations

Ellen Levine

When our first son, Danny, was three years old and I was five months pregnant, it seemed like the perfect time to escape on a last-chance, pre-baby vacation with my husband. Our plan was to head for the remote lake region of Canada on a fishing trip. Leaving Danny with my parents and a serious babysitter (that's what we called nannies back then) was our insurance policy.

Being separated from our only child did not bother my husband at all, but boy, did I feel guilty. This was before the cell phone was invented, so on our third night we drove miles to a roadside booth and called. Big mistake. Danny was crying. He had a fever and a sore throat. My mother assured us that she had taken him to the pediatrician and that it was only a cold, not even tonsillitis. I wanted to fly home immediately, even though I knew our child was in good hands. But they weren't my hands, and he was my responsibility. My husband, the doctor, reminded me that I tended to imagine the worst and that Danny was fine. He was right on both counts.

Conventional wisdom holds that it is easier to leave than to be left. But it may be time to retire that adage. Separating from my children and leaving them at kindergarten, camp, or college had always been hard for me. My husband, watching my performance that day, predicted a severe future case of empty nest-ism. But now I realize the source of my fishing-trip agony. I was the one doing the leaving, and I felt guilty. Good mothers, I reasoned, did not abandon their children. In the great debate about vacation with children versus vacation without, I had made the wrong choice.

To this day I have trouble packing to go away. And I don't mean picking out what to wear. Whether I'm off for a four-day business trip or a brief junket, it's unsettling to leave behind the people who depend on me. My husband. My grown-up children. The grandkids. And I don't need Woody Allen's therapist to figure this out. My parents went away often and under frightening circumstances when I was a child. My dad was drafted to fight in World War II right after I was born, and my mom had a very hard time emotionally. After he returned, when my sister and I were toddlers, Mom had several long hospitalizations that were never explained to us. First he was missing, and then she was. And it didn't feel safe without our parents. Those were the days when families kept secrets, but kids always sensed when something bad was happening. And it was terrifying. Having no information was worse than the truth, whatever that was. The message I absorbed: Do not do unto your children what has been done to you. I plead guilty to overreacting.

But when the boys finished college and left us for good, it didn't feel like a loss to me. It was a pleasure to fall asleep at night without worrying about when they would get home. No more lectures necessary on the subjects of grades, girls, or sexually transmitted diseases. And my husband had forgotten his forecast about how much I would suffer. I did not have an identity crisis. No "who am I now that I am not a mommy?" Maybe it's genetic. Maybe it's because I had a big career that kept me busy and fulfilled. But let me state here for the record, it's not because I wasn't attached to my sons. Motherhood dictated everything for me, right down to my daily commute. No public transportation for me; I always drove in from the suburbs, just in case I had to get home in a hurry.

When we took them to college, I made their beds. When they moved out permanently, I stripped their beds. And what about my husband? When the four of us became just the two of us again, he never looked back. That was not so surprising, I guess. What gave me pause is that I never looked back either. Almost without realizing it, many women absorb a sense that certain life passages are emotionally devastating. The advance reviews on empty nest had been gloomy. For me, it has been a lot better than advertised. But then again, so was menopause. Even as a member of the media I wonder from time to time if an event can ever live up to the advance press.

And I have to cop to the fact that I enjoy alone time. Always have. After freshman year, while other girls were jockeying for roommates, I requested a single room. It is almost embarrassing to admit now, but as a college student, I found the musings of Kahlil Gibran in *The Prophet* to be, well, prophetic. My parents were struggling to keep me at home when it was time for me to fly. I would quote passages to them. "You are the bows from which your children as living arrows are sent forth. . . . Let your bending in the archer's hand be for gladness; For even as He loves the arrow that flies, so he loves also the bow that is stable."

THESE MEANDERINGS DID not impress my parents; in fact, Gibran infuriated them. But I remember those instructions all these years later as I think about the process of letting my sons leave. It's not that we don't miss them; we do. Their need for us has diminished, and I have finally convinced myself that need and love are not always conjoined. A conversation with one of my daughters-in-law straightened me out. I was chumming for sympathy and whining a bit that my son didn't call much to talk anymore. She just told me the truth. "He talks to me now. He relies on me. But he still loves you." And as annoying as it was to hear that spoken with the utmost confidence and honesty, of course she was right.

We know they love us. When Dan married he moved to California, where he now lives with his wife and sons; that hurts. Peter lives here with his wife and daughter; that's a relief.

Years ago, I learned another lesson about separation. It wasn't easy, but I convinced my husband to visit friends of my parents who in their seventies had retired to Scottsdale, Arizona. Their home was jaw-dropping. From the enormous pool to the guest bungalows, the place could have passed for a six-star hotel. And then I spotted something that was a little weird in this deluxe setting—a trampoline. Seeing me stare, our host smiled and reminded me that their four children lived all over the United States. "Build a better mousetrap and your kids will keep coming home," he said.

His mousetrap was an amusement park. We think of ours as a bird sanctuary. Birds make hundreds of flights to ferry straw and grass to construct their nests. After the eggs have hatched and the chicks have flown, they rarely return. For some species, though, if the nest has been secure and "remodeled" from time to time, the birds do come back.

That's what we want now. For the birds to come back with their babies, the grandchildren. That's what we need. And here's the biggest surprise: We call them every day, but not to speak to our grown children. We want to talk to the toddlers, even if we can't understand what they are saying. We'll promise our sons and their wives almost anything to go away and leave us with the kids. But history repeats itself. The moms just have such a hard time leaving their children alone, even with us. The dads . . . no problem.

Without a Net

Jon Carroll

My younger daughter, Shana, became a trapeze artist when she was eighteen years old. It was a surprise to all of us; it was a surprise even to her. She walked backstage at the winter show of the Pickle Family Circus in San Francisco, and she changed her life. She changed all our lives.

The first thing people ask me is: Aren't you scared? The answer is no. I was scared at the beginning, but I saw how careful she was, and how serious. She's a slender blonde—five foot five, 120 pounds—and I sometimes forget how strong she is until I put my arm on her tricep to steer her across a crowded room. It feels like gripping a railroad track. Her delicate white hands are thickly callused; close your eyes and shake hands with her, and it's like you're meeting a lumberjack.

Occasionally, she takes a vacation, and when she gets back to work, she has to build up the calluses again, which involves a lot of bleeding. She has calluses on the tops of her feet, too, because that's where trapeze artists get them. She has had various athletic injuries over the years—shoulder, back, knee—but she never takes pain pills on the day of a performance. "Pain is information," she says. Her body will tell her when to skip a trick in her routine.

Shana does solo trapeze, which is not to be confused with flying trapeze, which is the kind where people do somersaults in the air and are caught by a strong guy hanging from his knees. Another way to look at it: Flying trapeze is the one that has the net. Shana uses a belt called a longue (probably from the French word *allonger*, meaning "to lengthen") which is attached to a belt that goes through several pulleys; its other end is held by her trainer. I have seen her fall in performance; it's extremely embarrassing for her and worrisome for the audience, but it's not dangerous.

For me, the trouble with the life of a trapeze artist is not the danger; it's the separation. Circus is by nature an itinerant profession. Shana trained for two years in Montreal and one year in Paris; she toured for nine years with the Saltimbanco iteration of the Cirque du Soleil show: Europe, Australia, Japan, Canada, hardly ever North America. She came home from time to time, and every time I was reminded that she has a real gift for intimacy; when she returns, it seems as though we pick up the conversation where it stopped months or years ago. It's nice, but it doesn't make it any easier when she's gone.

I was somewhat used to missing Shana; her mother and I had divorced when she was six (and my older daughter, Rachel, was ten); I saw both of them every other weekend and half the summer and at selected holidays spelled out in a document that resembled, in complexity, the Treaty of Versailles. I was fortunate in that my second wife, Tracy, shared with Shana something that no one else in the family possessed: physical courage. They would sit at the edge of a cliff dangling their feet over; I'd be fifteen feet back, wanting it to be over. I am sure that Tracy's closeness to Shana made it easier for me to stay close to her while she was finding her place in the universe.

My daughter Rachel and I went through a rough patch, a patch that started in adolescence and lasted into her early twenties. We are a lot alike, she and I, both stubborn and secretive, and we had to work out how to talk to each other. Eventually, though, she decided to stay in Oakland and, even more eventually, to raise a family. So now I have a granddaughter, adopted from China, and I see my older daughter a few times a week, and we have become friends—although we have not stopped being father and daughter. Every so often, she asks for advice or wisdom, and I am happy to give it, but I am careful about what I say—pontificating is a trap that fathers too frequently walk into. We talk about her child a lot; she is a single mother, so sometimes I think of myself as Daddy 2.0.

More family to add to the mix: Tracy's mother is Ruth. Ruth's husband died in 1997, and she moved up to Oakland from Santa Barbara to be close to the rest of us—Tracy has no siblings, and Ruth's only sister is two thousand miles away. Ruth moved into a high-rise "life care" retirement home. She was and is a remarkable woman, who has maintained her sense of humor and her interest in others while enduring the usual indignities of age. The story I am about to tell you happened in 2000; as I write this, in 2006, Ruth is ninety-four. She's slowing down but she's not stopping.

Here's a Ruth story: She has a small balcony outside her twentieth-floor apartment. On the balcony is some sort of potted plant, a bushy thing with thick, dark green waxy leaves. Ruth discovered somehow that she could write on the obverse side of the leaf. Below her apartment is a sidewalk; across the street is the path that goes around Lake Merritt; it's used by walkers and joggers at all hours and in all weathers.

Ruth took to writing one word on the back of a leaf and dropping it off her balcony. The words were things like *courage* and *peace* and *hope*. She thought maybe one leaf would fall at the feet of someone who needed a message, someone who needed to be reminded that hope was possible, that love was everlasting, that courage was necessary. That person would pick up the leaf, and it would be like magic, and the magic might help.

Distance made it impossible for Ruth and Shana to get really close—they first met each other when Shana was six, but for all of Shana's childhood, Ruth lived four hundred miles away; now they don't even live in the same country. But still, they shared something. Just recently, Ruth has had a lot of trouble retrieving words from her in-brain data bank; it happens, as they say, to everyone. She was embarrassed by it, and I think the rest of us were, too. We'd wait while she struggled for the name of a common object or ordinary emotion; we'd pretend nothing was wrong.

When Shana came to town and visited Ruth, she said exactly the right thing: "It's like a game show!" And she'd proceed to guess the word, using funny examples some of the time, turning the whole thing into hilarious sport. That says a lot about Shana, and a lot about Ruth.

In 2000, five years into Shana's tour with Saltimbanco, the troupe filled a blank space in its schedule with a month of shows in Seattle and Portland. Tracy and I had seen Shana perform a lot, because we had traveled to Montreal and London and Perth to see her. But most of her friends and family had not. Trapeze is difficult to explain beyond the word *trapeze*.

The trouble is that a trapeze act is virtually impossible to capture on videotape. The performer is too distant; the focus changes too abruptly. An accurate cinematic rendition of a trapeze act would require a sound stage, three cameras, and three days of shooting. So it is very hard for people to understand what Shana does until they see her do it.

Shana came back to her native land, and Ruth made the uncomfortable journey to Seattle to see her perform. Shana and Ruth had by that time known each other for almost a quarter of a century, so it was a pretty big moment in the family narrative.

We had front row seats, courtesy of Shana, because Ruth has some vision problems. Saltimbanco is a big show, raucous and teeming. Shana's act is one of the few quieter moments. Her solo was the second number in the second act. At intermission, Shana came out onstage to set up and check her rigging. Professional trapeze artists check their own rigging for the same reason that professional skydivers pack their own chutes. Safety first.

Mostly the milling crowd did not notice. Shana was dressed in black like the other stagehands; her fiddling with ropes and bars was not noticeably different from the other preparations. But I enjoy seeing her do it; I enjoy watching the litany of good luck rituals she goes through when the rigging is finished.

I was not nervous about the performance—I'd seen her perform dozens of times, and I trust both her skill and her prudence—but I was nervous about how Ruth would perceive it. Circus performing was not until very recently a respectable profession; I could not imagine what opinions Ruth was keeping to herself.

We stayed in our seats and watched the warm-up, and there was something about the preparation that profoundly moved Ruth. "I am surprised by how emotional I feel," she said. "I just think of little Shana, six years old, turning somersaults. I just see her like that."

"She turned somersaults into an entire career," I said.

"Yes," said Ruth, "but it's . . . just look at her there." At that moment, Shana walked to the ring curb and blew a kiss to Ruth. Ruth blew one back, her hand extending in an almost longing gesture. Shana reached back, and for a moment they almost touched.

"I should pay attention to this emotion," said Ruth. "That's how I learn who I am, by paying attention to emotions that surprise me."

Half an hour later, Shana came out in her tight blue costume, looking elegant and calm and princesslike, which was the point. The performance went well, with applause in all the right places, and Ruth expressed the usual amazement at the beauty and danger of it all. After the show, we went backstage, and Shana greeted everyone and gave us a tour of the practice tent, the dressing rooms, the eerie room where the masks and head-dresses are kept. Then we all went to the on-site café.

Shana and I bustled around, getting drinks for everyone. Over by the coffee machine, I repeated to her what Ruth had said.

"Well, yeah," she said. "I was having the same thoughts. The time, all the time past, and then to have you in the front row, which is so weird right there, and it was kind of hard to concentrate a little. The time . . ."

She busied herself with the cups. I realized that her eyes were filling with tears. I touched her back and made a circular motion with the tips of my fingers. "It's good that she could finally see you," I said.

"Yes," she said, almost fiercely. And then we walked back to the table, and Ruth and Shana sat across from each other.

And I thought: This is why we do it. This is why we put up with disagreements and defects and disappointments. This is why the work of family is worth going through. There are moments of grace and satisfactions too deep for words, and we should all be so lucky.

3GRLMOM

Martha Schuur

There are rows and rows of white folding chairs baking on the lawn under the graduation-day sun—as there had been for Courtney's two older sisters, and for me, thirty-two years earlier, and for my mother, another thirty-two years before that. By the end of the afternoon, five of the women in my family will have graduated from the same Los Angeles girls' high school: I'd be watching Courtney as her mother, and as an alumna, and as a history teacher here, as well. Who would have thought I'd end up a teacher? Wasn't I one of the girls who took joy in tormenting their teachers? And how did time fly so quickly, when inside I still feel like a twenty-five-year-old looking for the next adventure, the next door of opportunity to open up for me?

It is time to take our seats. The girls have lined up in their long white dresses, holding their bouquets of fresh flowers.

The strains of "Pomp and Circumstance" are about to begin. How odd, that the ceremony that alters my life the most is the thing that has changed the least, at least on the surface. The real change is that this time is the last time for our family. In a few hours, I will be the mother of three college-age daughters.

I sit in my front-row seat and watch the girls struggle not to cry, wiggle, or giggle. What self-assured, confident young women they are. Courtney is headed off to the Culinary Institute of America, probably the only graduate to go to what she happily calls a "trade school." She loves being different as much as I do—we're square pegs, thriving on how we do not fit into round holes. I couldn't be more proud of my independent daughter—of all my independent daughters, actually, since each one of them has struck out in her own direction.

With three graduates in the space of four years, though, I get a lot of questions about the darker side of these departures. With Courtney, it's gotten worse—how will it feel, people ask, when the last one goes? Yet why would it make a larger dent in my life than the others had? Didn't our first daughter's birth change our life forever? Didn't the second one's birth force us to work on our divide-and-conquer skills? And didn't Courtney's arrival teach us humility, now that we were officially outnumbered? The departures are just as different, and just as individually significant as the arrivals were. Still, people press me for an answer: How do I feel about the empty nest?

I must admit that I'm completely looking forward to it. When I say this to my younger women friends, it gives them hope. When I say it to my peers, they say they thought I was closer to my children than that. When I say it to older women, they give me the same knowing smile I used to get when the girls were in their terrible twos, or threes, or fours, and I wondered to a more seasoned parent if it ever would end. Those older women knew something then, they know something now, and I look forward to learning it: peace in my house, a safe haven from the hectic life that surrounds me. My husband and I will have uninterrupted conversations at the end of our long workdays, and I will be able to do what I want to do after work. After twenty-one years of raising daughters, spontaneity will return to the household.

Myth or reality? We shall see. What I really think, as graduation begins, and with it, another transition, is that this is going to be something like childbirth—enormous pain, and then great joy.

MY ELDEST DAUGHTER, Casey, is a bold sunflower who breezes through life, so dropping her off at college started out as a lot of fun. She and I drove and talked and laughed our way across Arizona, New Mexico, and Texas, and then we spent a few days getting her settled into her new room. We even enjoyed going to Wal-Mart; no sadness, just busy fun. My husband flew in after a few days, to make the drive back home with me, but there were still new people and places to keep us busy. We were fine until the morning when we had to say good-bye.

I had not anticipated this much uncontrollable crying, on all sides. How could I leave my firstborn in a strange place? Who would she talk to late at night? Who would encourage her, support her, and love her? For that matter, who was going to wrap their arms around me in the particular way she did? But I knew that the longer we lingered, the more painful it was getting, so we drove away—silent aside from our tears. We got to Amarillo around dinnertime, happy to have the distraction of where to eat and what to order, and how about that great smell of Texas barbecue?

The restaurant hostess didn't know why we were there, of course, so she sat us next to a young couple with a new baby. That did it. I started to cry, I lost my appetite to the pangs of a broken heart, and it was all I could do not to lean over and say, "Enjoy every minute, you have no idea how quickly it goes." Women had said that to me when our girls were little, and I never believed them.

We were busy enough when we got home, between work and the two daughters we still had with us—but each one of us invented a coping mechanism that we use to this day. I spent a lot of time cleaning up Casey's room: I changed the sheets and made the bed, I straightened the photographs on her desk; I counted up all the happy, smiling pictures and tried not to worry too much about whether she was that happy now. I made the room ready for her to return at a moment's notice—and having done that, I was ready to get back to living. If I couldn't yet call her without crying, I would send her e-mails. I would find ways to handle this.

As for Bob, he dealt with Casey's departure in a slightly different way. Every morning, when he woke up, he went to her room, stood for a moment in the doorway, and heaved a pensive, sad, soulful sigh—and then he, too, went on about his day. The sighing went on for about a week. The rest of us lay in bed and listened to him.

KELLY IS THE sentimental daughter, the one who went out with her friends the day Casey left and rushed home just in time for farewells, because she couldn't handle a whole day of good-byes. A year later, when it was time for her to leave, I borrowed that tactic. I couldn't run away from home, in the weeks before she left for Syracuse, New York, but I could keep busy with her, repainting her bedroom a tranquil, calming pale blue, occupying myself with helping her to pack. Kelly feels things deeply, but she does not allow others to see it, and it has taken me a lifetime with her to learn to read the signals. She is pure goodness, always there for friends and family. Who would be there for her now? Who would see past her bravado? I asked myself these questions, and others for which there were not yet answers, and then I tried to distract myself with paint, with suitcases, with things to do.

I thought it was a good coincidence that my school year started at the same time that Kelly's did, preventing me from going with her; I felt myself lucky, leaving the trip to Bob this time. I had no idea my heart could break again without even being on the scene. Bob called on their first night in Syracuse to announce that he had never felt such pain, and to wonder, in retrospect, how I held it together in Texas at all. I assured him that I understood. I only hoped, for his sake, that the strangers who sat next to him on the plane did not have a baby.

When he returned, we did what we do: I cleaned up Kelly's room to make it ready for her return. Bob stood in her doorway and sighed—and then he stopped in front of Casey's doorway and did the same thing, as though he were breathing out sorrow and breathing in memory. Room-cleaning and sighing were our departure rituals, and we seemed to be getting rather proficient at them.

COURTNEY WOULDN'T TOLERATE it. One morning she heard her father stop at Kelly's bedroom door, and she yelled out, "Dad, you still have one here!" That shook us out of our self-indulgence. We had to cope for Courtney's sake, and I chose to celebrate the fact that she was still at home and still needed us. The last time I had one child was the first year and a half of Casey's life. I would have to learn the appropriate balance between smothering and mothering, for this last year of Courtney's life at home.

Courtney has always been very independent, or so she seemed, determined to convince me that she didn't need much from me either emotionally or physically; maybe it's a third child's survival strategy. So I tried to anesthetize myself at the beginning of her senior year by working, occupying myself with new students and new courses, which made it easy to work too many hours. But I was making a mistake: She missed her sisters, her best friends and lifelong playmates, and she didn't quite know what to make of the two grieving adults who were her parents. She was happy to have me around to talk to, as long as we didn't spend that time moping together. For that matter, she was happy to embark on a food career when everybody else was sweating college applications. She was not intimidated by change—in fact, she seemed to welcome the chance to deviate from the status quo.

And that gave me my first glimpse of what lay on the other side of this process. I had always worried that my relationships with my daughters would never be the same—which turns out to be true—but I didn't see past that to the next truth, which is that they get even better. I no longer would have to focus on the daily management of their lives, but on the pure enjoyment of them. I had two adult daughters who chose to be with me, who chose to share their thoughts with me, and if Bob and I stopped cleaning and sighing and driving Courtney mad, we would soon have a third. What a gift. Choice is what's powerful here. When change happens without choice, then it can hurt terribly. That is not what's happening to us.

I should have known it; I wasn't paying attention to history. My family may look like a perfectly straightforward nuclear household, but we took a circuitous route to get here. I was the vice president of a medical corporation, working what seemed like hundreds of hours a week on the corporate path to success, when I got pregnant the first time, and I figured I would hire a nanny, take a long weekend off to have my child, and get on with my career. I enjoyed the illusion of control, and then I surrendered it to a first miscarriage, and a second, and a third. I decided that if I were ever lucky enough to have a child, I would overhaul my life to be a mother. And I made good on that promise to myself—when Casey was born, I quit. I got pregnant eight months after that, and then again eight months after Kelly was born, and suddenly I was a completely different person, a full-time mom with three little girls.

I hadn't planned it that way, any more than I had planned on becoming a tennis pro out of college, or getting an MBA at night to become a medical administrator, or subbing for one of my daughters' teachers, or deciding to switch to teaching full-time. What I had taught my daughters, by example, was that John Lennon was right: Life is what happens while we're making other plans.

By the time we got to Courtney's graduation, I had spent her senior year doing my best to live up to my own example. For years I had been driving a minivan with my priorities spelled out on the vanity license plate: 3GRLMOM. When the lease on the minivan was up, I traded for an appropriately named Ford Escape, and then I did the single most offensive thing I have ever done, at least in my girls' eyes: I gave up the vanity plate. I probably wouldn't have done it if I had known that it would have upset them so; they liked knowing that everyone behind us in traffic saw that outward statement of our bond, but to me it is always there, and it doesn't need proving.

No, I confess, getting rid of it was part of my break with the past, and that gesture was as important to me as the license plate had been to them. Over twenty years ago, I threw myself into motherhood completely, and now I was getting in position to throw myself into the vital-fifty-year-old-woman stage of my life. I installed a bicycle rack on top of my new Escape, and I started saving for a pink kayak I've had my eye on, which will fit nicely onto that rack. I even have a new baby—a Labrador puppy, that is, who is full of life. We'll go through one more round of room cleaning in the fall, and I imagine that Bob will sigh his way along the hallway for a week or so—but then we will have lots of new things to do.

Will I suffer a form of postpartum depression anyway? Probably. But I have my whole life to look back on, one that shows me that pain can bring strength and growth, if we let it. In a funny way, I started preparing for this long before I ever had children. My life has always been about the open door.

The Dog Waiting by the Door

Andrea L. Chambers

The ritual began every afternoon around three, with a great sniffing and shuffling and repositioning. Mina, our thirteen-year-old Rubenesque bichon frise, would hunker down, her ample left flank scrunched up against the front door of our Manhattan apartment, as if her soft (perfectly groomed, I might add) fur was somehow attached to the wood. Her deep breathing would soon transcend into a subtle snore, more of a wheeze and a whistle than anything terribly annoying. Each time the elevator stopped on our floor, Mina's head would shoot up, awaiting the familiar footstep and key in the lock. When the steps moved on, Mina would flop down, resume her pose, and add a little twitch mixed in with the wheezes.

Finally, sometime between 4 and 6 P.M., depending upon the vicissitudes of after-school sports and social life, the boots or sneakers would halt at our door. Mina was up like a rocket, prancing and circling and whining with desperate little mews, more like a cat, really, than a respectable dog. "Watch out, Mina," I would yell on the days I witnessed this command performance. But our daughter, Abigail, knew to open the door gingerly before hurtling her backpack like a projectile missile onto a chair and throwing herself on the floor, feet straight up in the air, dog scooped up on her chest. Then Mina would cover her with kisses, as if she had been gone for weeks, even months, instead of hours. The two would eventually settle down to do homework, Mina sprawling all over Abigail's assignments, claiming her turf. Come bedtime, Mina would settle down on a nest of pillows tossed at the foot of Abigail's bed. "Doesn't her snoring wake you up?" I occasionally asked, even though I know that a teenager's sleep is inviolate.

Then, one September day three years ago, the only footsteps stopping at our door were mine or my husband, Bill's. Mina greeted us with kisses and wiggles because she loves us, too— just not as much as she loves our daughter. When I swept Mina up as Abigail used to and cuddled her, she kept looking over her shoulder, puzzled. "I wish I could have prepared her," I told myself, knowing how silly that was. There is preparation. And then there is Preparation. The former had taken place that summer after high school as Abigail and I roamed the aisles of our local Bed Bath & Beyond and Linens 'n Things, stocking up on egg crates, extralong twin sheets, shower caddies, underbed storage chests, and so much more. Often, on light shopping days (hand towels, say, or bath products), we would bring Mina along, tucking items around her as she snoozed on a velour throw in the shopping cart. Mina and I were determined to send Abigail to college with her every need met. My daughter would not be rushing off to the local Wal-Mart to pick up things we had carelessly forgotten. She would be as equipped as an Arctic explorer.

That preparation was easy. The other one, the one that involves sending your only child off to college, is arduous at best. Yes, I dutifully attended all the college prep lectures Abigail's school offered for parents, but on some level I simply refused to believe that our eighteen-year idyll was about to end. From the first moments I began toting Abigail around Manhattan in a Snugli, she and I were best buddies. We had survived—even thrived on—the rigors of my being a typical Manhattan obsessive parent and her an overprogrammed kid. She reveled in all the Mommy and Me classes that morphed into museum visits, riding lessons, and flute concerts. I managed to hold down a full-time editing job in those days and still keep up with the program. We were a high-energy ("high-maintenance," my husband would add) duo determined to do it all.

The same forward momentum eventually propelled us on nonstop college visits during Abigail's junior and senior years of high school. Bill and I learned the art of freezing our faces in Botox-like masks to hide our own feelings and let the impressions and the ultimate decision be hers. In typical Abigail fashion, she weighed her options, selected her first choice, applied, and got in early decision. We were blessed. We were even spared that horrible senioritis year I am convinced God sends to parents as a way of making them ready—ecstatic, really—to ship their kids off to college. Abigail didn't throw tantrums, stay out until dawn, or even call me the *B* word. I knew about these things only from the parent coffee klatches that quickly descended into therapy sessions.

No wonder I was in total denial that extended all the way to the day Abigail and I took the train to her college a few hours from home. We directed Bill to drive alone so that he could have the entire car for Abigail's Bed Bath & Beyond booty, plus four seasons of clothes—just in case. That day, poor Mina was relegated to the kitchen of our apartment. Moving-in day was not for dogs, only for great bursts of parental energy that masked the pain. I remember reading that even Hillary Clinton lined Chelsea's drawers with contact paper, her Secret Service agents observing closely. As for me, I carefully trimmed and smoothed the ribbed plastic stuff that is now considered the product of choice, and unpacked the boxes my husband hauled up the stairs. When it was time to leave, he did not say, as Bill Clinton did, "Can't we stay for dinner?" Even I, to my credit, knew it was time to go.

Reality set in slowly in the days and weeks to follow as I looked at the clock each afternoon and began wondering when Abigail would be home; old habits die hard. By the time she started college, I worked at home, writing and editing—but I did not turn her room into a home office or exult in my free-dom from preparing her quirky, semi-vegetarian meals. I ob-sessed, rearranging the stuffed animals she left lined up on her window seat and tidying her closet one more time. I snapped at my husband and resented cooking meals. If the three of us weren't having dinner, why did I have to bother? The only good news in those early days was the "walking-to-class-call-your-mom" syndrome. This is a bona fide condition, something that should be noted in the psychiatric literature. College students call home when they are bored, rushing to class, or even on their way to some late night bacchanal. Abigail checked in frequently, often daily, by phone or e-mail, chatting about her classes or her roommates and asking me to send things like more skirt hangers or a closet light. Yes, this meant that my preparations had been flawed, but secretly, I smiled.

While I had my little snippets of Abigail time, Mina did not. Her foul mood permeated the house. She sulked, splaying her hind legs out behind her, laying her head on her paws and looking lugubrious. She dragged herself along on her walks, head down, disinterested in her old friends Lola and Goldie. I cuddled and coddled her, but she remained morose. Each afternoon, she would amble toward the front door, look at me a little quizzically, and then settle down to wait. Only the smell of dinner cooking would lure her from her perch and her unrequited love. Once in the kitchen, she picked at her food like an anorexic Hollywood star. Mina continued this behavior for weeks. Then, one day a month or so after Abigail left, she slowly eased herself down in the lamb's wool dog bed I had placed in the hallway *near* the door, but not in front of it. From then on, this would be her new perch, her compromise position and her bulwark against disappointment.

At bedtime, Mina made her feelings known from that first empty night. Trotting purposefully past Abigail's open bedroom door as if the room were haunted, she collapsed into the dog bed at the foot of my husband's and my bed. (I must confess that Mina has a place of repose in every room, plus her own dog sofa.) In fact, Mina rarely entered Abigail's room from the moment she left, and then only if I happened to toss her favorite squeaky caterpillar there in a game of catch.

Throughout these first weeks and months, I watched my husband go about his business, even-tempered, philosophical—and infuriating. He missed Abigail, I knew, but he was able to view her departure as a rite of passage and not a wrenching void, to be dramatic but not untruthful. "Don't you miss her?" I would practically shriek. "Of course I do," he would answer. "But what do you want me to do?" That only made things worse.

Christmas vacation was a turning point—and the beginning of the ebb and flow I now realize is part of the long, slow saga known as "sending your child off to college." This is not a one-note, a command performance, an isolated event, or a milestone. It is a work in progress that begins one Indian summer day with a lonely dog in the kitchen and inches along for the next four years, shedding and adding, twisting and turning, changing and staying exactly the same. That Christmas I had my first inkling that I was dealing with a continuum and not the end of a chapter. Fall break and Thanksgiving didn't really count. They were brief, filled with friends and family, and unreal—cameo visits, but not a homecoming. Mina showered Abigail with kisses but retained her cautious distance during those visits. She slept in her lamb's wool cocoon during the day and with my husband and me at night. "Mina is acting weird," Abigail noted but didn't seem too upset by it. College students are resilient.

Christmas, however, was a different story for all of us. The self-confident young woman who arrived home with what seemed like a semester's worth of laundry looked different, more mature. She sounded different, too. "She has her college voice," I would whisper to my husband about the somewhat haughty and impatient tone that would creep in. *"Didn't I tell you that already?"* Abigail would ask. I was often "Mother" now, not "Mummy" or "Mum."

In retrospect, I'm sure Abigail was terrified of losing her newfound independence, of falling back into the parental clutches. I, of course, wanted to resume the old relationship, asking her to call me when she arrived at or departed from various destinations—as parents of the "New-York-is-a-jungle" school of thought tend to do. She rolled her eyes at these gentle reminders, but she complied. Mina watched all this warily, maintaining a certain aloofness the first week. By week two of the three-week break, she had inched back into Abigail's room at night, reclaiming her nest of pillows. Then, come the middle of January, the house was suddenly quiet, the pillows tucked neatly on the bed at night, and Mina brooding again, though less intently, I noted. Pretty soon, meat loaf could lighten her mood. She was accommodating to the ebb and flow, as was I.

By the next summer, the rules and the rhythm were slowly shifting. My daughter informed me, firmly but gently, that I was lucky she chose to work at home for the summer, and that she did not need to call me with her every move. An inner voice told me that she was right. We arrived at a little entente cordiale, an accommodation that was a combination of behavior therapy and necessity. I had to let go, and I knew it. We navigated our way through this new territory, each maturing in different ways. Before I knew it, fall, that dread season, was here again. Naturally, there were a few more refresher visits to those houseware emporiums and the now familiar packing and hauling. This time, we took Mina with us on moving-in day, parking her on Abigail's bed, where she watched the drawer lining process, eyes at half-mast. That night, when my husband and I returned home, she knew the drill: Abigail's room was off limits again. Her snoring at the foot of our bed woke me up.

I must admit that this second departure was easier. My inner clock no longer ticked with the same urgency, reminding me that Abigail should be home from school, or ready for dinner. I actually began to enjoy certain freedoms, such as cooking what my husband and I liked, or going to movies or plays in the middle of the week. Mina pouted for only a week or so, and this time, she didn't even bother waiting by the door. I did notice that she seemed sluggish and slept more than ever. As it turned out, that had little to do with Abigail's departure.

All in all, things were going reasonably well until Thanksgiving. "What's wrong with Mina?" my nephew asked when she didn't paw everyone's knees and whine for turkey at the dinner table. I was struck by two things: how Mina had become so much a part of the family that everyone knew her peccadilloes—and that she spent the meal sleeping behind the sofa, hiding from the throng. Abigail gently tugged her out, then proffered a piece of dark meat, usually Mina's favorite. Mina sniffed at it with heartbreaking disinterest and slunk back to her hiding place. In the days that followed, her lethargy worsened. She tottered to the hydrant like an old lady and had accidents in the house. Meat loaf might as well have been sod.

The Monday after Thanksgiving, I dialed the number I knew by heart: Mina's veterinarian. Poor Mina might have a bed in every room and all the love and pampering in the world, but none of that quite compensated for her medical traumas. Her cute little knees had given away twice to torn ligaments, leading to two major knee surgeries. A metabolic imbalance meant that she developed bladder stones and had suffered through three operations to remove them.

Over the years, we had grown accustomed to rushing her to the vet, and this time was no different. I was shocked, however, at the diagnosis: "Mina has diabetes," her vet informed us after a barrage of tests. We were swiftly given a lesson in how to poke a syringe filled with insulin into the soft skin of her flank. Twice a day this needed to be done, we were told, on a carefully prescribed schedule of eight-hour intervals.

Poor Mina. Poor me. The thought of sticking her with a needle every morning and night for the rest of her life made me physically sick. I had a headache, a stomachache. From afar, Abigail was a wreck, as well. "So?" she would text message me from class, and I knew that translated into: "How's Mina?" Both of us spent our spare moments on the Internet learning way too much about the downside of doggie diabetes.

"She'll be fine. She'll be her old self again soon, and she'll barely notice the shots," my wise husband told me, and he was right. Thanks to special-order, short baby needles, Mina didn't even look up at the pinch. The next task was showing Abigail this new household routine. At Christmas, I gave her a needle lesson. With her usual competence, Abigail quickly mastered the task. That holiday season, she hung around the house a lot, hovering over the patient, watching for any signs of an insulin reaction and exulting over how much better Mina was getting.

Pretty soon, taking care of Mina absorbed a great deal of my time. No more evenings out at the theater or even sleeping late. I rushed home to give Mina her insulin at 7 P.M. and made sure I was up for the morning shot. I regulated her diet, walked her every three hours, and thought about my mother, who was left to care for our aged dachshund, Honey Lee, after my brother, sister, and I went off to college. In those days before the advent of pet spas, Rover room service at hotels, and dog whisperers, Honey Lee was just a canine. She slept in our old playpen in the basement "so that she won't piddle on the rugs," my mother explained. Still, I remember my mom huddled against the cold on Honey's walks, and it seemed to me that my lot was the same, only amplified. I also began to suspect that all that overprotective mothering I had used on Abigail during her childhood asthma attacks—and let's face it, during her childhood in general—was getting transferred to Mina. Was I alone in this? Did other mothers shift their nurturing to pets when their nest emptied? I'll leave that one to the bloggers.

When I received an offer to return to work full-time, my first thought was: "I can't leave Mina." Bill gave me a withering look and Abigail sprang into action from afar, suggesting dog walkers, bringing Mina to work, and other solutions. Finally, I hired two lovely women Bill calls "Mina's au pairs." They walk her, watch over her, and call me with regular reports. When Abigail is home, she takes over some of these duties, showing a solicitousness and concern that delight me. She and I have definitely entered a new, improved phase.

Thanks to the wonders of insulin, Mina's health is holding up, though she now has cataracts and is losing her hearing. In her dotage, she has developed a certain wisdom and serenity. Mina seems to understand that Abigail will burst through the door one day and then she will leave again, that there will be great crescendos of activity and tummy rubs and twirls in the air—and then there will be stillness. "It's okay, Mina, she'll be home soon," I tell her. She cocks her head and goes back to sleep, comforted, as I am, by that thought.

We are now nearing the end of this college continuum. Abigail is a senior, a confident and mature young woman with crystal clear goals and priorities. During the summer after her junior year, we agreed that she could pretty much come and go as she pleased with little or no monitoring, though some things will never change. If I see her heading out on the streets of New York in an outfit I deem too revealing, I give her "The Look." Usually, she grabs a sweater or maybe changes into a tad longer skirt. But not always. And I still lie there at night when she is out past midnight, listening for the key in the lock. Mina is no longer right by the door, of course, but she is still waiting, as am I, from a respectable distance.

In Twos

Grace Saltzstein

Everything in my life has come in sets of two: two marriages, a very short early one, and a second one that has lasted for thirty-one years; two sets of two daughters, the first my stepdaughters from my husband's first marriage, and then our two girls, who are twins; two houses, one for us to raise the girls in and one chosen because it's easy for everyone to get to; and two careers, my husband's and my own. We have had our share of college drop-offs, of graduations, of daughters marrying, moving farther away, and starting families of their own. The only consistent thing, I guess, is surprise— and the chance to learn from our mistakes.

I was a terrible stepmother. I was twenty-five when I married Alan, he was thirty-five, and his daughters Anneke and Sylvia were six and eight. I was in graduate school and he was teaching, and all summer long, and most Christmas holidays, these two very active little girls would be with us in California. Then they'd go back to Texas to their mom, and to school, and we'd have to maintain contact through phone calls and letters. I loved kids, I was always good with kids—but when it came to being a stepmother I was too intense. I tried too hard.

It wasn't always easy, especially in those first few summers. Alan taught summer school, and we had no money, and we were in this dinky little condominium in inland Orange County with no air-conditioning. It would get so hot that the girls and I would lie on the kitchen floor for an afternoon nap, because the tile was so cool. We hardly knew anybody in the neighborhood, and I couldn't take them swimming because I don't know how to swim. Who would keep them safe? Even if I could swim, we only had one car. Too often, I felt like the Wicked Witch of the West—and yet, of course, I adored them, I wished I were doing a better job, and I missed them the moment they left. And they always had to leave—usually just when we felt like we were starting to make this family thing work. It was terrible; the only way I could deal with them leaving our nest at the end of the summer was to get frustrated with them, get upset about how they weren't doing this or they weren't doing that, because otherwise it was heartbreaking. I needed to think that I was ready, eager, for them to go.

OUR TWINS, JENNIFER and Rachel, were born in 1978, and by then I had more of a plan. I came of age in the late 1960s and early 1970s, and I spent my entire working career wanting to be a good feminist, to have a life outside of the home in conjunction with a full family life—so I finished graduate school and went on to teach political science at UC Riverside, while Alan first directed a master's program and then chaired the political science department at Cal State Fullerton. We were an academic couple, which made life seem fairly predictable. I thought I could see how the future would unfold; we had it all laid out.

With the financial security of a second professional income, we were able to buy a fixer-upper when the younger girls started grade school and the older girls came to California for college. We cheerfully told people that I would retire when Alan retired, so that he wouldn't have to wait another ten years to have some free time with his wife—and then someday, we would die in this house. For now, the extra income from Alan's first stint as department chair paid for the older girls to go to college, the extra income from my tenure as department chair would pay for the twins, and if everything went according to plan, we'd have enough left over for a little dream we'd always had—a small place, outside of Southern California, convenient to our scattered children, where we could get together for holidays and vacations.

But first we had to raise those twins and send them off to school—at which point the plan began to dismantle itself, as long-range plans so often do. The girls weren't going so very far—Jennifer was headed to UCLA, and Rachel had chosen the University of California at Davis, no more than seven hours away—and yet, having spent the last twelve years refining the process of juggling work and family, I couldn't figure out how I could be available to them in the way I wanted to be now while continuing to work at all. The girls and I would be on the same UC course schedule, which meant that I wouldn't be there if one of them had something bad happen, or faced a particularly stressful week. Suddenly, all my talk about retiring when Alan retired seemed like a bad idea. I wanted to stop working now, even though it would be another seven or eight years before he was ready to step down.

I took an unpaid leave of absence for a year—but I knew in my heart that I wasn't going to go back. The twins graduated high school in 1997, and my leave began that July. The summer was a blur, to some extent; I was finishing up my research, the girls were working to earn their spending money for school, and before I knew it, it was time for them to leave. Rachel was moving into a dorm at Davis, but Jen didn't want any part of dorm living, so she signed up for a cooperative apartment at UCLA, and then things got very complicated. Jen was supposed to move in on a Saturday morning, and Rachel was supposed to arrive at Davis the next day—so we loaded all their stuff into our minivan and drove to Los Angeles for lunch with Anneke and Sylvia, who had been through this with us years ago and were there to provide moral support.

Jen's two roommates had arrived at the apartment ahead of her, and the room was crammed full of their stuff. They'd left her the top bunk, they smoked like chimneys, there was only one empty drawer left for all of her things, and we were all freaking out about this but trying to appear calm. As soon as we got out of the apartment, her half-sisters said, "We can't leave her there! How can we leave her like that?" And then Jen came out to say her final good-byes at the curb. She and Rachel embraced, and the rest of us stood there bawling.

All I could think was that there is so much chaos involved in getting ready to go, but there's that one point where you think, Oh my God, wait, what are we doing? The girls are going to be apart for the first time in nineteen years. How will they get through this? But there was no time to dwell on that, because we had to get back in the van to drive up to Davis.

We unloaded a second set of belongings on Sunday and took Rachel out to dinner—and afterward she said, "Well, I can walk back to the dorm from here, so, bye," and she turned and walked away. Just like that, we had no more children at home.

I must've cried half of the way back, on top of being pre-menopausal, which meant that I spent the whole drive having one hot flash after another. I thought that was symbolic: Life was changing everywhere I looked.

WE GOT THE first call from Jen the night before classes started, and you could hear the frat noise, loud, loud music, in the background.

"Mom," Jen said. "This is terrible."

And then, that same night, around midnight or so, Rachel called.

"Mom," Rachel said. "It's too far from home."

In Jen's case, she ended up coming home almost every week-end that entire first year. She was done by noon on Friday, so I would go over and pick her up, and Alan would drive her back on Sunday night, and that return trip kept edging up later and later. She was in performance music, so we went to any performance, and we'd take her to dinner; we saw a lot of Jen.

With Rachel, if she called to say she'd had a bad week, or if I was just missing her, I'd offer to come up. I figured out pretty quickly that if I left at five in the morning I could be there by noon and miss the traffic both ways. We'd go to a movie, or I'd take her to lunch or dinner, but it's hard when you visit like that. When they're at home and they get tired of you being around, they can get away from you, but what do you do when you've come all that way? After a while, Rachel would say that she was really glad I was there—but could she go take a nap? So we'd go to lunch, and then she'd go back to her room to take a nap, and I'd do a little shopping, or go back to the hotel to read.

At the same time, Sylvia, who had married and moved to Albuquerque a few years earlier, had her first child, so I'd go to help her out, and my family was in Texas, so I'd see them there, and I started to think about how everyone was starting to scatter, with more changes coming once the twins finished college. How nice it would be to have that little place Alan and I had always talked about. Now that I had retired officially, I was visiting everyone, and loving it, but I worried that the family would lose its center unless we made it easier for us to be together.

WE'D ALWAYS TAKEN lots of driving trips, from the time the twins were little, often to Albuquerque, which by now was home to Alan's sister, to Sylvia's new family, and to our nephew. We loved the Southwest—and every time we took a trip we'd always say, wouldn't it be neat if we had a place in that area, a jumping-off place for family trips, a place where we could be together even as the family spread apart. We were always ruling places out: We'd stop in a pretty little town, but there would be nothing there, and we'd wonder, how could we see movies? Where could we go to eat? One summer we went to Durango, Colorado, and picked up some real estate brochures, but for several years all we did was look. Every time we went back, the prices had gone up, and we had to start figuring all over again.

The twins got acclimated to college, and finished college, and we were still looking. And then, on a trip when we weren't looking, it happened. We took a new route from Albuquerque to Durango, through Rachel's new home, Santa Fe, past Abiquiu, where Georgia O'Keeffe lived and worked, and we got to a little town called Pagosa Springs, about an hour east of Durango and four hours northwest of Albuquerque. It was noon, and we couldn't check into the hotel in Durango until four, so we walked down the main drag to get some lunch, and everywhere there were those little real estate flyers. Right away we saw a half dozen places we liked, and then we decided that since we weren't in any rush, we'd stop in someplace to get directions to some of the houses.

But the place we picked to stop was a real estate office, and it wasn't like they were going to give us directions; one of the brokers was free, and so she would take us around.

We fell in love with the first place we saw. No matter what else she showed us, Alan would say, "But what about the first place?" We put in a bid that afternoon, and they called us on my cell phone as we were driving home, two days later, to say that we had the house. For two years after that I was in charge of getting that house put together—because I was the one who had retired early, and Alan was still working. It was very time-consuming, and it was wonderful. At home I had always lived by lists, day after day, lists and then lists of lists, master lists and sublists. But once the house in Pagosa Springs was done, I could go there and have no lists at all. I relaxed completely. I was never good at that whole business of separating work from home, of turning work off when I got home at the end of the day. In Pagosa Springs, it was different.

I did the reverse of the stay-at-home mom; I had a twenty-year career and then I got out. I still get hung up about it periodically. I'm not doing anything to save the world, anything that's fundamentally worthwhile. But we have four adult daughters now. Jen just got married and is on the East Coast working toward her PhD. Rachel's engaged and in Montana, working on a teaching credential. Anneke is a lawyer in Santa Monica; and Sylvia and Cliff do a yeoman's job in juggling two careers while bringing up our three wonderful grand-daughters. As for Alan and me, we want what we've always wanted—to be able to see everyone frequently, and not the way it was when Sylvia and Anneke were little, where we stayed put and they came and left, came and left.

Alan has retired now, so there's nothing to keep us in Southern California if the girls feel like heading to Pagosa Springs—or even if they don't, and it's just the two of us. Indeed, the idea of dying in our California home doesn't hold the allure it once did now that our mountain retreat beckons. Our newest plan is for Alan and me to go to the little house every year for the Fourth of July, and to stay through Thanksgiving, and to have everyone come there to visit, and for us to come and go from there to visit the rest of our extended families. We haven't been there for such a long time so far, yet we already are starting to ask, "What if . . . we lived there full-time?"

None of this is what I expected I would do with my life. None of it is what I used to think I wanted. But somehow family brought us to a little house in the mountains, for any and all of us to use, whenever we can get there, in combinations that will change throughout the years. We have hung up a little plaque in the house in Pagosa Springs. It says IF YOU'RE LUCKY ENOUGH TO BE IN THE MOUNTAINS, YOU'RE LUCKY ENOUGH.

A Rotten Enough Parent

Douglas Foster

Near Numbi Gate, the entrance we're using into Kruger National Park, a man who sneaked past the rangers was chased down and mauled to death by lions just yesterday. "That's so *harsh*," Jake says, buzzing his window back up a notch for our trip through knobthorn and acacia on our winding way south. It's the cusp of spring in South Africa's largest wildlife refuge. The morning highveld chill gives way to a magnificent sun.

An hour down that road, without another car in sight, springbok appear, tufts of taupe fur brushed up against the breeze. Herds of zebra, klatches of giraffe, and a couple of rhinos go about their business, unimpressed by the father and son pair peering out the windshield. When we pull over, I shut off the engine to sneak sidelong looks at him, as if he's a particularly rare species of wildebeest.

It's been about nine months since we've seen each other. So at the end of a reporting sojourn in Africa, I've offered him this trip as an early birthday present, his twenty-fourth. My son has grown into his lean frame and carries himself now with a new air of composure. The only hitch in his style is the brace he's wearing on his right arm, the memento of a recent skateboarding accident. I can't help myself, blurting out something parental: "Maybe you're getting a little old for boarding." Instead of rolling his eyes, he says: "Maybe you're right."

Jake lives in Los Angeles now, and I teach in Chicago when I'm not reporting from Africa. In the five years since that life-altering day when he packed up his sound system to set off for college, we haven't seen each other nearly enough. We've never fully mastered the technological fixes for separation, either. I hear his voice mostly on the answering machine these days.

So when we met up a few days ago, it felt like a kind of revelation. When we're apart for long stretches, I tend to fall back on stock images of my son—the blond toddler at four, the stocky intense baseball pitcher at eight, the teenager all sharp elbows and knees, the college student home on vacation, dressed in prison-shaped dungarees and balloon-size T-shirts, cranking the volume on lovely trance "music." Being back in his presence provokes a swift correction: He's in my blood and bones, yet I haven't captured the true current measure of him. Perhaps that's a father's fate—finding oneself perennially behind the curve in considering his own child.

———

WE PULL OUT, meandering down the road again. Around a curve we come across a family of elephants. The matriarch thumps in our direction, a vision of overlapping leathery wrinkles. An astonishingly long trunk snakes like some independent appendage toward the dust, beneath small, sad eyes. I share the little I know about her remarkable ability to remember distant water holes that sustain the herd. Behind her, three young elephants gambol, jockeying trunk to butt against one another, their Dumbo ears flapping.

They remind me of the times, shortly after his mother and I divorced, when Jake was only three, when he and I used to go "elephant hunting" in Tilden Park, through the hills east of Berkeley. Those adventures two decades ago helped take the onus off the troubles we were living through as he shuttled back and forth between two houses that were set, for a time, against each other.

His mother remarried, and Jake had to move from one house to the other several times a week. That was a common enough experience in a state known for its embrace of joint custody. In Jake's case, though, it meant navigating between two increasingly dissimilar worlds—one with a conventional nuclear family that soon included a new addition (a baby sister), and the other with a single father who proved less conventional by the day.

I tried to turn the new arrangement into something prosaic, and to appear unflappable in the face of differences over everything from our custody schedule to where Jake would go to preschool. But I was frankly struggling, too—not least because, in the wake of my breakup with his mother, I began to date men for the first time. All at once, Jake had two households, a step-dad, a new stepsister, and a gay dad. His world suddenly seemed like a surprisingly unsteady place, in all sorts of ways.

It helped enormously to hike up the trail in Tilden Park, pretending to listen as herds of phantoms skirmished in the Northern California redwoods. It may seem like mystical thinking, but I think there weren't so many elephants in the room at our house because we so regularly chased them off in our imaginations. Sometimes it was easier to talk about what was bothering him when we were off in the woods.

There wasn't anything he was forbidden to discuss, and nothing was decided about his life until he'd had his say. In that overwrought, egalitarian way of raising children common to California, he was always fully enmeshed in conversations about his fate, even if sometimes the burden was a little much.

He was only four when I consulted him one evening about an offer I'd received to become an on-air television correspondent. Jake cocked his head quizzically, asking me angrily, "But who will take me to *school* then?" before weeping inconsolably. It turned out that he was worried I'd never be restored to my full size once I shrunk small enough to get into the box. Happily, I didn't last long on-air, and there was no lasting size-related damage.

NOW THREE LITTLE elephants, quite real ones, charge single file toward us. Their bellies are bloated, and their necks droop, billowing folds of skin leaving plenty of room to grow into. "Man, look at those little guys," I say. "Hey, remember when we used to go elephant hunting in Tilden?" Jake narrows his eyes over the top of his sunglasses, regarding me the way you'd consider a wacky uncle.

"We ever catch any?" he asks.

The matriarch, as large as a house, huffs close to the car, angling her body to protect her young. You have to admire her stamina, and envy her clarity. Excuse the anthropomorphizing, but I doubt she keeps herself awake at night wondering how she measures up as a parent.

What I wouldn't have given, years ago, for a glimpse of this reunion of ours and a whiff of reassurance about who we would become to each other once my son left home. I used to torture myself with mental lists of all the myriad ways I'd failed any conventional test of parenthood—working impossible hours at overly demanding jobs, regularly venturing off on reckless reporting trips, longing for him to return from time he spent in his mother's house, and pressuring both of us to make up for lost time once he did.

When Jake was little, I sometimes comforted myself with passages from *Good Enough Parent*, by the since-discredited psychologist Bruno Bettelheim. He argued that children of parents who relaxed a little, striving not for perfection but rather to be good enough, would develop a stronger sense of autonomy. I imagined producing a companion volume—a screed called *A Rotten Enough Parent*—for those of us even more evolved, in which the ways we failed our kids could be seen as advanced character-building exercises.

———

WHEN IT WAS time for Jake to go to college, I helped him load his blankets and heavy sweaters into a trunk for the two-thousand-mile flight away from home, and then I discovered the need for a little character building of my own. Since my son had lived with me much of the time during his final three years in high school, his departure seemed all the more searing. Perhaps this common rite of passage reverberates with a special intensity for a single parent. A family-of-two was suddenly one again. It felt to me like an erasure of identity.

Within a few months after college started, my son's absence shouted down the hallways of our house like an errant wind. I'd wake three or four times each night, listening for the car, bending my ear for his muted thumping around the kitchen, waiting for the reassurance that he, too, had gone to sleep. I found myself on too many mornings, many months after he'd left, banging downstairs to wake him—why couldn't the wretch get himself up?—before realizing, with a start, that he was probably sleeping past the alarm in a dorm thousands of miles away.

I missed my opportunities to grump at him, to tell him how to behave and what to do. I missed more the chance to make amends for all my grumping by cooking up Sunday breakfasts for his hulking friends, as the eggs went by the dozen and potatoes by the sackful. I even missed that cagey game parents play with their teenagers, where you manage at last to pry some scrap of information from their grimy, privacy-obsessed grasp.

Now I struggled to keep my hands off. I tried to restrain myself from calling every half hour and quashed the impulse to keep him under an electronic thumb. Long, repetitive, philosophical e-mails were sent along only every third time they were drafted. These messages usually ended on a practical note. Was he eating right? Drinking too much? Taking the wrong drugs and too often?

In retrospect, it's a miracle that he didn't move to another country without leaving a forwarding address.

Jake came back to live with me the summer after his freshman year. I'd waited, like an overeager suitor, for his return all spring. Instead of the perfect reunion I'd longed for, with lazy chats and hunts for elephants in Tilden Park, we slid past one another, as if he couldn't fully come home again. Suddenly we were speaking different languages. He'd joined a *fraternity*—and it will be impossible to explain the depth of my sense of betrayal unless you, too, are an anti-Yuppie Californian.

I did my best to ignore all the ways in which he'd become a foreign entity, arguing with myself that he was old enough to make his own decisions. As soon as he returned to school, though, I rented out our house.

Until then, I'd held out the hope that my lover at the time, and his two children, might move in with me. It seemed possible that they'd fill the place back up, and I'd compensate for missing my son by becoming a parent to someone else's children. But the relationship had begun to unravel, and suddenly I couldn't stand any longer the idea of staying in that house.

I can see now that this was the moment when the rest of my marbles fell out. I chose a studio in Oakland so small that I couldn't put the futon down and still walk around it. Friends couldn't hide their perplexity. Several came to visit, looking in on the room like those children Keane used to paint, eyes wide in horror. My closest friend stood at the threshold, peering in, glancing at me, peering back in. I explained my decision to her with impeccable logic: I needed to save money to pay my son's tuition.

In retrospect, there was more than dollar logic going on. It felt oddly comforting to bring everything so close—one bookshelf, two chairs, a single small dresser. No more pretending any longer that my life belonged in a large, normal-looking house on the street where I'd put my son through high school. If I could have moved into a tin can, I would have liked it even better.

It took me forever, or at least until Jake's third year in college, before I tumbled at last onto the fact that I needed not only a new kind of relationship with my son but also a new kind of life for myself. They were flip sides of the same Frisbee. Having the patience to let my grown-up child decide how to find his way back to me also meant challenging myself to tilt life forward.

Finally I began to understand that he didn't need me in the same way anymore—and slowly allowed myself the pleasure of being freed from that yawning need.

NEAR SUNSET ALONG the lazy Sabie River, we pull over again, ceding the road to the hyenas. In a lagoon nearby, hippo ears dot the water like little ducks. Such perky ears can fool you, covering for mountainous forms just beneath the surface. During the past few days, my son and I have excavated plenty about the past. On a walk along an endless summer's beach at Jeffrey's Bay, he's told me what the divorce meant to him, why he chafed so much against the constraints I laid on him in high school, and even what was happening during his college years when he fell for long stretches into silence.

I've offered up only current news—a new relationship, an idea for a book, the twists I've encountered in starting my career all over again in my fifties. He listens closely now, more attentively than he's ever seemed to listen before. And he asks good questions, a lot like those I ask of him. Is there a new romance? Is the work interesting? What's the next adventure?

He asks for my advice about the job offers he's gotten, and when I veil my answer with a neutral list of pros and cons, he interrupts to add, "No, I mean it—I want to know what you really think, and I'd like you to help me decide what to do."

The sun, a blood-red orb, hovers above the pond. There's no horizon. Tumbleweed, flame lilies, and bush willow pock the landscape. I always yearned for this kind of adventure with him, this depth of comfort with my boy. For so many years I harbored too little faith that it would be possible.

Baobab trees run on and on, downcast like brooding old men. The water in the pond swirls around unseen forms. An uninflected silence falls, the kind you sink into because there's no tension left on the line. In the water, two hippos the size of dinosaurs lift their giant heads, revealing their enormous bodies. They draw together, opening their mouths to each other, vamping like cats.

Epiphanies of the Empty Nest

Letty Cottin Pogrebin

I t's been almost twenty years since the last of our three kids moved out. Though this entitles me to pontificate at length on the impact of the Empty Nest on a long-married couple, my findings boil down to simply this:

- You lose a kid, you gain a sex life.
- Not having to worry about where your children are at two in the morning frees you up to worry about global warming.
- Just because they've been out of the house for a couple of decades doesn't mean they won't bounce back.

The sex epiphany, first. My husband, Bert, always jokes that I couldn't make love unless our children were outside the city limits. He exaggerates. The truth is, I couldn't relax unless they were well out of earshot and unlikely to stroll in unannounced. My libido was grateful when they spent the night at a friend's house, or better still, the summer at sleepaway camp. I have good reason for this quirk. As a small child, I once padded into my parents' bedroom in search of comfort after a nightmare only to see them thrashing about on their bed, not a pretty sight when you're six. I thought they were hurting each other, and even at six had my doubts when they claimed it was chilly and they'd been rubbing their bodies together to get warm.

Wanting to spare my own children what psychologists call the trauma of the primal scene, I may have bent over backward to control my erotic impulses while we were under the same roof. Periodically, however, Bert and I went somewhere romantic, just the two of us, and consummated the marriage at will, which is precisely what the Empty Nest made possible 24/7—except when our grown-up children return these days for a weekend visit. Then I'm back where I started, cautioning Bert to pipe down and keep the bed from telltale jiggling. To my mind, censoring our amorous activities is worth it if it means we can spend more time with our kids, especially since they now come equipped with our remarkable grandchildren.

Bottom line: Though we wept like babies the first night our babies moved out—and we still miss the intimacy of family life, the daily fun, the chance to assess their moods firsthand and be there to buck them up when needed—Bert and I were able to move on to the next stage of life with no permanent scars. Happily, we're healthy, have lots of friends, work we love, and a good marriage, so we don't need our kids to provide care or entertainment. Moreover, we soon discovered that the perks of Empty Nesthood can go some distance to compensate for the loss of parent-child togetherness. Besides having sex as often and as noisily as we please, we could wake up when we were good and ready, leave the house and arrive home any old time, make dinner at eight or nine (because adults don't necessarily get hungry at six), eat in a restaurant or see a movie on the spur of the moment, do laundry once a week instead of once a day, have an uninterrupted conversation, make and receive calls without having to negotiate access to the phone line, and know that when there was a mess in the sink or a wet glass left a ring on the dining room table, we had only ourselves to blame.

Then, too, for the past couple of decades, we've been able to talk to each other about our children without fear of them eavesdropping. It's counterintuitive, but the fact is, the older they get, the more we seem to have to say about them, and it's probably just as well that they can't tune in to our unabashed pride in them (and get swelled heads), or overhear our deep concern when things aren't going smoothly for them (and feel even worse that they've made us worry).

Which leads me to my next epiphany—about worry. My husband and I have always had a functional division of labor: he was in charge of worrying about ordinary threats to our children's well-being—high fevers, poison ivy, sore throats that might turn into strep—while my department was natural disasters and freak accidents. (They could get stampeded by a surging crowd at a rock concert or struck by lightning during a sudden storm in Central Park. Anything was possible, right?) But since we live in New York City amid all kinds of strange folks and unpredictable temptations, we both took on the job of worrying about where they spent their Friday and Saturday nights, a concern we alleviated in a way friends tell me was unique.

We didn't give our teenagers a curfew. This is because we raised them with a clear moral and ethical compass, and we felt we could trust them to behave accordingly no matter what time it was. Put another way, a kid can do drugs, booze it up, or have unprotected sex at four in the afternoon, so we saw no reason to fetishize nighttime. But being "progressive" parents did not mean we were unconcerned about their safety. We made up for being laissez-faire about curfews by imposing the following stringent rules:

Whenever you leave the house, we have to know where you're going and which kids will be with you. If there's a party, we want to know at whose house and whether a parent will be present. And most importantly, when you change locations, we expect you to call in and report your new whereabouts. (Perhaps I should emphasize that this was long before cell phones and text messages, so they had to seek out a public phone or call from someone's house to fulfill their obligation, but that's exactly what they did.)

On any given weekend evening, our daughter Abigail and her buddies might decide to leave the high school dance and go to the ice cream shop on Lexington Avenue, then traipse over to her friend Julie's house, then up to her friend Robert's apartment, then finish the night hanging out on the steps of the Metropolitan Museum (the Manhattan equivalent of a suburban mall), in which case, my husband and I would get four phone calls from Abigail—maybe the last of them at I A.M.

That same night, we would field two or more calls from Robin, who was likewise traveling around the city with her pals, and from David, who would report in from here and there, each child phoning at different times to register her or his new destination. In those years, five or six calls per night was par for the course.

This policy, which significantly reduced both our hours of sleep and our worry quotient, also yielded other interesting by-products. It kept us abreast of the identities of our children's friends—the kids they spent the most time with, who therefore presumably had the most influence on them—and under what circumstances they were socializing. We could, if we had to, reach any of those children's homes because when our children changed locations, they also gave us the phone number. I'll never forget the night when the mother of one of David's friends called in a panic at about two in the morning. Her son was supposed to have been home an hour ago. Might he possibly be at our house? No, he wasn't, we said. "But, we can tell you he's at Stacey's house on Riverside Drive and Eighty-third Street. And here's the phone number."

Curfews sound like an effective means of parental control, but when you think about it, they're kind of silly. Johnny Jones, obeying his parents' dictates, might please them by walking in the door before 1 A.M. But what they'll never know is that, until 12:45, he'd been drinking at some local bar that routinely serves underage patrons without checking IDs.

Since city kids don't drive, city parents were spared the pre-eminent worries shared by most suburban parents: a kid involved in a DWI arrest or an auto accident. A couple we know in Westchester thought they'd solved the problem by giving the car a curfew. Their daughter could stay out, but the car had to be in by twelve. Dutifully, tires screeching, the girl would swing into their driveway as the clock struck twelve, but at the same time some other kid would drive up in his car and open the passenger door for their daughter, who'd hop in and zoom away.

Our no-curfew policy struck Bert and me as a logical compromise and a fair trade-off: the kids got their freedom in return for accepting accountability. We were seriously sleep-deprived on weekends until the last of them moved out, but in return, we got peace of mind. I wouldn't have had it any other way. And now that our son David is living with us temporarily, I wish we could revive the policy.

Which brings me to my final epiphany: They bounce back. About seven months ago, David left his marriage of eight years. Since the housing market is extremely tight right now, we cleared out the closet in his old room, which had long since been transformed into a TV-and-guest room, and he moved back in. Our son, incidentally, is delightful company, great sense of humor, neat in his personal habits—and no strain on his parents' sex life this time around. First of all, Bert and I are older and somewhat less randy, and second, David's work schedule is such that he and we are like ships that pass in the ocean. As the director and general manager of a Manhattan restaurant, he sleeps late, leaves for work around eleven in the morning and comes home at all hours. And therein lies the problem. . . .

All these years, since the kids left home, we've been blissfully unaware of whatever they chose not to share with us, a condition I call "Empty Nest Oblivion." Having no knowledge of their exact whereabouts, we had no reason to worry about them. Certainly, neither of us knew what time David put his key in the lock when he lived in his own apartment. But now, and for however long he might remain under our roof, we know exactly what time he comes home. If I wake up in the middle of the night—as people my age are wont to do—and I see he's not in his room, I immediately imagine the worst. The restaurant was robbed and he was shot. Someone on his kitchen staff had a temper tantrum and stabbed him with a steak knife. He was mugged on his way home. Had an aneurysm. Tripped on a curb, hit his head, and is lying unconscious on the sidewalk being ignored. (Sadly, New Yorkers have a way of passing by homeless people who bed down in our streets; how will anyone realize he's hurt and not just asleep?)

It's 3 A.M. for God's sake! Where is he?

Trust me—you can't ask a thirty-eight-year-old to call in when he changes locations. You can't probe too deeply as to who his associates are or where he spends his time. You can't readily assess his state of mind, or expect him to be comforted by the words or hugs that did the job when you were parenting a fourteen-year-old.

Our nest, fortunately, is still roomy enough to welcome a grown-up child, and both David and we are comfortable with his returning to his childhood home for as long as he needs shelter before he can set himself up in a new place. But the situation is not the same as it was when he last lived with us. Back then, we had some parental power; we could demand phone calls, lose sleep but keep our peace of mind.

Now we have neither power nor oblivion; we just lose sleep. We've diverted a large chunk of brain cells from worrying about global warming and the conflict in the Middle East to worrying about our son's happiness. It's a different trade-off— but as long as we're able to come through for him, I wouldn't have it any other way.

A Mile Ain't What It Used to Be

Brenda C. Roberts

The word *mile* used to mean something—distance that could not be overcome easily, a silent space between lives.

Technology has changed that. We now have at our disposal an arsenal of devices that can make a mile evaporate with stunning ease, creating an intimacy unimaginable just a couple of generations ago.

And though the United States is one of the last holdouts against conversion to more efficient metric measurement, the mile inevitably will go the way of ragtime and railway stations, to America's sepia half-world of reminiscence.

Our older daughter, Gisele, chose a college nearly 3,625 kilometers away—some 2,253 miles of roads, mountains, and rivers to cross. She went there with no thought of geography: A world in which a mile has the power actually to separate parents from children is not her world.

When we brought Gisele to Ann Arbor to begin her freshman year, the fever of things-that-must-be-hooked-up consumed us. Wires. Cords. Plugs. Ports. Remotes. Memory cards. Outlets. Surge protectors. Ethernet.

Like thousands of other hovering parents, we dealt with our separation angst by obsessing over the networks Gisele would use to override geography. They simply had to be in place and functioning before we left her. Once we had deposited our dark-eyed darling, we had to be able to reconnect with her instantaneously. California was seven or eight states to the west of Michigan. We had to be satisfied that we had conquered the geography problem.

The last half hour before we pulled away from the curb was freighted with anxiety, hers and ours, with excitement, with admonitions spilling out and tenderness spoken and unspoken, love, confusion, and the irresistible urge to linger.

It took Gisele to recognize the moment that pulsed with "this is it, this is it," like a defibrillator going off in the core of our little circle. After a last set of hugs for us and her sister, Hayley, she abruptly pivoted and marched across the sidewalk, straight up the broad steps and into Couzens Hall, chin up, no glancing back. We stood rooted in shock, stupidly studying the empty space between us and the dorm doors, beyond which was Gisele, already engulfed in a life invisible to us.

Back in the rental car, my husband's cell phone jingle broke the heavy silence. We had her voice again, right there with us.

Don't recall what it was about. Wasn't important. We could hear her, almost touch her. Everything was all right. When we got back to California, there would be more cell phone calls. And e-mail. And instant messaging. And text messaging. The network was in place, already trumping the miles.

For earlier generations of my family, the notion of such a network would have been hard to fathom. For them, most farewells were final.

AT SIXTEEN, MY grandmother Sarah Waller had steady work as a general maid for a white family headed by the fellow who ran the local operation for a large, prosperous outfit called the E.E. Jackson Lumber Company. It was 1919, maybe 1920, and the money she earned—any money she could earn—helped keep the Wallers fed.

Black families in rural northwestern Louisiana could not afford idle hands, no exceptions. But there was just so much work to go around in the woods and farmland where they lived, in Natchitoches Parish. The Reverend Waller and his wife, Emily, had had to accept it when Sarah's older sister, Martha, left for Shreveport and later moved to Alexandria, to find work and send money home if and when she could. Emily's death followed, dealing another blow to the family, but the teenaged Sarah, her younger brother, Buddy, and their half sisters, Daisy and Dorothy, helped Reverend Waller keep the household afloat.

What could be hunted was hunted, what could be coaxed

from the soil was coaxed, what could be pulled wriggling from the Cane River was pulled. But without having Emily to help with all of it, enough gave way to just enough, and just enough to barely enough. When Sarah could, she brought home "extra" from the white family's table. As the oldest child living at home, she made sure a plate was waiting for Reverend Waller when he came in. Too tired to talk, they would sit on the porch, eat in quiet, and watch night cover the woods and fields.

Bad got worse for the Waller family with the news that the E.E. Jackson Lumber Company was pulling out of Louisiana. My grandmother's employer, the mill boss, was ordered to follow the timber to Alabama. A substantial house would be provided for him in Riderwood, a tiny indentation in the piney woods of the state's southwestern sector, a long dark country road's ride thirty miles east of Meridian, Mississippi. The man's family was to accompany him: wife, toddlers, infant . . . and Sarah.

In those days, my mother tells me with a matter-of-fact shrug in her voice, southern families carried their maids with them wherever they moved.

Martha already had become invisible to her father, living an unknowable life about seventy miles away. And now Sarah was to leave the state entirely. What must have passed through my great-grandfather's thoughts?

Sarah would be entirely dependent on her white employers, he knew. If anything were to go wrong, any pattern of mistreatment were to develop, she would have literally no way to return to her father in Louisiana. No fare, no friends in that strange place. The Jim Crow South left little maneuvering room for teenaged black females. And what were the white folks like in Alabama? As bad as in Louisiana? Worse?

Sarah was so young. Reverend Waller would have thought long about her responsibilities, not only in caring for the father and mother but also for their toddlers and the baby. She would do the cooking, the sewing, the washing, ironing, and cleaning. She would now live full-time with the family, available all day and on call through the night.

Would she be lonely? Sarah's whole world had been a few square miles of pastures, cotton fields, live and water oak, pecan and locust trees, and of course the Cane River. He and the other children loved her and kept her company. Now she would have no one close. . . .

And how would life feel for him, without Sarah in the house? Her gentle ways had helped fill the space where his wife and older daughter had been. Her absence would be hard on him, but it had to be borne; such as it was, this was her chance.

Reverend Waller was essentially unlettered, so communicating by mail did not even enter the picture. Sarah could read and write, but barely; she had not had the luxury of schooling beyond the early grades. She had never had to write a letter. Composing one would be an ordeal requiring hours of free time, something she would hardly ever have.

As my mother recalls it, my great-grandfather had to spend every day—except Sunday, when he preached—working or in search of work. There was no time off, on the day Sarah left, to escort her to her white family's house. In the soft predawn gloom, father and daughter walked together only as far as the woods' edge.

There was no lingering good-bye. All that had been said and done the evening before. Besides, the thought of Sarah's white family, all packed up and waiting for her in front of their house, made her nervous about being late. She had a few miles to cover, and she wouldn't have wanted morning light to hit her only halfway there.

At a time when living was more like surviving, stoicism was a trick Reverend Waller had mastered early. Bitter, sweet, it all goes down the same way, our family sages used to observe when calamity, disgrace, or separation came to pass. Savor the sweet; it won't last. Swallow the bitter down fast.

The pastor swallowed the woods' sharp piney breath and walked away fast. They were leaving; it had begun. First Martha, now Sarah. His second daughter was on her way to the unseen side of the moon.

FAMILY LEGEND HAS it that Will May instantly made up his mind that Sarah would bear his name and children when the small shy new girl from Louisiana walked into the Riderwood lumber mill yard, probably carrying a covered hot lunch for the mill chief, her employer.

A valued stoke man at the mill, Will kept the fires burning in the boiler room to make the steam that moved the saws that cut the trees. He was, my mother says, the best stoke man in the county. Everyone said so.

Will May was proud and stern, but with a deadpan sense of humor whose sting sometimes took a minute to raise a welt. My mother heard people say that, in a match of wits, Will could best his mill bosses and most if not all of the cotton and truck farmers in and around Choctaw County, Alabama, even on an off day.

Despite the lack of a formal education, he was a crack mathematician whose natural gift for surveying and crop yield estimation brought many local farmers to his door, pickup truck engines running, to pull him away from his dinner for a look at a field under cultivation.

He was a ravenous reader. Anything he could scavenge— mostly almanacs, day-old newspapers, government journals, anything white folks left lying around at the general store— went home with him to be devoured.

Will got his way, married Sarah, and discovered the joy and agony of rearing six children—four girls, two boys—during the Great Depression. Alert to the quick mind and confidence of his oldest daughter, Loubertha, he determined early on that she would finish what he couldn't—go to high school, maybe even become a teacher.

Like virtually every other black family in Riderwood, the Mays had a daily struggle on their hands: Will haunted the woods for secret stashes of ginseng root to be dried and mailed in matchboxes to pharmaceutical companies in Montgomery. He set traps for squirrel and rabbit, and occasionally he caught supper. He and Sarah kept a truck garden and raised chickens. Sarah, who had left the mill boss's family to work as cook for the only doctor in the area, now and then was able to bring a little extra home for the six May children. Their windows had no glass, they had no electricity, no plumbing, no phone.

But Loubertha had a fine intelligence, had once won a summer scholarship to the Tuskegee Institute, and damn if Will wasn't going to send her higher than anyone in his family had ever been.

He must have overlooked, ignored, or discounted the effect of his daughter's sassy repartee and auburn hair on the young men of her acquaintance. He certainly underestimated the slow smile of Booker T. Banks, who had been finding a fresh reason to be in the Mays' yard, smiling, every Sunday unless it rained.

World War II was reaching into Riderwood and draftees were marrying hastily before leaving home. Booker T., too, had been called up. Will May reluctantly gave him permission to marry Loubertha, but not without exacting a solemn promise. "You got to make sure my daughter finishes high school," he told him.

The promise had a price: Loubertha's separation from her parents, sooner than they wanted or expected. At sixteen, she was a student at the Choctaw County Training School in Lisman, but the school did not allow married women to attend classes. With Booker T. stationed in Aberdeen, Pennsylvania, the only way Loubertha could graduate from high school was to move nearby to Pittsburgh to live with Booker T.'s sister Dot and her husband Zeman, who were moving there from Alabama. There was a high school in Pittsburgh where she could complete her studies.

Preparations for Loubertha's departure did not take long. Sarah had a hat box her daughter could use as a suitcase; a couple of cardboard boxes were adequate for her other belongings. Sarah packed baked sweet potatoes and jelly biscuits for the trip in the Jim Crow railroad car, since black passengers were not allowed to buy food at train stations en route.

In spite of herself, Loubertha's excitement flashed in her eyes. Riderwood had no traffic lights, no sidewalks, no paved roads. She was going to Pittsburgh, a city full of automobiles, lights burning through the night, women with slouched hats, men wearing suits on weekdays. A city more than 850 miles from her hometown.

Will watched her, his face grave.

The mail hack, whose white driver accepted riders for a fee, came to a stop on the dirt and gravel road down the hill. Black passengers were permitted to sit on mail sacks under a canopy in the back of the hack. Dot and Zeman, already on board, had picked out two fat sacks. They sat tolerating the blanket of August heat, shifting in their make-do seats.

Sarah leaned under the canopy to give earnest instructions to them about taking care of Loubertha in "that place." Will helped Loubertha climb into the hack but could not bring himself to look at her. He had not imagined giving her up so soon, to make his dream for her come true. Instead, he looked into the woods, or at the red dust on his shoes.

The mail hack with the scowling thick-jawed driver would be Will's only connection with his daughter once she went away. The gravel below would crunch, the horn would honk, and someone would have to scamper down the hill in a hurry to get the letter before the driver got tired of waiting in the heat.

It would be more than six weeks before Will and Sarah could expect to hear from Loubertha, counting train travel and the fuss of settling into a boardinghouse in Pittsburgh. When they would see her again or hear her voice was even less certain. There was no travel money.

Without warning, the hack pulled away. The younger siblings shrieked and ran after it a few steps until the gravel began to bite their bare feet. Loubertha waved through the dust. The smile on Sarah's face had crumbled like dry bread, but she waved back, chopping at the swirling air with splayed fingers.

Will stood with his hands in his pockets until, obscured by bushes and trees, the hack passed out of sight down the road about a mile.

Sarah had been sixteen when she left home for a new life some 350 miles away. At the same age, Loubertha put more than twice that many miles between herself and her home. Next, it would be my turn.

IT WAS A fairly audacious notion in the mid-1960s, that a sixteen-year-old black girl from a Sacramento neighborhood only one generation removed from the rural South could go live and study in some unknown country, farther away than anyone in our family had ever been, except for the men who went overseas during the war. But I was Loubertha's daughter, and she wanted me to fly high.

Loubertha (in my twenties, I began calling her by her given name, woman to woman, to underscore my independence) and

I filled out piles of American Field Service application forms, hoping to win for me a scholarship to study abroad. We rushed around getting signatures. Finally, we mailed everything in.

Life rolled on and we stopped thinking about it until a day toward the end of June, a time of year when all of my friends attended summer school in the morning, some to get a jump on coursework, some just to get out of the house to keep their summer day from spoiling in the heat like fruit split open on the ground. It was already so hot in Sacramento that the tang of tar in the asphalt streets went up my nose on the way home from class.

I found Loubertha on the patio. She was peeling peaches in the shade, next to where the sun was burning a perfect square on the concrete bordered by our house, the garage, and the rented back house. I headed for the refrigerator and grape Kool-Aid, but her expression was so odd it made me wait.

"This came today, for you." She handed me a crisp envelope, a letter peeping out of it. It was from the American Field Service, addressed to me and to Loubertha and Booker T. Banks. I read, but something about the sun and heat interfered with my understanding.

I read it again: Switzerland. I was to go there. A family waited for me there. Here were their photos. The youngest daughter was one year older than me. They lived near a town called Schaffhausen, where there was a beautiful waterfall and a castle and the Rhine.

I could not seem to think.

"Do you want to go?" Loubertha's voice and eyes were complex. I would not understand what they were asking me and telling me until, more than thirty years later, it was my turn to let my own daughter go.

I was excited in spite of myself. It would be hard to leave my parents, the room where my sisters and I had fought and dreamed together, the storytelling around the dinner table, my troublemaking brothers. Part of me wanted to stay put, holding on to all of them, reassuring them that time and distance were without meaning for us.

But there was to be an ocean voyage, a new language, goats and cheese and icy mountains, yodeling and snow and some kind of dirndl I'd probably have to wear. It was irresistible. So my family, my one improbably plaid suitcase, and I made the trip to the San Francisco airport with its crush of travelers and the constant echo of news about boardings and departures. I was intoxicated with the sense of adventure.

An important blue carpet led to the passengers' boarding entry. We milled around at its edge. When the last call echoed over our heads, there were hurried hugs, "Don't forgets," and shoves from my brothers. My father held me tight. I spun around in a state of conflict and headed down the blue carpet.

"Did you forget something?" Loubertha's voice somehow floated over the din in the boarding area; she had followed me for a few steps and then called out. In my hurry to get on the plane—my first flight—I had nearly missed her embrace. Once in the air with no turning around, the regret and loss would have been overwhelming for me. I ran back to her in such a rush I nearly knocked her over, aiming to kiss her cheek but missing that altogether and planting one instead on her neck.

I would cross the continental United States, the Atlantic

Ocean, and several European countries before I got to Switzerland. There would be no calls en route or even after I arrived;
long distance was too obscenely expensive to be considered.
But letters and photographs were our connection, every week,
over more miles than many in my extended family back home
could comprehend.

My parents must have had second and third thoughts about
to whom and to what they were sending me. There would be no
one like me there. Would I learn to make myself understood?
Would I be lonely? A year and that many miles; a lot of time
and silent space.

I looked back. Nearly all hands were waving, but Loubertha's arms were folded tight across her chest. After my plane
lifted off, I am told she walked out of the airport and back to
the car very fast, the family huffing to keep pace with her.

For me, those first miles stretching over the shimmering San
Francisco cityscape led to school and eventually to work, marriage, and motherhood; my husband and I raised two daughters
in Los Angeles. When it was their turn to leave, our California
girls gave up the golden coast for colleges in the Great Mid-
west. Gisele chose Michigan, and three years later our younger
daughter, Hayley, struck out for Chicago. Visits back home
from then on were just that: visits. New flavors, new loves; a
different music was in their ears.

Helping them prepare to leave us was a study in ambivalence; our hearts brimmed with pride, but a current of longing
ran right through it. With every sock lovingly tucked into the
trunks came the sensation that we were aiding and abetting
their escape into the wilds.

But we were able to do it: help them prepare, pack, leave. We had all those electronic devices, after all. We could hear, laugh with, fuss at, instant or text message them every day, sometimes several times a day, at will. It helped.

I am descended from people who did what they had to do and did it without the promise of even a phone call. In their lives, distance was a hand that came and snatched your child in the dust or in the predawn gloom. It was something to fear, but something they had to accept. "That was just how it was," my mother says.

My people had their reasons. Economics. Hopes that their child would catch a break, not miss an opportunity. The intrusion of a slow smile, the inevitable upheavals that come with love and war. Whatever the reasons, they gave us up, shaping the family history like a river carving canyons.

Would I have had the strength to let my daughters go the way Reverend Waller did, or any of the others? I can't say. Because I live in times in which the meaning of a mile grows ever more faint, I have not had to discover the answer. I hope I've at least had the good sense to pass on to my daughters their ancestors' relevant genes. Because when it comes time for them to help their own children leave, they still will need a measure of stoicism in their veins, no matter how wireless the world.

Leaving the Island

Martha Tod Dudman

Thirty years ago, at age twenty-three, I stepped onto the dock at Little Cranberry Island with a knapsack, a carton of Lucky Strikes, a light green Hermes typewriter, and the confused determination I'd had all my life—to be a writer.

I'd come to that small Maine island for the summer, but I spent the next four years there. I supported myself with odd jobs: working at the general store, babysitting, painting houses. My mother sent me some money. I tried working as stern man on a lobster boat one fall, but the long days spent hauling traps and stuffing bait bags on the choppy sea were too hard and too cold. Most of the time I was writing, or squinting, with what I hoped was literary concentration, through clouds of cigarette smoke at the sea. The island is tiny—only a mile by a mile and a half—but I almost never felt bored or lonely. Though I'd grown up in Washington, D.C., and gone to college in Ohio, I'd been spending summers on Little Cranberry since I was five or six, and it felt like home to me.

There were eighty-seven people on the island, about half of us under thirty. In addition to the older married couples, mostly fishermen and carpenters and their wives, there was a crop of handsome young lobstermen and a handful of artists and writers—part of the urban outflow of the 1970s. We were in search of authenticity and life.

On summer evenings we built enormous bonfires on the back beach and sat around drinking beer and cheap red wine. Moonlight glinted on the black water that stretched out toward what I thought was Spain. The night air was chilly away from the fire, but hot by the flames. The smoke billowed up and dark waves lapped the shore, dragging the stones back and forth with a rattling, comfortable sound. I could have stayed there all night.

IN THE COLD fall, I got up early. The air was clean and bracing, the floor frigid, my determination intense. From the window I could see the fishing boats heading out of the harbor. The lobstermen were wonderful with their strong arms and tanned faces, and they handled the boats, the traps, and life itself with infinite grace—swinging their heavy traps up onto the side of the boat, hurling the short lobsters back into the ocean to grow larger for another year's catch, the sparkling sea all around and the dark blue mountains of the mainland set against the clean, pale sky.

The Fernalds, one of the original island families, had a big house in the middle of the island. The fishermen's voices came crackling over the old CB radio in the kitchen, where we women gathered in the afternoon for tea and hard gingerbread or leftover muffins from breakfast.

Evening came early in winter. The houses were quiet, woodsmoke curling from the chimneys and the day's work done. As I walked home at twilight, I'd meet Warren Fernald coming up the road in his big boots, carrying some crabs he'd caught in his traps for his wife, Anna, to pick out. She'd sell the crabmeat pound by pound and in this way pay for a car eventually, a long white car she kept parked on the mainland and learned to drive at forty.

I thought I would live there forever.

There's something about living on an island that small. While you become intimate with the place itself—each tree, each curve in each path in the forest, the line of rocks exposed at low tide on the shore—you also become part of a close-knit community. I found I could recognize someone a quarter mile away. Long before I could distinguish their features, I knew it was Arthur by his blue jacket and his slightly bowlegged walk, or Hazel, leaning forward in her tidy brown coat, hurrying to the post office on a winter morning. Everyone knew everything about me, but that knowledge was contained somehow—the water around the island a safe shield that held us all together and kept the world at bay.

It sounds kind of corny, I know, but the island community really is like one big family. A quarrelly, cranky family some days. A family with a nasty old aunt who says inappropriate things and has that unfortunate mustache; a family with a grouchy grandpa and a spoiled little niece—but a family that looks after its own. And so, if there's fire, or trouble, or a child gets sick, or a boat gets lost, or a family falls on hard times—the whole island rallies, comes close, bearing corn bread and soup, jelly and pickles, casseroles and comfort and care.

I STAYED ON the island almost four years. Wrote two books and many stories, but I published almost nothing, and I began to feel as if I'd come to the end of something. Maybe I wasn't ever going to be a writer, after all. Maybe I'd just been hiding out from life there, hunkering down and feeling too safe. Wasn't it time I went back out into the world? Talked to people I didn't know inside and out? I didn't realize at the time that this was the way my life was always going to be—periods of solitude and quiet followed by flurries of gregariousness and action. And I didn't know how seductive each could be—how long times spent alone and writing would send me hurtling into outside adventures, hungry for talk and lights and heedless conversation, and then how all of that would send me back where I could be alone. I didn't yet understand the contrary pull that would dog me all my life—I only knew it was time to leave.

I didn't go far—just across the water to Mount Desert Island, which is only an approximation of an island, connected, as it is, to the real mainland by a bridge, with access to movies and restaurants, Bangor and malls and the highway beyond. I could drive to Portland if I wanted to, I could drive clear through to Quebec or Montreal or New York City. I was only three miles away from Little Cranberry by boat—a half-hour ride—but an eternity removed in spirit, and though I came to make the new town home, it was never home the way the island was.

I gave up the island and I gave up writing. I was twenty-seven now—a grown-up, or trying to be. I decided it was time I became a responsible adult, so I started taking night courses in education at the University at Orono, got a job in special education, and then another job at a residential treatment center for adolescents. I fell in love, got married, and had two children. But the marriage didn't work out, and so, in my mid-thirties, I got divorced and took a job working at the radio stations my family had bought in Ellsworth.

Within a few years I took over the business and bought a third radio station in Bangor. Now I knew what the world was about—or thought I did. I had to make money, learn about business, join the Rotary, be a success. And if sometimes I felt I was living someone else's life, well, I was doing the right thing, wasn't I? I was supporting my children. My ex-husband was still in the area and he loved his kids, but he wasn't much help financially. It was up to me. I was doing what I had to do.

I missed it, though—the writing, the interior conversation, the construction of combinations of words on the page. I missed the island, too: the quiet desolation and the tides; the sense of peace and timelessness; the way I knew each island house so intimately: the layout of the rooms, the colors of the wallpaper, the halls.

The island wasn't far away. My parents still had their house there, and I often took my children out in summer on the mail boat. I wanted them to experience the sun on the field, the cry of the gulls, the sound the rocks made when the receding tide pulled the small stones down and back, down and back, and we lay on the sun-warmed rocks dreamily thinking of nothing, smelling the warm smell of sunshine and seaweed and summer.

My children loved the island. They picked blueberries, as I had, in the field out front of the house. Heard the same ting! ting! as the berries fell into the same tin pan I'd used when I was a kid. I took my son down the woodsy path back of a neighbor's house to see the old rusty truck with the square, old-fashioned windshield still intact, and I made up a story about the man who had driven that truck deep into the forest and left it there long ago.

During the sad first years after my divorce, I brought my children out to the island in winter, too. We borrowed a house for a few days and made raisin bread in the gas stove and sat by the fire to read. Outside the full moon rose, enormous, over the trees. We took long walks in the snowy woods and slid on the icy pools. I wanted them to know how the field looked covered with snow; the woods mysterious and silent, the wide marsh a frozen tundra. "Let's pretend we're in Russia!" we'd cry and march out across the white expanse in our big boots and fur hats. I wanted them to know how it felt to sit in the Fernalds' warm kitchen eating cookies Anna had made, listening to Warren's jokes, exchanging compliments and stories and gossip and good-natured insults with those dear old friends.

———

IT'S NOT EASY growing up in Maine. It's not easy growing up anywhere, and Maine has its own set of circumstances. The rural dreaminess so seductive to adults, and so magical for young children, can be boring and dangerous to a teenager. And if you're smart and a little bit different, if you have a divorced, single mother who works all the time and would rather be writing, if you live in a town full of rich summer people and resentful year-round folk, and you don't quite fit into either category—it can be very hard.

My children had an untidy adolescence. Neither one was happy in school. My daughter took to drugs; my son, to the sea.

My daughter found her own dangerous way out and back and then away again. Everything was blown apart during the two or three years that my daughter was taking drugs, stealing, getting into trouble, running away for days at a time and then reappearing, dirty and sullen after her wild nights. I finally sent her out west, first to a wilderness program, and then to a residential treatment facility, not so different from the one here in Maine where I had worked years before. During that difficult time I found that nothing I had thought so important really mattered anymore. The only thing that mattered during those dark days was that my daughter would stay alive.

She did stay alive, and we both changed and grew. I reconnected with writing stories, beginning with my own. In the midst of the tumult, I had sold the family radio stations, and now I found myself with a pocket of time—my daughter in treatment, my son just finishing school—the house quiet and orderly for the first time in years. I wrote a book, *Augusta, Gone*, about what had happened to us—and it was that book that allowed me to give shape to what we'd gone through and finally, truly express to my daughter how much I loved her.

SHE LIVES IN California now, where she says she belongs. She's shed her Maine childhood like an ill-fitting coat. She's in college full-time in San Marcos and working, too. She calls me from her cell phone as she barrels down the highway in her silver Element. She's got an appointment, she tells me, in San Diego. Just got her business cards. She's switching her major to sociology and she's taking a wonderful class. She still loves to come here in summer, when it's spangly, bright, and warm, but "not in the winter, Mom," she tells me firmly, and tries to tempt me westward with tales of how I'd love Palm Springs— "You can hike," she tells me, "and there are lots of older Jewish men. You'd love it."

She calls me often. I know more about her life now than I ever did when she was younger and living at home. I've learned not to tell her what to do; and I've learned not to be afraid to tell her what I think. Sometimes it amazes me—how much we sound like each other when we talk. Sometimes I think she is me and I am the one with the long blond hair flying back, soaring along the highways of California, jabbering into a cell phone, radio turned up loud. She's me without all the weight of my life upon me.

I've gotten used to having her far away, and when she comes home I have to get used to having her here—the chaos in the living room, the TV on, the music blasting, her odd hours. But then, when she leaves, I have to get used to being alone all over again every time. I like both ways of being—the quiet order of my single life, and the cozy camaraderie when she is here.

My son lives on Little Cranberry Island. Early on, he was entranced by boats. He earned the money to buy his first one at eleven—a fiberglass skiff named *Bombay*. When he was a freshman in high school, the principal, who'd loved boats himself at that age, helped him get a job as crew on a boat delivery to Florida. He learned navigation and did a report for school credit. By fourteen, he was fishing—stern man to an old friend from Little Cranberry, who was a young fisherman himself when I lived out there.

My son had his captain's license by the time he was eighteen, had finished high school, moved out to the island, and was hauling a few traps of his own from a nineteen-foot outboard. Now, at twenty-two, he fishes out of a thirty-six-foot, forty-year-old lobster boat that he bought himself and completely rebuilt. It's called the *Georgia Peach*, after his sister.

He called me one evening, late in the fall. "Go out and look at the northern lights, Mom," he said. He'd been out on the back beach, and he wanted me to see them, too. So a friend and I walked up to the top of Schoolhouse Ledge here in town. It was beautiful, it was amazing, but it wasn't the same as being on the island—I knew what he'd seen out there—the great shafts of light over the ocean, the pulsing pink- and green-colored streaks in the inverted bowl of the sky.

Sometimes the solitude and lack of single women get him down, but he loves it on the island. He's joined the Cranberry Isles Fishermen's Co-op and the Volunteer Fire Department, never misses a community supper at the Neighborhood House or the school play, performed by the seventeen kids at the two-room island school. In winter he hauls out his boat and heads west, leaving his car in my driveway under the basketball net—where he used to shoot hoops on spring evenings, while I washed the supper dishes, watching him from the kitchen window. I'd be tired and cross from a long day at work, but I remember being moved, almost stunned, by the elegance of his leaps, his grace. When our children are removed from us, even by a pane of glass, they can seem miraculous.

He spent a couple of winters in California near his sister; got a job building houses in La Jolla. Then last year he went to Costa Rica to learn Spanish, and traveled through Panama and Nicaragua. This winter he's in South America, deep in the Amazon jungle, a place I visited myself at his age. He travels, as I did, alone, but he makes friends everywhere he goes, because he expects to.

He used to be shy, my son, as a little boy, but he's become the man he is now on the island. And he goes out into the world, expecting the world to welcome him, the way the island has.

I think when you have the safety of a true home you can go anywhere. When you have a safe anchor, you can drift a bit without fearing you will lose your way entirely and be washed up, helpless, on some rocky shore.

I still live in the house in which I raised my children. I've taken down the posters, painted over the walls once pocked with thumbtacks and tape marks. Their favorite toys are in the attic, but most of their books are still on their shelves. After my daughter's whirlwind visits, she always leaves behind a trail of sequins and high heels and torn paperbacks. My son's size-

fifteen shoes stand by the door. I have their photographs everywhere at many ages—the babies that they were, the two fine
grown-up people they've become. They don't belong here now.
They're in their lives. And when I miss them most it's that I
miss the children that they were—the time we had together
when they were little.

My daughter will finish college soon and wants to open an
art gallery in California. She's spent the last few summers at
home in Maine, working at the restaurant on Little Cranberry.
She says she'll always come back here to visit, but she couldn't
live here now. "Are you kidding, Mom?" she says to me in mock
outrage. "Snow?"

My son doesn't know, he says, if he will fish forever. He has
a lot of ideas—things he might do. I know he has written some
stories. He likes to build houses. He loves to travel. He can do
anything. I am convinced of it, and he is, too.

That's maybe what an island does for you, if you live there
awhile. It gives you a place you can always go back to. It gives
you a sense of self. It gives you a quiet little nest of memories
and impressions, of pictures that you can always take out and
look at—no matter where you are—at a busy meeting somewhere in a city; speaking to a roomful of strangers; in a tiny,
strange South American hotel. If you are in a bad marriage or
a no-win business negotiation; a hospital bed; a fight—you
will always have it, tattooed on your heart—the sight of the
ocean opening up before you, the sun on the rocks, the wind in
your face, and the wide, impenetrable, dependable sky.

Good-bye to the Sunset Man

Lee Smith

Once again my husband and I line up for sunset cruise tickets on the tall vintage schooner *Western Union*, which sways in its dock at the end of William Street, Key West, here at the end of America.

"How many?" The handsome blonde in the ticket booth looks like she used to be a man.

"Three," I say.

"Two," Hal says, turning around to look at me.

"So how many is it?" She drums her long nails on the wooden counter.

"Two," Hal says. He gives her his credit card.

She slides over two tickets for the sunset cruise and two coupons for free drinks, which we order on the roof of the Schooner Wharf Bar where we wait until time to board. This year we are here without my son, Josh, who died in his sleep this past October 26. The cause of his death was an "acute my-ocardiopathy," the collapse of an enlarged heart brought about, in part, I believe, by all the weight he had gained while taking an antipsychotic drug. He was thirty-three; he had been sick for half his life, doing daily heroic battle with the brain disorder that first struck while he was in a program for gifted teen musicians at the Berklee College of Music in Boston, the summer between his junior and senior years in high school.

Back in Chapel Hill, we'd started getting wilder and wilder phone calls from him about "birds flying too close to the sun," reports of all-night practice sessions on the piano, strange encounters in the park, and no sleep—no sleep, ever. He flew home in a straitjacket.

Then the hospitalizations began—first a lengthy stay at Holly Hill in Raleigh followed by a short, heartbreaking try at returning home to normalcy and Chapel Hill High; then long-term care at Highland Hospital in Asheville, where he lived for the next four years, sometimes in the hospital itself, sometimes in their group home, sometimes in an apartment with participation in their day program. For a while he was better, then not. All kinds of fantasies and scenarios rolled through his head. He moved, talked, and dressed bizarrely; he couldn't remember anything; he couldn't even read. We brought him back to UNC Neurosciences Hospital. They referred him to Dorothea Dix Hospital's test program for the new "wonder drug" clozapine, just legalized in this country.

Up on that beautiful, windy hill looking out over the city of Raleigh, Josh started getting truly better for the first time. At twenty-three, he could participate in a real conversation; he could make a joke. It was literally a miracle.

He was able to leave the hospital and enter Caramore Community in Chapel Hill, which offered vocational rehabilitation, a group home, and then a supervised apartment—as well as a lot of camaraderie. He came in with some great stories as he worked with the Caramore lawn and housecleaning business . . . my favorite being the time the housecleaning crew dared one of the gang to jump into the baptismal pool at a local church they were cleaning—and then they all "baptized" him on the spot. Before long he graduated into a real job at Carolina Cleaners. Against all odds, Josh had become a "working man," as he always referred to himself; his pride in this was enormous.

Though other hospitalizations ("tune-ups," he called them) would be required from time to time, Josh was on his way. He lived in his own apartment, drove a car, managed his weekly doctor visits, blood tests, pharmacy trips, and medication. But as the most important member of his own "treatment team," he steadfastly refused his doctor's eventual urging to switch to one of the newer drugs, such as olanzapine, risperidol, or geodon, in hopes of jump-starting his metabolism. Clozapine had given him back his life, and he didn't want to give it up. And in spite of his weight and smoking, he seemed healthy enough; physical examinations didn't ring any warning bells.

Josh became a familiar figure in Chapel Hill and Carrboro, with friends and acquaintances all over town—especially his regular haunts such as Weaver Street and Caffe Driade, where he went every day. Josh worked at Akai Hana Japanese Restaurant in Carrboro for the last seven years of his life, doing every-thing from washing dishes to prep work to lunchtime sushi chef. He was the first one there every morning—he opened up and started preparing the rice. It was his favorite time of the day, as he often said. He played piano at Akai Hana every Sat-urday night: a mix of jazz, blues, and his own compositions.

The live music produced by the Wharf Bar's Jimmy Buffett wannabe band is way too loud, and our drinks, when they come, are a startling shade of red, with umbrellas in them. Hal raises his plastic glass high. "Here's to the big guy," he says. We drain them.

Josh considered the schooner trip a requisite for his annual Key West experience. He loved the ritual of it all, beginning when the crew invited the evening's passengers to participate in raising the mainsail. He always went over to line up and pull, passing the halyard hand over hand to the next guy. He loved to stand at the rail as we passed the town dock and Mallory Square, where all the weird pageantry of the sunset was already in full swing: the tourists, the guy with the trained housecats, the flame swallower, the escape artist tied up in chains, the oddly terrifying cookie lady. The aging hippie musician on board invariably cranked up "Sloop John B" as we headed out to sea while the sun sank lower on the starboard side. The sun was so bright that I couldn't even face it without sunglasses, but Josh never wore them. He just sat there perfectly still, star-ing straight into the sun, a little smile playing around his lips.

What thoughts went through his head on his last voyage, a year before he died?

Perhaps more to the point, what thoughts did not go

through his head, in this later stage of schizophrenia characterized by "blank mind" and "lack of affect"? Gone the voices, gone the visions, gone the colored lights, to be replaced by . . . what? Maybe nothing, like the bodhisattva, a person who has achieved the final apotheosis, beyond desire and self. Here he sat, an immense man in a black T-shirt and blue jeans, silent, calm, apparently at peace. He no longer seemed to know what he had lost.

Some call this a "blessing," and some days I am among them; but most days I am not, remembering instead that wild boy of seventeen who wanted the world—all the music; all the friends, BMX bikes, and skateboards; all the poetry; all the girls—all the life there ever was.

Now the captain is blowing the conch shell from the deck of the *Western Union*. We stand. The sun slants into our eyes. A breeze is coming up. I pull on my windbreaker, fingering the little bronze vial of ashes in my pocket.

It's time.

THAT LAST JANUARY, Josh and I flew into Key West together, arriving late on a cool and blustery Tuesday night around 9 P.M. Wind rattled the palm fronds as we walked out onto the brightly lit but somehow lonely-looking Duval Street. Only a few people scurried past, their shoulders hunched against the wind. We passed the funky Chicken Store, a "safe house" for the much-maligned chickens that have overrun Key West. We passed the Scrub Club, an "adult" bathhouse that usually featured its scantily clad ladies blowing bubbles over the balcony rail, calling out, "Hi there! Feeling dirty? Need a bath?" to the amused passersby. But it was too cool for bubbles that night, and the girls were all inside behind their red door. The wind whipped paper trash along the street.

We crossed Duval and went into the friendly-looking Coffee and Tea House, where big trees overhung an old bungalow with a porch and yard filled with comfortable, mismatched furniture. Josh was very tired. He had that out-of-it, blank look he sometimes gets, almost vegetative, like a big sweet potato. We walked up the concrete steps and into the bar with its comforting, helpful smell of coffee brewing. People clustered at little tables, on sofas, in armchairs in adjacent rooms, talking and reading the newspapers strewn everyplace.

The bartender's long, gray hair was pulled back into a ponytail. He came over to Josh and said, "What can I get for you, sir?"

"Well, I'll tell you," Josh said in a surprisingly loud voice (maybe it even surprised him), shaking his head like a dog coming up from under the water. "I'll tell you, buddy, I don't know what the hell it is I want, and I don't know where the hell it is I am, and I don't know what the hell it is I'm doing!"

Heads along the bar swiveled, and the bartender burst out laughing. "In that case, sir, you've come to the right island!" he announced as everybody applauded.

Josh had found his Key West home for the next week. At bars or beaches, he talked to everybody; you never knew what he was going to say next.

He told a great version of the Christmas story, too, conflating the Bible with O. Henry: "Once upon a time there was a young girl who was very sick, and somehow she got the idea that she would die when all the leaves fell off the tree that grew just outside her bedroom window. One by one they dropped. She got sicker and sicker. Finally there was only one red leaf left on the tree; she was just about to die. That night while she was asleep, Jesus flew up to her window. Jesus was a French artist. He wore a red beret. So he brought his box of oil paints with him and painted red leaves all over the window, finishing just as the sun came up and the last red leaf fluttered down to the ground. Then he flew away. Then she woke up, and she was well, and it was Christmas."

Answering the question of whether or not he believed in Jesus, Josh said, "Well, I don't know. Every time I'm in the hospital, there are at least three people in there who think they're Jesus. So sometimes I think, well, maybe Jesus wasn't Jesus at all—maybe he was just the first schizophrenic."

Josh's eventual diagnosis was schizo-affective, meaning partly schizophrenic (his mind did not work logically, his senses were often unreliable, his grip on reality sometimes tenuous) and partly bipolar—actually a blessing, since the characteristic "ups and downs" allowed him more expression and empathy. But diagnosis is tricky at best. The sudden onset of these major brain disorders usually occurs in the late teens or early twenties, and it's usually severe. But all psychosis looks alike at first. There's no way to distinguish between the "highs" of bipolar illness, for instance, and the florid stage of schizophrenia—or even a garden-variety LSD psychosis. Reality had fled in every case. The best doctors make no claims; "Wait and see," they say.

———

A YEAR LATER, my husband and I sit discreetly at the very back of the *Western Union*, right behind the captain at the wheel. He has given the order; the crew has cried "fire in the hole" and shot off the cannon. We have covered our ears. We have gotten our complimentary wine, our conch chowder. We have listened to our shipmates talk about how much snow they left behind in Cleveland, how many grandchildren they have, and how one guy played hockey for Hopkins on that great team in 1965. Then we duck as, with a great whoosh of the jib, we come about. We sit quietly, holding hands, hard. Now there's a lot of wind. All around us, people are putting on their jackets.

Independent of any of this, the sky puts on its big show, gearing up for sunset. The sun speeds up as it sinks lower and lower. The water turns into a sheet of silver, like a mirror.

Like Hal, Josh was a major sunset man, always looking for that legendary green flash right after the sunset, which nobody I know has ever actually seen, though everybody claims to have known somebody who has seen it. Here, where sunset is a religion, we never miss the moment. In Key West the sun grows huge and spreads out when it touches the water, so that it's no longer round at all but a glowing red beehive shape that plunges down abruptly to the thunderous applause of the revelers back at Mallory Square.

"Get ready," Hal says in my ear. "But look, there's a cloud bank, it's not going to go all the way."

I twist the top of the vial in my windbreaker pocket.

The sun glows neon red, cut off at the bottom by clouds.

A hush falls over the whole crowd on board the *Western Union*. Everybody faces west. Cameras are raised. It is happening.

"Bon voyage," Hal says. Suddenly, the sun is gone. The crowd cheers. I throw the ashes out on the water behind us; like a puff of smoke, they disappear immediately into the wake. I say, "Good-bye, baby." Nobody notices. The water turns into mother-of-pearl, shining pink all the way from our schooner to the horizon. The scalloped edge of the puffy clouds goes from pink to gold. The crowd goes "aah." Good-bye, baby. But no green flash. The crowd stretches, they move, they mill around on deck. The light fades and stars come out.

I don't agree with the theory that mental illness conveys certain gifts. Even if this sometimes seems to be the case, as in bipolar disorder's frequent association with creativity, those gifts are not worth the pain and devastating losses the illness also brings with it. Yet sometimes there are moments. . . .

I am remembering one starry summer night back in North Carolina, the kind of breathtakingly beautiful summer night of all our dreams, when Josh and I took a long walk around our village. He'd been staying with us for several days because he was too sick to stay in his own apartment. He'd been deteriorating for months, and his doctor had arranged his admission to UNC's Neurosciences Hospital for the next morning. Josh didn't know this yet. But he was always "compliant," as they call it. We were very lucky in this. My friend's son wouldn't take his medicine and chose to live on the street; she never knew where he was.

Josh liked the hospital. It was safe, and the world he'd been in that week in North Carolina was not safe, not at all, a world where strangers were talking about him and people he used to know inhabited other people's bodies and tables turned into spiders and all the familiar landmarks disappeared so that he couldn't find his way anywhere. He couldn't sleep, he couldn't drive, he couldn't think.

Yet on that summer night in Hillsborough, a wonderful thing happened. We were walking through the alley between the old Confederate cemetery and our backyard when we ran into our neighbor Allan.

"Hi there, Josh," Allan said.

Instead of replying, Josh sang out a single note of music.

"A-flat," he said. It hung in the hot honeysuckle air.

"Nice," Allan said, passing on.

The alley ended at Tryon Street, where we stepped onto the sidewalk. A young girl hurried past.

"C sharp," Josh said, then sang it out.

The girl looked at him before she disappeared into the Presbyterian Church.

We crossed the street and walked past the young policeman getting out of his car in front of the police station.

"Middle C," Josh said, humming.

Since it was one of Hillsborough's "Last Friday" street fairs, we ran into more and more people as we headed toward the center of town. For each one, Josh had a musical note—or a chord, for a pair or a group.

"What's up?" I finally asked.

"Well, you know I have perfect pitch," he said—I nodded, though he did not—"and everybody we see has a special musical note, and I can hear every one." He broke off to sing a high chord for a couple of young teen girls, then dropped into a lower register for a retired couple eating ice-cream cones.

"Hello," another neighbor said, smiling when Josh hummed back at him.

So it went all over town. Even some of the buildings had notes, apparently: the old Masonic Hall, the courthouse, the corner bar. Josh was singing his heart out. And almost— almost—it was a song, the symphony of Hillsborough. We were both exhilarated. We walked and walked. By the time we got back home, he was exhausted. Finally he slept. The next day, he went into the hospital.

Josh loved James Taylor, especially his song "Fire and Rain." But we were too conservative, or chickenshit, or something, to put it on his tombstone, the same way we were "not cool enough," as Josh put it, to walk down the aisle to "Purple Rain" (his idea) while he played the piano on the day we got married in 1985.

I say the song to Hal as the light fades slowly on the water behind us, with that last line about seeing you again. Well, I won't. I know this. But what a privilege it was to live on this earth with Josh, what a privilege it was to be his mother. There will be a lessening of pain, there will be consolations, I can tell. But as C. S. Lewis wrote in *On Grief*: "Reality never repeats. . . . That is what we should all like, the happy past restored" . . . as it can never be, and maybe never was. Who's got perfect pitch, anyway? Yet to have children—or simply to experience great love for any person at all—is to throw yourself wide open to the possibility of pain at any moment. But I would not choose otherwise. Not now, not ever. Like every parent with a disabled child, my greatest fear used to be that I would die first. "I can't die," I always said whenever any risky undertaking was proposed. So now I can die. But I don't want to. Instead, I want to live as hard as I can, burning up the days in honor of his sweet, hard life.

Night falls on the schooner ride back to Key West. I clutch the bronze vial that held some of Josh's ashes, tracing its engraved design with my finger. The wind blows my hair. The young couple in front of us are making out.

"Let's get some oysters at Alonzo's," Hal says, and suddenly I realize that I'm starving.

"Look," the captain says, pointing up. "Venus."

Sure enough. Then we see the Big Dipper, Orion, Mars. Where's that French artist with the red beret? No sign of him, and no green flash, either—but stars. A whole sky full of them by the time we slide into the dock at the end of William Street.

The Shuffle

Jan Constantine

For years my life went absolutely according to plan. I had a husband and three children, I had a career as a corporate attorney, and I had a hobby, which was singing. Everything moved forward at a predictable pace—my first child went to college, my second child went to the same college, and I assumed that when my third child, Elizabeth, was a senior in high school, we'd go through the process again in preparation for her departure.

Except Elizabeth decided when she was a sophomore that she wanted a change of scene—quite a change, in fact, since she wanted to spend the second semester as a foreign exchange student in Australia. Admittedly, my motherly responsibilities had been waning since Elizabeth began her adolescence, and I had expected that they would continue to do so until my sole function was to be a human ATM machine, dispensing money on demand. But Australia? That was speeding up the process a bit.

Elizabeth was a very independent child, with a talent for attracting a gaggle of close friends wherever she roamed, and we had traveled as a family, so the idea of her spending six months so far away didn't scare me. We found a program, threw a farewell party at an Outback restaurant, just to get everyone in the Down Under mood, and sent Elizabeth to Tasmania to live with a family and attend a vocational high school for six months.

Free at last, sort of. What would I do with six months of a temporarily empty nest? My husband didn't have much time to spend with me, since he was buried nose-deep in an antitrust trial. I didn't have much free time, either, since being a corporate lawyer ate up its share of nights and weekends. But I had some time, and I thought I ought to use it well. I was a member of the City Bar Chorus, a singing group made up of lawyers, paralegals, anyone associated with the legal profession, and we sang for audiences in nursing homes, children's hospitals, and fire stations. I loved running the sing-along, leading the audience in old favorites. What if I tried doing a show on my own?

Eureka! I had found my project. I decided to take a cabaret performing workshop, to test my mettle as a solo performer. Elizabeth had extended herself beyond the normal boundaries of her life, and I would take inspiration from that.

I auditioned right after she left, for a class that began a month later, in the spring. Everyone in the class was like me— people who did something else for a living and wanted to try a new outlet for their creative juices: doctors, lawyers, executives, students, actors, retirees, an accountant. All of us were aspiring performers who were willing to pay $600 to spend three hours a week learning how to deliver a song in the intimate setting of a cabaret. And there was no way out. The eight-week class culminated in a performance at a New York City cabaret, where each one of us could invite friends and family to watch us strut our stuff.

What a thrill this was for me; I had happy memories of singing as far back as sixth grade, when I was one of two students chosen to represent my elementary school at a local songfest. When I thought about it, this had always been a passion of mine, one that had been shoved to the side to make room for real life—I'd sung in school choruses in junior high and high school, I'd been a member of an a capella group in college, and I sang my kids to sleep with show tunes. I sang in the car, I sang in the shower, and I sang with my synagogue's adult choir. The class was a chance to take something that was very important to me and bring it center stage, at least temporarily.

I loved everything about the amateur cabaret scene: the fragile egos of the performers, the polite detachment of the accompanists, the techies on sound and lights, the talented waiters who hoped that they, too, would be discovered someday. There were even cabaret groupies who came to all the shows with the expectation that other performers would feel guilty enough to come to their shows in return. I got the camaraderie of the uninitiated; we all got mutual respect and admiration for daring to go public, and solo, in front of paying customers, even if the customers were sympathetic friends and family of the performers on that night's bill.

By the time Elizabeth returned from Tasmania, a month before her junior year began, I had one show under my belt (two songs) and was about to move up to the intermediate class (three songs), on my way to the advanced workshop (five songs!). I dragged my parents, my cousins, my high school friends, my college buddies, and my legal colleagues to those shows, cajoling them to shell out twenty-two dollars to hear me and some strangers sing our hearts out. My half year of childlessness had turned a hobby into a miniature career.

I was feeling brave, so I decided to work up an act with a classmate and fellow lawyer, Susan Elicks. Sue has a beautiful voice and prefers ballads, while I go for the specialty songs, fast and funny, but we are a great team. We hired a director and accompanist, booked another cabaret venue, and started to work on a show for June 2005. Elizabeth would graduate from high school, and I would graduate to the ranks of working singers.

I was thrilled when my two worlds collided—several mothers of Elizabeth's friends had seen me perform, and they invited me to sing at a senior class wine-tasting and fund-raiser for the parents. The venue was the glamorous school lunchroom, but I thought it was a great idea.

Elizabeth was not so sure. In fact, she was completely mortified at the notion that I was encroaching on her territory; she was not at all pleased that I had agreed. She managed to be away the day of the show, looking at prospective colleges, and, since none of her friends got to see me, she recovered quickly.

As for me, I was delighted at the way all the threads of my life seemed to be so comfortably woven together.

A week later, I got fired.

It was one of those management shifts, where people from the old regime move out and people from the new regime move in, but that was little comfort. I had no recourse, so I focused instead on keeping the rest of my life as stable as possible. It wouldn't be fair to Elizabeth if I left work immediately. These were the last months of her senior year, and I didn't want to be underfoot when she was home with her friends, doing what high school seniors who have been accepted into college do during their last semester—nothing! So I set up my severance to make sure I didn't leave my job, officially, until the end of June.

Then I threw myself into rehearsals for the cabaret show. Suddenly, singing took on a whole new importance in my life. Those rehearsals kept me sane. I was about to lose my identity as a full-time working woman and mother for the first time since my son was born, in 1978. I was grateful to have something to do rather than sit around feeling dazed and upset. College was now only months away for Elizabeth, and I had to figure out who I was going to be without children and without a job. Empty nest is one thing. Empty life was totally unacceptable.

But I'd been working forever, so I had no answer to the question, What next? I'd never thought about it. For the second time, I looked to Elizabeth for inspiration. After graduation, she returned to Tasmania to visit the family she'd lived with, and when she came home she explained her plan for the rest of the summer, which involved relaxing and pleasurable pursuits. Life was going to be downhill after this, she said, with school and jobs and other hassles too numerous to imagine. For once, I agreed with her. I decided that I, too, was in between obligations at the moment, having graduated from my last job, having to consider my next one. My summer should be similarly footloose and fancy-free; I vowed not to seek another job until Elizabeth left in the fall.

We coexisted for a while, Elizabeth sleeping until two in the afternoon and me doing some volunteer work. I went back to piano lessons, which I'd abandoned when I was fourteen. There were bicycle rides in Central Park, museum afternoons, lunches with friends who still had jobs. If I craved an office, there was a small but cozy nook at my husband's firm. After a few weeks, something dawned on me: This life change wasn't so bad after all.

In the scheme of things—Elizabeth in Tasmania, me out of a job—her departure for the University of Wisconsin seemed more manageable than it might have been when life was still an orderly enterprise. My husband and I accompanied her to Madison, and I have to be frank: I don't know which of the two of us, Elizabeth or I, was more relieved to see the other one leave. For all the anticipation, I didn't have a twinge when she left; in part, I guess, because I'd already had two children leave for college. I was ready for Elizabeth to follow suit. And we'd gotten to the point where we were butting heads—not because we were having trouble with each other but because we are so very much alike. She needed to be on her own, and I imagine that she, like me, had begun secretly to crave the excitement of not knowing what to expect next. Life can take interesting twists and turns.

In my case, I was offered a part-time position as general counsel for the Authors Guild, and, to my surprise, I took it. Elizabeth's early departure, and my professional upheaval, and my singing, had all conspired to teach me a new lesson. I had developed a real appreciation for a little bit of spontaneity in life, something that had been missing in my existence until now. I'd had a taste of a different balance between work, and family, and me, and I'd come to like it.

So I embarked on my empty nest journey a very different woman than I expected to be, less defined by my job, more committed to a variety of things, with some experience of living in an empty house. Along the way, I learned the best secret, which is that "empty" is a temporary state, whether it applies to family or to work. Life fills up again: My son, who had an apartment for his first year of graduate school, while Elizabeth was in Tasmania, came home for his second year, and his girlfriend spent many nights at the homestead with him. When they got engaged, and started spending most of their time together in Brooklyn, our apartment felt like a morgue—but just as I was starting to feel too alone, a family friend moved in for four months while she finished her graduate studies.

By the time she was ready to move out, I was in rehearsals for my second cabaret show with Sue, aptly entitled "Ready to Begin Again." I'm taking a tap-dancing class. My son's wedding is on the horizon. My other daughter, who's been in San Francisco, has just announced that she misses home and plans to head east for graduate school. And Elizabeth visits us with her old friends from high school, and her new friends from college, in tow. We don't have an empty nest, ever, for very long. It's really a modified empty nest, and between family and friends, that's what I expect we'll have for the rest of my life.

It's a lot of change. I used to think that I understood the balance of my life, the meaning of family, and career, and music, the percentage of every day that was to be devoted to each of them. But the family nest changes unpredictably, and the work nest? Sometimes that changes unpredictably, too, and you're the one who gets emptied out. Along the way, I learned flexibility. Empty? That's just what happens right before the nest fills up again. Someone will always be there for me to preen over, to protect and defend.

Legacies

Roger Wilkins

She's gone. College was over last year. Now she has finished her postgraduate fellowship year as well and she has gotten herself a job—in New York. It is a job that requires a car and also requires an apartment shared by other very young emancipated adults. She also has a boyfriend—a very nice, well-educated young man who has a wonderful smile and is as comfortable and friendly as an old collie. He too will be working in New York. As I said, she's gone.

So, my wife and I now have an empty nest. It is a subject that my wife has been discussing, confronting, and wrestling to the ground for the last five years. Patricia is energized by change. She addresses it, ponders it, slugs it, and deploys her troops (me) to make the appropriate adjustments.

I hate change. I try hard to ignore it, but I can't ignore The Force Arrayed Against Me, so while carrying out my orders I fight rear-guard skirmishes designed to protect as much of the status quo as possible.

For example, when Elizabeth graduated from high school back in 2001, The Force began gathering. Instantly there was a lot of chatter about how burdensome the stairs were in our four-story Washington town house for "people our age." "We need to start downsizing," said The Force, who is ten years younger than I.

"We need to get an apartment and live on one floor," she would continue. I took this less seriously (as it now turns out) than I should have. And so when it became clear that my feints, jabs, and assorted other evasions were all being briskly swatted away by The Force, I rolled out my howitzer.

"You can't just abandon the only home our child has ever known (Elizabeth is our only child, but I have two older off-spring from my first marriage) the minute she goes off to college," I said. "That's a very powerful, not so subliminal message: 'We couldn't wait for you to leave, you little rascal, you, and don't come back no mo, no mo!'"

The Force turned that over in her head for a day or two and then, typically, came back with a crafty counterproposal.

"Okay, we can stay in this house if we renovate. It's really impossible the way it is." Knowing that it would be imprudent to gamble away the concession I was being offered, I caved—cravenly. And soon Steve, the brilliant architect, designer, and all-around-change-of-life guru came into our lives. Presto! We had a plan, which included moving Elizabeth's room up to the fourth floor and converting her old cave into a dressing room.

Not long after we had told Elizabeth of these plans, she reported a conversation she had with some of her dorm pals about what their mothers had done with their rooms when they went away to college.

"One girl said that her mother had cleared out all her high school memorabilia. Another said that her mother had replaced all her furniture and created a dainty little sitting room. A third chipped in with the fact that her mother had repainted the room with a color that the girl hated. So I said," Elizabeth continued, "my mother *demolished* my room."

We lived in our house during the renovation. It was during the time of the anthrax scare, when a couple of Senate office buildings—not far from our house—were closed. And, of course, anthrax was the talk of the town. One night at a dinner party I stared grimly across the table at The Force and blurted, "Anthrax, hell: It's plaster dust that's gonna kill me."

But the fact is that Elizabeth got a good deal in that renovation. She got a bigger room—one in which all her doodads collected over the years could be displayed—and she also got a very nicely redone bathroom, all on the fourth floor, which the rest of us rarely visit. In essence, she had something akin to a very attractive little apartment. Looking at it as I passed through from time to time, seeing so much of the stuff of her life so neatly displayed, warmed my heart. It was such a nice place for her to come home to that the empty-nest discussions—unavoidable in our set—rolled over me with no apparent effect.

Then reality struck. During her New York fellowship year, Elizabeth said offhandedly—"well, I really *don't* live in Washington anymore." When The Force repeated those words to me, the rickety architecture of my denial was destroyed instantly. The reality struck me like an unerring rifle shot from the deep past. There was, once more, an irremediable absence in the house where I lived.

The first time that happened to me was when I was a child, in Kansas City, and my father was either hospitalized, or at home but gravely ill. During my first four years (when I don't think I ever saw him in person), he was at a Missouri state tuberculosis sanitarium for Negroes somewhere out in the country. My mother and my grandmother talked about him a lot, and so did family friends who came to visit. He was always a shining, brilliant person in their telling of it. Much of that talk, I think, was to help make my father real to me, but all it actually did was to make me feel his absence even more.

Then, when I was almost four, when the doctors had taken a lung to save his life, we were told he would soon be home. I remember that my mother had put his hat on a table by the front door so she wouldn't forget to take it when she went for him. I remember thinking: "Tomorrow night he'll walk in the house and he'll be under that hat." It was probably the happiest thought of my childhood.

My father was a journalist; a writer, thinker, reader, and talker. He loved language, and drilled it and reading into me. He got me books, and when he was strong enough, he would come out of his bedroom and sit in a chair in the living room. He would read his book and I would read mine; I remember one special night when he was reading *King Lear* and I was reading *King Arthur*, the two of us, together. When he was really feeling good, he would take me down to the newspaper office and would sometimes let me push the button that started the roaring and clanking press. For a little boy, that was better than Christmas. When we made those visits to the office, all the people came around and made a big fuss over him and me. When he was very ill and confined to bed, he would sit up with a Royal portable typewriter on his lap and he would write stories and send them to publishers, hoping for some checks that would help the family.

He typed on yellow paper, and when I was out back burning the trash in our big barrel, he would zip slick yellow paper planes out his window at me. But after a few years at home, he got pleurisy in his remaining lung, and then he died, before I was nine. After that, I couldn't help looking at the window when I was outside—but of course, there were no more little yellow planes.

That was sixty-five years ago. There hasn't been a single day since then that I haven't thought about him and felt my emptiness. When Elizabeth made that comment about not really living in Washington anymore, the emptiness rushed at me, bigger and more consuming than before, because now I knew what I was missing.

MY FATHER'S ABSENCE has almost everything to do with how I think about myself, both in the larger world of work and within my first and second families, all of which is intertwined. Until I was forty, I followed a traditional young lawyer's trajectory: I practiced in New York and then gravitated toward the Kennedy administration in 1962; I was President Kennedy's assistant to the director of the foreign aid program, and then I stayed on through the Johnson administration as assistant attorney general. I left the government when Nixon became president, and I went to the Ford Foundation—again, that's what a lawyer like me did, went from the government to someplace else where you work on the same things you worked on before. Then, when your party comes back into the White House, you go back into government.

I didn't, though. The *Washington Post* asked me to join its editorial board in 1972, and I leapt at it, because in all of my jobs, the one aspect that I liked the best was writing, and that was because of my father. I was taking a little cut in pay, but I worked for three papers, the *Post*, the *New York Times*, and the *Washington Star*, all told about nine years. And I served on the Pulitzer Prize Board; one of two of us who broke the color bar there. I ultimately chaired the group for a year—and the day I sat down to chair that committee for the first time, I said silently to myself, this is for you, Dad.

It was as close as I could get to the daily detail of life with him that I would have observed and absorbed had I really known him. I have only three or four clear memories of us together that I've used so much, cherished so fervently, and revered so religiously I fear that my yearning and overusage may have brushed the truth out of them. And, of course, he couldn't have been perfect, but nobody told me about his mistakes and false starts.

It was harder to absorb his legacy as a husband and a father. I know that there was guidance that I needed from him—that my mother, my grandmother, my uncle, and my stepfather couldn't supply. I know that I needed to know my father better than I did. I deeply believe that I would have been a far better man than I have been had he lived to guide me through puberty, college, and early adulthood judgments.

Through the bliss and strain of early fatherhood, and stress, separation, and divorce, I tried to be an insistent presence in the lives of my two older children: Amy, who was born when I was twenty-seven, and David, born when I was thirty-two. They were about thirteen and eight when my first wife and I separated, and within two years I was working in New York, while they stayed with their mother in Washington, D.C. I saw them at least once a month, sometimes more frequently, but I was miserable. I adored them—I did and I do—and I felt terrible guilt and enormous pain when we were apart. I knew what it was not to have a father—and as I look back at that period now, I think I must have been clinically depressed. I know I drank too much. It was a very, very bad time, and I don't think I fully stabilized until after I met Elizabeth's mother, Patricia, and we started a new family. I wasn't always a good father to my older children, but they know I've tried, and they know that, at the times of their crises, I've been there with my hands on them and their souls.

They know me deeply. They hoard exceedingly funny stories, and whenever strangers exhibit the slightest inclination to puff me up, they always manage to pull out in full plumage some dumb daddy story that has us all rolling instantly. They know me as I wish I could have known my father.

Elizabeth is a different case: I was fifty-one when she was born, and I was terrified that I would die before she really got to know me and also before she could actually feel the contours of my spirit on her life. Having a child at fifty-one is not a normal thing. It can't be taken for granted as the next logical step in life as it is when you're in your twenties and thirties, and everybody you know is doing the same thing. People made the normal adjustment at the incongruity of a gray-haired man nurturing a toddler. A friendly-looking maternal woman put it best when she encountered me and a dawdling two-year-old Elizabeth on the street one day.

"Come on, Elizabeth," the woman heard me say with exasperation as my child examined with minute care the progress of a leaf being blown gently along the sidewalk.

"Mind your grandpa, Elizabeth," the woman put in with a warm and generous smile.

Then there was the fiendish girl at summer camp, whom everyone in the cabin hated. When she learned that Elizabeth's father was sixty-one she exclaimed for all the other ten-year-olds to hear: "My God, when you're twenty, he'll be over seventy."

The thing about being so old was that I thought about being a father much more carefully than I had at twenty-seven or thirty-two. This time around, it was different. For example, there was an interminable wee-hours night when Elizabeth was an infant and she could not be kissed, consoled, hugged, read, or sung to sleep. There was no escape. Patricia was taking a well-deserved night off and the yowling was driving me up every wall in the house.

What the hell am I doing here, I wondered. I'm comforting and rocking this tiny creature who knows me, if at all, only by smell. She knows no language, and she's beyond any alternative method of communication I can think up. Why all this tenderness for this little monster who's torturing and terrorizing me? "Stupid," I responded, "this little noise box is a person, and though she doesn't know your name, she depends on you. So what if she is grouchy and doesn't want to go to sleep? You got her here. You and Patricia decided to bring her into this world, and she is dependent on you. If you can't meet this, your most sacred responsibility—even in the most trying and heartbreaking times—you're not much of a human being." And after a while she stopped yowling, and her ragged and tired old father finally got some sleep.

The age gap haunted me. I was determined that she would get to know me as I had not known my father. I figured that I'd better create some memories for her to summon up when she needed a sense of me. So I created a silly game in which each of us tries each day to pop the other on the head first, crying: "First bonk of the day," as loudly as possible. And I'd often help her practice kicking her soccer ball in the dining room when Patricia was cooking dinner. The fact that we had a glass dining room table didn't deter us at all. Stories of this and other games are now staples in the cluster of stories that my young adult daughter laughingly tells about her childhood.

Another thing I did to set myself in her memory was to walk her to the school bus every morning. As she got on, I'd invariably say: "Use this day well, Elizabeth." Many years later, when I walked into her freshman dorm room on parents' weekend at college, I saw a handmade sign she'd posted above her bed. It read: USE THIS DAY WELL, ELIZABETH.

————

THE OTHER DAY, The Force and I took the train from Washington up to New York to attend the ceremony marking the end of Elizabeth's postgraduate fellowship year. We observed warm and loving exchanges among a group of extraordinary young adults who had forged deep bonds during their year together. Our daughter—clearly in her element—was absolutely radiant through the evening.

The next morning, we took Elizabeth and her boyfriend to brunch at a fashionable restaurant she chose that was on Fifty-third Street between Fifth and Sixth avenues. We all bantered, and she told her boyfriend some of her favorite "Daddy is a dope" stories. After we had dined fulsomely and enjoyed one another immensely, it was time for Patricia and me to make our way back home. I hailed an empty cab, we exchanged quick kisses and hugs, and then we climbed in after our bags. Elizabeth and her friend waved and walked away, holding hands. Once Patricia and I got settled in our seats, I turned around, just in time to see them join the mass of humanity on Fifth Avenue. A moment later, they turned the corner and were gone.

Like her sister in Washington and her brother in Baltimore, Elizabeth had merged into the adult world. I had the feeling that their grandfather would have doted on each one of them.

I reached out and took Patricia's hand as our cab turned down Seventh Avenue toward the train station and home. My nest was empty but my heart was full.

Keeping Him Safe

Rochelle Reed

L
ast September, as my friends were sending their kids off to Berkeley or Stanford or UCLA, I drove my son, Evan, to a nearby armed forces recruitment center where he joined the U.S. Army.

I'd never noticed the recruitment storefront sandwiched into a corner of our supermarket shopping center. Yet there I was, handing over the infant I'd nursed, the toddler I'd cuddled, the teenager I'd taught to tie a Windsor knot, to a roomful of slick government salesmen in camouflage uniforms and lace-up boots. Full of military braggadocio, they stepped over one by one to shake my hand and assure me gravely that my only son, whom they hardly knew, was "a good man."

I'd promised Evan that I wouldn't cry. It would be too hard on both of us, he said. I kept my vow as I stood in that grim office full of metal desks, the windows and walls hung with posters devised, as far as I was concerned at that moment, to entice guileless young men and women: "Helping myself, my country, my future. It all makes sense."

Only one thing made sense to me: This was definitely not the way things were supposed to turn out.

Despite his boyhood collection of G.I. Joe action figures, never in a million years did I imagine my son would join the army. Nor did Evan. In high school, he'd hang up on recruiters who called the house. He'd blurt, "Get away from me!" to the ones who trawled the local hangouts. Our home was liberal Democrat and antiwar. A ten-year-old when this country was on the verge of the Gulf War, he colored posters saying "No Blood for Oil." Now at twenty-one, he was a Michael Moore fan. The night before he left, he spent his time reading *Angry White Men*.

Sending my son off to war seemed completely absurd, but I wasn't there to argue or lament. It was too late for that; he'd already taken his tests, passed his physical, and now it was time for him to leave. I smiled, I nodded, I managed to laugh and joke, yet all the while my mind kept flashing to the day we brought Evan home from the hospital. Even as I sat in the front seat, I awkwardly reached back to keep my hand on the tiny new body buckled into the regulation car seat behind me.

Now I wanted to touch him again as he stood beside me, almost six feet tall, shoulders back instead of in their usual slouch. But I couldn't, of course. I sensed how awkward he felt with his mother at his side in this roomful of soldiers, but he was determined to push through and introduce me all around.

He needed to show off to me his peers in this tough new life he was entering, almost as unencumbered as that baby in the car seat, only a small blue duffel bag holding the few personal belongings—underwear, socks, a Mach 3 razor—he was allowed to take with him to boot camp.

When I tell people Evan has joined the army, their reactions are almost always the same: Their faces freeze, they pause way too long, and then they say, "I'm so sorry, I'm so sorry for you." I hang my head and look mournful. But as it dawns on them that Evan wasn't drafted—Vietnam still clings to my generation—their expressions become suspicious, then disbelieving, sometimes disdainful. I know what they're thinking: *Why in the world would any kid in his right mind choose to enlist when we're in the middle of a war?* I start telling them the story, desperate to assure them it wasn't arrogant patriotism or murderous bloodlust that convinced him to join. What finally hooked him was a recruiter's comment that if he thought the country and the army was so screwed up, he should try to fix it.

And on a deeper, personal level, Evan signed up hoping that after five years of anger, sadness, and misdirection, somehow the army would help him fix himself. Just as I was counseled that Evan, then sixteen, was "at risk" for alcohol and drugs, his father filed for divorce. His sister, Lainey, twelve at the time, was able to cope. Evan was far more troubled, trying desperately to be the man of the house. He went to school, worked thirty hours a week, and zealously watched over his sister. But alcohol and drugs soon filled the void left in his heart. We moved away, and he got better, until he met up with the wrong crowd in our new town. His sister and I tried reasoning, anger, and tears, but nothing worked until he hit bottom, got some help, and turned himself around.

He'd never had anyone to teach him what it meant to be a man; that was how he explained to me his decision to join the army. At twenty-one, he'd been almost two years clean and sober, but life wasn't as interesting as when he'd lived on the edge. He couldn't concentrate on college courses, he was resisting promotion at his job, and he not only wanted but needed challenge and discipline, he said. The only way to get it, he'd decided, was to pit himself against drill sergeants, armed insurgents, and Improvised Explosive Devices. If he could do it, he told me, he'd have the self-assurance he hadn't found in his old life.

Even when Evan and Lainey were small, I'd braced myself for someday facing an empty nest. I just didn't expect that their dad would be the first one to fly the coop. I read somewhere that the first thing to go when a father leaves home is the family dinner. And so it happened in our house. We dutifully assembled at the dining table for our evening meal, but we'd lost our appetites. Like watching a hologram, we could still see all four of us together. So we convened, but we usually ate standing at the kitchen counter or in the living room. On the rare occasions when we ate at the dining table, Evan sat in his father's place. Eating out was even harder. No matter how many coats and parcels we piled on the empty chair, a restaurant table was a painful reminder that a member of our family was gone.

Now it's Evan who has gone off to Iraq, leaving Lainey and me behind. I wake up early these days. I make coffee, retrieve the morning papers, and then compulsively read every story about murdered soldiers, beheaded soldiers, tortured soldiers, wounded soldiers, soldiers with missing limbs and damaged brains, soldiers who have gone berserk and raped and murdered innocent civilians. I purposely teeter on the edge of fear and grief, bracing myself for whatever the future brings. I hate surprises, so I plan for worst-case scenarios. I ponder whether to sell our two-story home and buy a one-story, in case Evan comes home in a wheelchair. Every time I take a trip, I wonder how the army will find me to tell me that he's dead if I'm out of town. I've promised Evan that if the worst actually happens, I'll bury him in a coffin next to my parents and grandparents in rural Wyoming. But would Evan really mind if I kept his ashes in an urn, so that I could have him close to me?

"Please, oh please, let him call me" is now my daily mantra. I breathe, I exhale. Put this in perspective, I demand of myself. Evan volunteered for the army. He wasn't conscripted like my father's father in Austria. Or my mother's father, who returned shell-shocked from the Great War after he watched his hometown buddies blown to bits as they sat smoking cigarettes in a foxhole in France. My father's mother sent four sons to World War II; one was eaten by sharks when his plane crashed during a South Pacific monsoon. My mother's only brother, a jovial test pilot I dimly remember, was killed at the beginning of the Korean War. Mothers throughout history have seen their sons off to war, I remind myself. I'm merely one of billions.

If only my thinking could stop here, but I must grow tough, tougher, toughest. Evan volunteered for this, I remind myself. He's promised to defend his country at all costs. My son may hesitate before he pulls the trigger, but he's promised to shoot to kill. He's donned the uniform, so whatever happens—ambush, rocket fire, mortar attack, IED, an insurgent's sword—he must face the consequences. Now I must accept that the son I raised to be a gentle, caring soul is somewhere in the Iraq desert, a loaded M3 in his arms. At this very moment, he could be exulting with his buddies that he killed the enemy, ending the life of another mother's son. If, God forbid, another mother's son kills Evan, will I share the empathy I'm willing to extend to my own flesh and blood?

Luckily, I still have Lainey here. Each day she brings me great joy. A sophomore in college, she might have been gone by now, but nobody in this family leaves according to plan. She's happy to live with me and attend the local community college. With her at home, my nest seems half-full. But I won't have her forever. She'll leave to attend a university next fall, and I know that while her room will still contain her things, I'll be alone.

I recently sat down and charted my life, marking off the years and what I've done in them. I've got a chunk of time left, so now I make a great many plans—I'll write a book, I'll travel around the world, I'll take an EMT course and volunteer as an AIDS worker in a foreign country. I'll become fluent in Spanish, I'll start my own magazine, I'll build a house with plenty of room for my kids and friends to stay forever if they wish. And if Evan comes home safely, I'll add on a big garage so he'll have a place where he can come over and tinker on cars.

If Evan comes home. *When* Evan comes home, I affirm. If he'd stayed here, I remind myself, he might have driven too fast and ended his life against a telephone pole. Or dropped out of

AA and died of an overdose. He could have been shot and killed while he tallied receipts at the Motel 6 where he worked as night manager. He didn't have to go to Iraq to risk his life. He could have been killed or maimed in any number of ways right here in our picturesque little town. This grotesque chain of thought becomes oddly soothing, because it reminds me that no matter how hard we try, we are never fully in control. Even though I reached back to touch my tiny infant in his car seat on the way home from the hospital, I sensed I could never protect him enough. Now, like my son, I must move forward with fear, and also with great hope.

When I was pregnant with Evan, I was sent to Santa Fe to write an article. Visiting the Museum of Indian Arts & Culture, I noted a plaque with a Navajo proverb that I've often repeated to myself: WE RAISE OUR CHILDREN TO LEAVE US.

And one way or another, they do.

The Shoes on the Stairs

Jamie Wolf

When our daughter, Kate, was young, she had extreme difficulties with separation. Until the age of three or so, she would sob piteously, "No leaving, no *leaving*," whenever David and I went out at night, or when I left the house during the day, and sometimes merely when people she was fond of went home from the park. Defying advice from people like my mother (who chided, "Why do you always have to say *good-bye*? Just slip out quietly, so she doesn't notice!"), we went through endless repetitions of "We go away, we come back," until finally, after many months, it ceased to be such a problem.

"A good mother is like wallpaper," was the slogan that one of my closest friends, herself the mother of two, proposed during this period. She meant this not to imply the desirability of being a doormat, but the importance of serving as a dependable background, rather than the primary focus, for the child, and being willing to undergo some personal inconvenience and discomfort in the interest of the child's eventual independence. I found her incredibly perceptive about these matters; besides, the philosophy was in sharp, salutary contrast to my own up-bringing, which most definitely had been oriented around my parents' wishes, and so I took the slogan to heart.

In its application, what the wallpaper concept involved was a conscious determination that whatever decisions we made on Kate's behalf were going to center around her. We would award genuine weight and respect to her preferences and inclinations, we vowed, even if they interfered with our own. It never oc-curred to us that this could be seen as abdication of parental responsibility—in fact, we believed that an emphasis on Kate's eventual self-reliance was what would end up being best for her in the long run, and thus represented parental responsibility at its fullest.

Sometimes—often about the most superficial things—this philosophy was harder to hew to than it was on other occa-sions. Kate's taste in clothes, for instance, was for a long time almost ridiculously unprovocative: She liked long, old-fashioned dresses and she liked to change them for dinner. In second grade, though, she entered a Madonna phase, featuring tight bicycle shorts and rhinestone belts, and for a number of years thereafter she went about looking pretty much indistin-guishable from the hookers on Sunset Boulevard. This was fol-lowed by an initial Salvation Army phase, characterized by a favorite floor-length, fluorescent, Marcia Brady-like pink-and-orange sundress, and then by a less comprehensible Salvation

Army phase—this one involving oddly colored polyester garments that looked as if they had been left behind by a deceased elderly man in his Miami condo. (It was here that I finally broke down and bleated, "But I don't understand the *aesthetic*"—although I never insisted, as my mother had done with me, that Kate go upstairs and change.)

Ironically enough, it was easier to avoid coercion and reprisals in the more significant areas of Kate's life. Homework was one of them. Kate was actually fairly conscientious until her midteens, so for a long while this wasn't an issue. But when she began to neglect her work—which, naturally, in her later teens she did—we both felt that it would be better for her in the long run to suffer the consequences of diminished grades than to get the work done through constant intervention on our part. Besides, who wanted to participate in all that nagging?

Family dinners were another area we didn't regulate. They hadn't been a regular event for David, and I had such hideous memories of the dinners of my own childhood, our spoons chinking interminably on the well-chosen china, that it seemed far more pleasant for us each to fix ourselves something separately, and then to congregate later on the couch in front of the television. The three of us spent lots of incidental time as a family hanging out; we had a regular weekly dinner with David's brother and his wife and their son, and fairly frequent dinners with my brother and his wife and their kids. We didn't think we needed to sit down together every night.

We were also fairly casual about chastity, drugs-and-alcohol, and orthodontia. When Kate, then a high school junior, came into our bedroom one night to inform us that her boyfriend would be sleeping over, our discomfort had more to do with the same "ick" reaction she'd displayed the time she'd walked in on us making love than it did with any outrage or real concern. She seemed pretty sensible to us; better, we felt, for her to be having sex in the house than in the back of said boyfriend's monster truck. The issue of drugs and alcohol was helped by Kate's having to accompany various friends to the emergency room for alcohol poisoning, and by her own early reaction to people when they'd been smoking dope, which was that they seemed stupid to her. (As far as other drugs went, and for alcohol later on, all we thought we could really do was to insist and plead, and plead and insist, about no driving when she or anybody else operating the car was under the influence.) And once the dentist told us that braces weren't functionally necessary, we were damned if we were going to enforce suffering for the sake of cosmetic improvement.

For all our efforts, we knew that teenagers were apt to become surly and difficult, and we were braced for the probability with Kate. In fact, from a Darwinian point of view, it seemed to us to make perfect sense. Human beings, unlike most other animals, don't have an instinct to drive their offspring from the nest. If, for the sake of their eventual well-being, kids need to individuate and leave home, the unpleasantness of their teenage behavior is probably the only resource they can realistically draw on for enlisting their parents' cooperation. If they stayed as endearing as they had been as children, how could any of us bear to let them go?

Kate's departure began before she even hit her teens, when I arrived one spring afternoon to pick her up from school. Gazing at me blankly, she asked, "What are you doing here?"—as though I'd violated the NO TRESPASSING sign in the parking lot. However, I'd prepared myself for this moment. And when I mentioned the situation to a friend later that day, she said soothingly that "it" had already happened to many of her friends, and they'd told her it was as if your children just disappeared for five years or so, and then one day they came back.

But as it turned out, we weren't braced enough. We hadn't expected that it would be so intense: the sulks and storms and wild crying in her room, and then the acting as if we were insane, or had been imagining things, when she came back downstairs and we asked if she was all right. We hadn't expected such violent rejection ("Go AWAAYYY," Kate would scream if you knocked on her door when she was sobbing)—especially not the kind that could turn into indignation if you didn't persist for the proper amount of time.

The truth is that in child rearing as in life, no matter how much you try to do the right thing for its own sake, usually you're secretly hoping for a payoff. With Kate, we believed that our reasonableness, our adherence to the wallpaper philosophy, would make the teenage kickback less harsh. We wouldn't have changed our approach if we'd known differently, but at least we wouldn't have been so blindsided. What we hadn't reckoned with is what seems obvious to us now: If you're a doted-on only child whose parents treat you with a certain egalitarianism, you have to push away all the harder to separate from them.

I mean, we knew children needed and wanted limits, if sometimes only to be able to refer to them as rationales for their own choices ("*Yell at me and tell me I'm grounded,*" Kate would whisper occasionally when a friend phoned to invite her someplace she didn't want to go), and we did set behavioral limits, which Kate more or less adhered to. But we didn't have a lot of hierarchical or psychological boundaries, and that's where the action occurred. Particularly with me. Every day became an endless series of lectures to me from Kate, an itemizing of my every flaw and failure—my undisciplined work habits, my absentmindedness, my tendency towards tears, my unkept promise to purchase a zebra when we moved to the new house ("But, honey, you were *eight years old* when we talked about that, you *knew* it was just pretend. . . ." "Then you shouldn't have promised!!"), my poor household management skills, my habit of kissing the dog openmouthed, my disproportionate attachment to objects, my tardiness, and so on and on and on.

This was especially hard for me to get used to, because Kate, as a child, had been so incredibly solicitous of me, so calm, so kind, so helpful and reassuring. "Don't worry, Mom, nobody's perfect," she would say, patting my hand when I got agitated about not being able to do something properly. "Now, Mom," she would suggest gently, if we were in a taxi approaching an airport, "it might be a good idea to start getting your wallet out now. . . ." Nobody, not even David (who I knew loved me deeply, but made it clear he did so despite my faults), had ever made me feel so bathed in love, so cared for and well instructed and so . . . *approved of* . . . as my own daughter.

Naturally, in those years before the incident in the school parking lot, there were fallings-out and irritation between us. For the most part, though, what I recall is a time of such immense, shimmering happiness, so full of harmony and mutual enjoyment, that even now, writing about it, I can't let myself reenter it completely. It's too scalding; it makes tears start to come.

For the months and years that followed, though, we were at loggerheads nearly all the time, and always, as Kate presented it, as a consequence of *my fault*—something I was or wasn't, something I did or hadn't done. I dreaded being around her and longed to be around her, and was always frantically trying to set things right, which made me anxious and fluttery and enraged her even further.

And her strictures grew more elaborate. It was no longer enough not to comment on something; to keep quiet, for instance, when Kate at fifteen appeared one day with her hair dyed bright red and cut in a bob, complemented by a style of makeup more commonly seen on mature European film stars. I said absolutely nothing about this for several hours, which I thought qualified as exemplary behavior. In fact, I was rehearsing to myself the disingenuous line I'd come up with; I could barely wait to deliver it.

"Why are you carrying on about my hair?" Kate asked, finally.

"Your hair?" I replied perkily. "Did you do something to your hair?"

"Oh, don't even try that," responded Kate, witheringly. "I saw the look on your face the minute you saw me."

So now looks were under scrutiny as well, and there were other rules that weren't apparent until you violated them. To hug her or not to hug her? Mostly if you hugged her she pulled away, but then she might get furious at you for not being demonstrative enough. Trying to figure out the pattern became a constant challenge. (The idea that there might not *be* a pattern was too dark and undermining even to contemplate.) If it was her task to make us feel relieved when she left home, she was certainly doing an excellent job.

DAVID AND I had been married for ten years before Kate was born; we'd been a couple for a number of years before that, and we'd always truly liked spending time alone together. Thus, when at last we deposited Kate at college—her final *"Fuck you!"* to me prompted by the insensitivity of my last-minute question about whether she was sure she didn't want to keep the cell phone we'd brought for her—I have to admit it was with nearly unalloyed relish that we found ourselves back to our existence as the primal triad, i.e., David and the resident springer and I, a configuration that in some ways felt more natural to us than our identity as parents.

Thanksgiving vacation with Kate passed pleasantly enough that first year, and so did Christmas, which was marked by our most recent springer spaniel devouring several gift-wrapped boxes of chocolates and having to be taken on Christmas morning to have her stomach pumped, thus creating a useful diversion. It began to feel as if the return my friend had predicted was indeed at hand.

But then came spring vacation, and with it a whole new set of bitter complaints from Kate. Why was I so *jumpy* around her? Why hadn't we insisted on her doing her homework when she was in high school? And why hadn't we had more family dinners? We volunteered to schedule them now . . . only to find there was something wrong with the evening or the restaurant or the proposed home menu every time.

And then that first college summer she stayed home, working intermittently at the bookshop job she'd had since she was sixteen, and she had time on her hands, and most of her dissatisfaction came to focus once again on me. My weight gain, for instance. I'd been prescribed a migraine-preventing medication with appetite-stimulating side effects, and by the time I was fully aware of its impact, I'd gained over forty pounds. Kate didn't care about my *appearance*, she was quick to assure me; that was completely superficial, but what about my health?

It was useless to explain that with this much weight to lose I needed to make it a nearly full-time project, or that the daily hour of exercise Kate was recommending would take years to have effect, or that I was so demoralized I found it impossible to get started. She was inexorable. And this was what was so insidious about dealing with her: She was so often right, and her ideas were invariably good ones. It's just that she never let up. To be in a room with her—with rare and wonderful exceptions—was simply to await the moment she was going to start.

In the years to come, there were occasions (usually on the telephone or in e-mails) when I felt such a strong surge of connectedness to Kate that I was sure our problems were over. There were times when she made a gesture that wiped out every hurt: She based (or so it seemed) a character in her senior-year fiction project on me, and in reading it I felt so uncannily understood and approved of that it was magical. But then she graduated from college and came back to work for a year in Los Angeles (she was living on her own, with a couple of roommates), and again our every interaction seemed to end with her ranting about some deficiency of mine, and me in tears, and her upbraiding me about being too reactive. And then she went off to New York.

This time, though, rather than bringing relief, her absence only made things worse. "Empty nest? *What* empty nest?" was how David phrased it. I was in perpetual despair about my relationship with Kate. It was like a layer of sadness underlying everything—my work, the cozy Sunday mornings David and I spent snuggled up together, my time in the garden. I felt trapped in behavior that seemed utterly surreal to me, because it was so at odds with my deepest feelings for her—just as I sensed Kate's behavior was at odds with her deepest feelings for me.

She lived in New York for another year, first in Brooklyn and then for a while in Harlem and then on the Lower East Side, doing a variety of jobs. Her trips to Los Angeles were briefer than they had been, and they swirled into an endlessly replicating pattern: our eagerly awaiting the sight of her; her taking over the house with her friends and her laundry and her elaborate, exotic meal preparations and, needless to say, her judgments and her complaints; our being exhausted almost immediately by her presence; eagerly anticipating her departure—and then missing her the moment she was gone. Every visit added to the accumulated wistfulness. *Wasn't all this supposed to be over by now?*

In point of fact, the situation was on its way to easing. It was

Kate, actually, who helped me finally move forward. She'd been in the middle of one of her familiar litanies, accusing us of both having given her too much freedom and attempting to control her life. As usual, there was an element of truth in what she was saying; as usual, also, there was a great deal of wild overstatement. Nonetheless, I'd let myself be drawn in and overwhelmed until I ended up wailing what I so frequently felt: "You make me feel I've never done *anything* right."

Kate muttered a few exasperated platitudes about not meaning anything as extreme as that. Then she turned to me and said, in a level voice, "You must have a lot of hostility toward me for making you feel bad so much of the time."

It was like a cartoon moment. I can remember looking at her silently, listening to my own thoughts clicking into place ... *That's true ... How perceptive of her to say that.* ... I don't remember the rest of what happened that afternoon, but during the next couple of weeks something did shift in me, emotionally. It was like some exaggerated illustration of addressing a dilemma through the simple device of giving it a name.

A month or so later I flew east for Mother's Day. Kate came up to my hotel room as I settled in, and before fifteen minutes had passed, she'd started in on me in the accustomed way. Suddenly, as I listened to her, something new occurred to me. *This is about intimacy,* I thought. She's used to lecturing me, that's what feels familiar to her. And, of course, whenever she's anxious and uncertain about her own life, it's easier for her to focus on what's wrong with me. She can't talk to anyone else in quite the same way—maybe that's bad, and maybe that's good, but that's the case. I'm safe—I *am* like wallpaper. To her, that's what my being her mother means.

It was another cartoon moment. It relaxed me enough simply to say "Hmmm," when Kate began to talk about her plan never to visit our side of town, once she moved back to Los Angeles for graduate school. And it may have been what prompted her to tell me then that she'd come to a realization: I, like her, was partly the stubborn product of my history—and possibly she could begin to adapt to me the way I was.

On her next visit out here, Kate cooked us a macrobiotic dinner with the garlic adjusted; it was delicious. She stayed in the pool house, an opportunity for diminished friction that we'd been urging on her for a long time, although she still watched television a couple of times in our bed. I was surprised at what a pang it gave me to think of her not even coming into the house at night, and so I was oddly comforted, the morning she was due to depart, to come downstairs early and see at the foot of the stairs a flat-soled, thin-strapped, multicolored, worn-down, 1950s-thrift-shop pair of her sandals.

What I'd been truly yearning for, I think—until then I hadn't really come to grips with it—was some kind of return to our very earliest days, when Kate was still a toddler, and she and David and I and our first dog, whom we loved as if she were our child, would lie in bed with our bodies touching late at night, and I would experience a feeling of such ... *completeness* ... at the thought that the three sentient beings I cared about most in the world were all here, pressed up against me in one small place, as if our bed were a raft floating through the universe.

I needed to recognize how impossible it was going to be ever to fulfill that longing. For just an instant, though, the sight of Kate's sandals in the hall (evoking her elongated feet, which at her forceps-assisted birth were the first glimpse of her we'd had) restored the pain and the exhilaration, the uncertainty and resolution, of her arrival—and the unadulterated happiness of the moment when the doctor had made his way closer to our end of the operating table to tell us: *You have a daughter.*

Afterwards

Roxana Robinson

When my daughter was fourteen she went away to boarding school. That was the year we sold the horses, so both the house and the barn suddenly were empty.

At that time we lived in a farmhouse on the side of a hill. Across the lawn was a big white ash tree, and beyond the ash was the barn. In the winter it was still dark when we got up, and the house was silent in the cold. Outside the windows the tall sugar maples were bare and gray against the snowy lawn.

During those years, when my daughter was still at home, we all woke early in the mornings. My husband got up first, to take the train into the city. He was dressed and gone before we knew it, his car crunching quietly down the drive. I got up next, and when I had dressed I went in to my daughter.

I had painted the walls of her room a pale summer blue,

with white cumulus clouds drifting between the windows. Over her bed I painted a big faint rainbow, arching over her as though she were the treasure, the pot of gold. Her bed was an old brass one that had belonged to her great-aunt, and my daughter slept deep in the middle of it, covered by the high light mound of her quilt, her head buried in the pillows. When she slept she was lost, she was fathoms below the surface, and rousing her was hard. I hated asking her to leave.

My daughter's school ended at ninth grade, so, after graduation, she had to go elsewhere. The local public high school was not academically challenging, and most of her friends were choosing to go off to boarding school. My daughter, too, wanted to do this. It was a familiar notion to me: I'd gone to boarding school, and so had my husband, and everyone in both our families. It was a fact of life: When you were fourteen you were sent off to boarding school. You knew that it was a new country, where you would lead a new strange kind of life. You didn't know what it would be like, this strange new life, but you knew it was one you could not lead at home with your parents. In some ways you looked forward to it, leading a life without your parents, and in some ways you dreaded it, because you had never done that.

On those mornings, when my daughter was awake, I went down with the dogs, racketing down the steep back stairs into the kitchen. There I made breakfast for my daughter, toast and eggs, or cereal. Oatmeal, if I got up early enough. As I worked I kept glancing nervously at the clock on the wall: The approach of the bus was ticking away in my head. Sometimes I went to the bottom of the stairs and called up again. When my daughter came down, sometimes she was still sleepy, still caught up in that dreaming web that had held her through the night. Sometimes she was still buttoning her sweater, or carrying her shoes. She sat down at the kitchen table and I put her cereal bowl in front of her. The window there faced east, toward the little garden and the wisteria-covered pergola. Beyond that was the rising hillside, where the horses grazed. In the winter, it was all gray, and the landscape was quiet.

While my daughter ate, I stood behind her and loosened her hair. It was long and thick and honey colored, and she wore it in braids; during the night these became fuzzy and matted. In the morning I disentwined the strands and shook them loose, and brushed her hair until it was smooth and shining. I parted it down the middle of her clean pale scalp and then I braided it again into two fat glossy plaits. I snapped elastics around the ends, leaving soft feathery tips.

When my daughter had finished her cereal, or even before, if we were running late, I urged her into her coat, grabbed mine from the mudroom, and we went out to the car. If she hadn't done eating, she carried the cereal bowl and her spoon with her. Our dogs—big black furry poodles—came with us, clambering eagerly into the backseat.

We drove down the dirt road to the corner of Mount Holly Road. There we parked. My daughter would finish her cereal, and I would read out loud to her. One winter I read *The Adventures of Sherlock Holmes*, so that, as we sat in our muddy red Volvo on our country lane, our big black dogs peacefully filling up the backseat, we were also drifting through the pea soup fogs of London, filled with horror at Moriarty's dastardly schemes, and admiration at Holmes's eccentric genius. My daughter listened with attention. She was a dutiful, beautiful child, with grave blue eyes. I read the dialogue in an English accent.

When the school bus rumbled down the hill and braked at the intersection with our road, the dogs stood up in the backseat, and I closed the book. My daughter gave me her cereal bowl, opened the door, and grabbed her schoolbag, so that by the time the bus had pulled out onto our road, rattled, and groaned its way around the corner and wheezed to a stop, my daughter was standing on the side of the road in her bright red parka, her fat glossy braids sticking out like flags. Sometimes she remembered to turn and wave to me just before she got onto the bus, but sometimes she climbed the steps without turning around, already part of the morning world of the school bus, which did not contain her mother.

When the bus had rumbled slowly on, I turned around and drove back home. The dogs bounded joyfully out of the car, and we set out across the lawn to the barn. Our barn was two stories high and set into the side of the hill. The whole upper story was the hayloft, its big doors opening directly onto the hillside, so the wagons could drive in and unload. In the lower part were the horses. A center aisle spanned the width of the barn, with a door at each end. On either side of the aisle were big box stalls.

The door facing the house was a heavy sliding door, and in the winter I shut this at night. Sometimes the door iced shut, and in the morning I had to bang it loose. The horses could hear me, and as I started rolling open the door they started whinnying and nickering. When the door opened they were all leaning out over their stall doors, blinking their long eyelashes in the sudden brightness, nodding impatiently at me, and making brief shrill noises in their throats. As I came inside I spoke to them, and said their names. I could smell their thick sweet smell, and the sharp smell of their urine, and I could feel the warmth made by their bodies and their breath in the barn all through the night.

As I was rolling open the sliding door my daughter was on a high slippery seat on the school bus, halfway to her school.

I raised the lid of the grain bin to scoop out breakfast, and the horses filled the air with high, tiny squeals of hunger. I fed my horse first, my clever, nervy Appaloosa, Jack Robinson, and then my husband's huge, gentle hunter, John Deere, and then my daughter's brown pony, Tresco Bay. Tresco, who was smaller than the others, had to poke his nose upward over the high stall doors. Tresco was an honest soul, good tempered and steady, with a great heart.

My daughter was a beautiful rider, subtle and elegant. She had started riding around six, and doing little local shows at around eight. In the short-stirrup classes she was successful— she and her pony were as cute as anyone else in the ring—but when she graduated to the equestrian classes, the competition became more difficult. The other girls were now on fancy, big-time ponies, fine boned and elegant, who cost twenty thousand dollars or more. My daughter was a beautiful rider, but our brave-hearted Tresco was not a twenty-thousand-dollar pony. Her teacher had warned us that she wouldn't be able to go on winning with him. Still, my daughter liked the challenge and decided to go on showing, and when the judges watched the riders instead of their mounts, she went on winning.

When she rode in shows, I stood at the rail. I watched her steadying Tresco as they came around the corner, I saw her turning to look at the next set of fences, her body balanced, her legs firm, her gloved hands steady on his neck. It was a marvel to me that she could be so poised, and in such control of all this—her horse, the complicated course, the big curve of the ring.

Those mornings, once the horses had food in their buckets they stopped squealing, and then the barn was filled with the peaceful sound of their chewing. I took their water buckets from the stalls to clean and fill. While one was filling I went outside again, up the hill and around the back to the hayloft. I opened the big door and stepped into the high dusky space of the loft. The air was still and silent, rich with the scent of hay. High up in the interior, hidden in the dimness, the bats moved about, disturbed by my arrival, speaking in their shrill mysterious code, reminding me of who owned the airways. In the dead of winter they were silent, hibernating, but they were still there. I opened the front window that looked out over the paddock, and I threw out flakes of hay, making three separate piles on the frozen ground.

Downstairs, the horses stood in their stalls, waiting for me to come down and let them out. They had finished eating their grain and were now patient. Jack Robinson put his head over the stall door and stretched his long nose toward me, ears pricked politely. I rubbed my knuckles against the center of his forehead, where it was always dusty. He liked this, and he closed his eyes and leaned his hard bony head against my hand. When I stopped, I lowered my head, and he blew slowly and gently into my face, and I drew in a long draft of his sweet meadowy breath.

By now my daughter was at school, off the bus, inside, among her friends. They wore uniforms, at that school, the girls in white blouses and pleated tweed skirts, the boys in khaki pants and blue blazers. They still had the bodies of children—slim and waistless, with loose, supple movements. The girls wore brown leather lace-up shoes, the laces raffishly unlaced, dragging on the floor behind them. The girls were mean to one another. When my daughter told me this I didn't know what to say to her. What is it that you should say? I thought it would be better when she went away. I hoped it would be better. You always hope things will get better.

When she was in seventh grade my daughter asked me to cut her hair. It seemed that the other world had begun to impinge on ours. It seemed that Princess Irene's long golden locks were no longer the criterion by which hairstyles were measured, or at least not by the other seventh-grade girls in her school.

By then my daughter's hair was very long; when it was loose she could nearly sit on it. She sat at the kitchen table and I brushed her hair out for the last time. I braided it neatly, as I had done every morning for the last seven years, and then I cut off the braids. We saved them, still braided, still bound with elastic bands. We wrapped them in tissue paper and put them in the top drawer of her bureau. That way, it seemed as though we could always go back and take them out again, if she were to change her mind about getting older.

THE DAY SHE left for boarding school, we packed the car early in the morning. The horses were gone by then—my husband had never really liked riding, I had taken on a project that would require traveling, and my daughter was leaving home—so there was no one in the barn to go out and feed. It was a Saturday, and we all had breakfast together—my husband, my daughter, and me. Her school was three hours away, and the car was filled with things my daughter thought she'd need, so far from us: clothes and lamps and bedspreads and posters and rugs. She didn't know what she'd need. It was a new life.

My husband walked restlessly around the kitchen, jingling the change in his pockets and asking me when I'd be ready to leave. I went into the pantry and opened a cupboard door and hid my head behind it and began to cry. She would never live at home again.

That last summer, before she left, one night my daughter and I were at home alone. My husband was traveling. My daughter and I were in my bedroom, sitting in the window seat that overlooked the lawn and the ash and the barn. The ash tree spread its high leafy canopy, and above it was a full moon. The dogs were asleep on the rug. We'd been reading; it was around ten o'clock, and we were ready for bed.

"Let's go riding," my daughter said.

I looked at her. We were bathed, and in our nightgowns. The

horses were fed, watered, and turned out in the field for the night. Riding at night is dangerous.

"All right," I said.

We pulled on our jeans, and the dogs stood up, mystified but eager. We ran quietly across the lawn, the dogs behind us. The night was warm and velvety, the stars close. The leaves in the ash tree moved mysteriously overhead.

We took the bridles from the tack room, and at the pasture gate we called to them, our voices low in the darkness. The horses were invisible on the hill, but they heard us. After a moment we heard them, their patient footsteps through the long grass. They came quietly down to the gate and lowered their docile heads. We slipped the bits into their mouths and swung ourselves up onto their summer-smooth backs. We rode up into the field and over the crest of the hill, through the narrow gate and down into the big back field. Beyond that were the black woods, deep, impenetrable. Down at the bottom of the field, we turned the horses around and set their heads toward the crest of the hill, the line of black trees along the fence.

"Let's canter," my daughter said.

One of the rules of riding is never to run when you can't see the ground. Another is never to ride without hard hats. We wore no hats, and we could barely see our own hands.

We pressed our blue-jeaned legs against the horses' smooth silky sides, and they slid at once into a rhythmic canter, rocking us through the darkened meadow grasses. The drumming of their hooves was like a mysterious signal in the night. The sky was wide open above us, the stars rose up in legions, and the air was sweet.

This was my daughter's idea. I would never have thought of it.

AFTER MY DAUGHTER went away to school, my husband and I still woke early. He still drove quietly down the drive, headed for the station. I still got up then, although there was no one to get breakfast for, no anxiety about missing the bus. There were no more pea soup fogs, no dastardly plots. The dogs watched me closely, ready for action, but there was no reason, then, to go out to the barn. The horses were gone.

After my husband had left I got up and went downstairs with the dogs. I made coffee and toast and took it into my study and sat down at my desk. I was doing research, then, for a biography, and I was working in the guest room. I had spread my notes across the white bedspread on the double bed. I wrote at a card table. The house around me was entirely silent. The rooms were empty, and when I went downstairs to get a second cup of coffee I was alone.

In the afternoon I heard the school bus groaning its way up the hill in front of our house. Before, the bus had let my daughter off there, at the bottom of our driveway, and then she climbed the driveway carrying her book bag, and then I heard the back door opening into the mudroom. After she left, the bus still stopped there, but now it was only to let off the neighbor's children. I heard it stop, as it always had, but afterwards there was no sound at the back door.

Sometimes, in those afternoons, I went out to the barn, the dogs behind me. The barn was empty, and the heavy stall doors stood open onto the aisle. The sweet smells still lingered there—the grain, the hay, the rich leather of the saddles, and the sweet, close scent of the horses themselves. Sometimes I stood in the dim, cool space and remembered the way the horses put their noses out of their stalls in the mornings, blinking at the light, the way they had called to me, when I pushed open the door.

Sometimes I went into my daughter's room, with its pale blue walls, the drifting white clouds, the faint glowing rainbow. The big brass bed was neatly made, the bedspread smooth, the pillows plump. I opened the top drawer of her bureau and took out the golden braids, wrapped in tissue paper. I held them in my hands.

They were so light. They were so thick, but they weighed hardly anything at all.

Conversations

Kit Rachlis

M y former wife and I took our daughter Austen to college together. Late in the summer, the three of us flew from Los Angeles to Boston and drove to Hampshire College in western Massachusetts. The drive, for the most part, was silent. Austen barely said a word. Her mother and I were keenly aware that we were doing something as a separated couple that we had always imagined we would do as husband and wife.

When we arrived at Hampshire, what followed was as ritualistic as kabuki. Children on the verge of independence snapped at parents for being overly solicitous. Parents nodded to one another in silent sympathy. We lugged Austen's stuff up to her room, said awkward hellos to her roommate, and followed her around as she filled out paperwork. There was a moment, after we left Austen on a long line in the administration building, when her mother and I found ourselves with nothing to do. It was a beautiful warm August day, and we headed for a court-yard. My former wife read the paper. Parents made small talk. I just sat in silence, arms spread out, head thrown back, letting the sun hit my face.

Suddenly I found myself crying. It caught me by surprise, but it probably shouldn't have. The three years of living apart, the uncertainty of how her mother's and my separation would affect Austen, had finally caught up with me. I was crying be-cause, for the first time in fifteen years, there would be no more taking her to school, no more long Saturday drives to batting practice, no more packing her lunch, no more writing messages on her napkin. This was as it should be. The whole point of be-ing a parent—at the risk of sounding sententious—is to help instill your child with the skills and the confidence and curios-ity to go out on her own. Knowing all that didn't stop the tears from coming down.

I hugged Austen good-bye later that afternoon. My last im-age was her sitting cross-legged on Hampshire's massive lawn with her orientation group. My former wife drove me to the Trailways station in Northampton. She would be taking the rental car back to Boston. I would be taking a three-hour bus trip to Vermont to visit friends. The only people who travel by bus in the United States are the young and the poor, and I hadn't done so since I was in my twenties. Squeezing down the narrow aisle, finding a seat toward the rear, sent me back to bus trips I had taken as a teenager through the South. Rather than filling me with romance and adventure, they invariably made me feel alone, acutely aware of the distance between me and everybody I loved.

To drop off your child at college is a modern rite, a universally accepted signpost that you have completed the longest and, you hope, most strenuous stretch of parenthood. You and your spouse are supposed to get in the car together, reassure each other that everything is all right, discuss how far your child has come and how proud you are, and in the silence and small talk of the long drive home or to the airport begin to sense what the next phase of life will be like. Instead, I was sitting in a nearly empty bus, the light outside fading, feeling like a teenager again, not sure whether being on my own meant freedom or isolation.

PERHAPS IF WE had had more than one child and had to juggle complicated schedules, I would have felt differently, but I never wanted to carpool. The drive to Austen's elementary school and, later, to her high school was about eleven miles. This added another twenty minutes to my morning commute, but those twenty minutes were my favorite stretch of the day. It was a chance to have unfettered, unpressured time with Austen. We had been keeping this time for ourselves since she was very young, and I wasn't about to give it up so I could get to work earlier.

My wife and I had stumbled on how to divide duties when Austen began day care—I'd be responsible for the mornings and lunch, my wife would take care of the late afternoons and dinner. This routine was so established that after we split up there was no question we were going to preserve its essentials. I no longer woke up Austen, but I continued to take her to school and make her lunch. Sometime when Austen was in kindergarten, I had begun to draw on her lunch napkin. "Draw" is an exaggeration. Doodle is more accurate: a daisy, a palm tree, a funny face. When Austen reached high school, the doodles had evolved (or, I suppose, devolved) into a note to her that always played off her favorite TV show, *The X-Files*. Sometimes I'd wish her luck on a test or make an inside joke or comment on something in the news. It was my way of saying hello to her in the middle of the day. But those drawings and those quotes were also about something else: They represented a direct line from my father through me to her.

After I graduated from high school, I took a year off. For most of the first nine months, I worked for a federal poverty program in rural North Carolina. In the spring, I decided I needed a paying job and returned home to New York City. I had not lived with my parents for an extended period since I had left for boarding school at thirteen, so this was a new experience for all of us. I had been out on my own for a while, but I was also in the last throes of adolescence. The line between parent and child suddenly was hazy. Did I have to let them know I was coming home for dinner? (Yes.) Did I have a curfew? (No.)

I don't know how it began, but my father started to make me lunch. My father loved to cook, and it's quite possible he just wanted to put the leftovers to good use. But I suspect there was another reason. Making me lunch was a chance to re-create a routine that we had lost out on when I went off to boarding school. It was a chance to connect in all the nonverbal ways that parents need to connect with their children, except it wasn't entirely nonverbal. Every lunch came with a paper napkin on which he had written a quote. Not a profound quote. Not a quote full of advice. The first one read: "No matter how thin you slice it, it's still baloney—Al Smith." The second one: "Without bread all is misery—William Cobbett." The quotes were silly, they were witty, they were literary. Many, though not all, alluded to food. My father passed his views of the world on to me in many ways, but never in all his years did we ever have a father-son conversation in which he'd put his arm around me and told me in a grave tone what he expected of me or what values I should uphold. Those values, I realized much later, could be found in the lunches he made me.

Lots of school counselors say that some of the most profound conversations between parent and child transpire in a car. It's the perfect setting: Both parties are trapped in an intimate space, but they don't have to look at each other. Austen and I spent an enormous amount of time commuting, just the two of us—twenty minutes a day, five days a week, for eleven years—and I can't recall a single conversation that was "profound." I can recall our listening to NPR and Monty Python tapes. I can remember her reading aloud from the front page of the *Wall Street Journal* when she was eleven, and my trying to explain each item. I can remember her recounting in detail the plots of the books she was reading or cramming for a test or filling me in about her friends. I can certainly recall our talking about movies and politics and sports and journalism, about the different ways to define success and how to grapple with disappointment. Most of all, I can tell you what those drives felt like: They were reassuring. Our conversation could be weighty or trivial or sleepy or incessant. It didn't matter. What mattered was that the conversation never stopped.

When Austen was fifteen, though, I moved out of the house. Her mother and I had been married for eighteen years. In the immediate aftermath, when I was staying at a friend's, I often found myself in the divorce section of bookstores, furtively scanning for advice. It was the British psychologist and writer Penelope Leach, who had shaped some of my former wife's and my ideas about child rearing, who provided the most practical suggestion: To make things as least disruptive as possible, the parent who has left should try to live within a reasonable distance of his or her child. In Los Angeles, where driving even short distances can consume huge portions of the day, this seemed both obvious and essential. I found a guesthouse a mile and a half away. Built on the side of a hill, it consisted of two rooms stacked on top of each other. The second floor—the living room/dining room/kitchen—was perched high above the street and looked directly into the crown of a tree. Friends said the apartment was my aerie. The image was more apt than they knew. I filled the two rooms with mostly borrowed furniture to make it homey for Austen, but it wasn't large enough for her to stay overnight. I was living in an empty nest, and the worst part was that I had created it myself.

After I moved out, our routine expanded. In addition to taking Austen to school, I picked her up two or three times a week and made her dinner before dropping her back home. We also spent almost every Saturday together. Austen, who played first base on the varsity softball team at her high school, had a standing appointment Saturday afternoons with a hitting coach. He lived deep in the San Gabriel Valley, thirty miles away, an hour-and-a-half round-trip, which is a lot even by L.A. standards. Those drives became an extension of our morning commute: a chance to talk, to listen to the radio, to just be together. If Austen didn't have plans for Saturday night, we'd usually see a movie. (A true child of Los Angeles, Austen made it clear at an early age that she wanted to make movies when she grew up.) There came a moment, of course, when she announced that certain parts of town were off limits; we might run into her classmates, and it would be too embarrassing to be seen going to the movies with your father.

It took eighteen months after I moved out for my wife and I to agree that the marriage was over. So I didn't start dating until the summer after Austen's junior year, and even then, I did it sparingly at first. One side of my family is Scotch-Irish Presbyterian, the other Russian Jewish, which means, I've often joked, that I'm a Calvinist Jew: I was born guilt ridden. It would be easy, in retrospect, to see my decisions as paying penance—the tiny apartment, not dating much, taking Austen to school and picking her up, the Saturday afternoons and evenings. Sure, I wanted her to know that even though I was no longer living in the same house I wasn't gone. But that puts it in terms of duty, and it never felt like duty. I enjoyed all that time with her. The irony of my moving out was that I ended up spending more time with Austen than if I had remained married. If it meant putting off my life, so what? Maybe, it was even a relief.

BY THE LATE fall of her first year at Hampshire, Austen was calling every Sunday morning in tears. The phone would ring precisely at eight-thirty in my Los Angeles apartment, and by the third Sunday I knew it was her before I picked up the phone. Nobody else would consider calling at such an hour. I was aware, though, that she was being considerate; she didn't want to wake me, but she wanted to speak to me as early as possible. The calls followed a similarly heartbreaking pattern. She was sure she had made a terrible choice. Hampshire was the wrong place for her. She didn't have any friends. She was convinced a professor was going to blame her for something she hadn't done. She wanted to transfer.

Austen's mother and I had figured out early on that the quieter she became the greater her anguish. At least the phone calls were coming, a good sign she wasn't keeping everything bottled up, that she was letting me—and her mother—know how unhappy she was. On the other hand, she was as unhappy as I had ever heard her. She wasn't suicidal, I was sure. Nor was she on the edge of paralyzing depression. But she was in agony, and there was only so much I could do to relieve the pain. I tried to reassure her (in all likelihood whatever she had done wasn't as bad as she feared), ask questions (where did she think she'd like to transfer?), and offer practical advice (if her advisor was as bad as she said he was, Hampshire had a system that encouraged students to switch to a new one). But mostly I listened and hoped that being at the other end of the phone would provide some consolation.

She was struggling, I knew, with homesickness, with being three thousand miles away, with being on her own. She was also grappling with being a fish out of water. Hampshire is one of the most progressive colleges in the country. In a culture of bohemianism, Austen was the straight kid, the kid who wore polo shirts instead of tie-dye, who thought Al Gore was a better presidential candidate than Ralph Nader. During one of those Sunday calls, between the tears and the despair, she said the problem with Hampshire was that there were too many boys who had nicknamed themselves Ché. It was a typical Austen remark—keen, caustic, and pithy—and it gave me hope. Anybody that observant hadn't entirely given up, hadn't totally given into her fears. At least, that's what I told myself.

In the summer before Austen left for Hampshire, I had started dating a woman who had moved from New York to Los Angeles. Her name was Maia, and she had two children who were a few years older than Austen. She was usually with me those Sunday mornings when Austen phoned. She was patient when the calls went long and shrewd about what Austen was grappling with. Over winter break, I told Austen about Maia. I was aware that she was still feeling shaky and that this news would be unsettling. On the other hand, she was eighteen years old, and she needed to know about my first serious relationship since her mother and I had split up.

Austen's response was mute, a nonresponse that was a response in itself. In February, after she was back at Hampshire, I called to say that Maia and I were flying to New York and invited her to join us. Austen's response was classic: She'd be happy to come down, but she had no desire to see "that woman." Maia, showing much more insight than I, refused to be hurt by any of this. Of course, Austen was going to have complicated feelings about her father going out with somebody, she counseled. Give it time.

The Sunday morning phone calls continued, but late in the spring I detected a change. When she discussed what she was doing, the same names cropped up. It was clear she was finding a coterie of friends. It was even clearer that professors adored her and were taking her under their wing. The date for sending in her transfer papers approached and passed. Austen said she wanted to stick it out.

Returning to L.A. for the summer, Austen announced on the phone one Sunday that she was willing to meet Maia. But, she said, there were certain conditions: The meeting had to take place at a dinner party, and she wanted to choose the guests. The guests she was thinking of were friends of mine who had taken a special interest in her over the years. She explained all this in her most adult voice. I was startled but then realized she was being psychologically astute. She wanted to be surrounded by grown-ups who loved her when she met the woman her father had fallen in love with. Austen arrived for dinner with her best male friend, a graduate from Northwestern who was five years older: the perfect protector. He came with flowers and presented them to Maia. Austen and I hugged, and as I turned to introduce her, Maia said, "You must be Austen. I've heard so much about you." They embraced and began to talk. That was six years ago. They've been talking ever since.

Trading a Business Suit
for Blue Jeans

Glynna Freeman

We have three magnificent kids: two boys, Crispin and Clark, and a girl, Cassidy, each five years apart. In my completely objective opinion, they are bright, beautiful, and really nice people, each of them out of the nest—and all of them settled within two miles of one another in Santa Monica, California, pursuing careers as performing artists. We raised our kids in downtown Chicago, primarily because my husband, Lee, and I are both lawyers who have spent the last thirty years specializing in federal litigation, which meant that we normally worked seven days a week, often ten or more hours a day. The only way we could see our kids and be available when they needed us was to live near our work; there was no time for significant commutes to the suburbs. But as the kids left for college, and home became someplace they visited, the importance of that geographical connection vanished. I gave in to a yearning I had had since the eldest was born: to reconnect with some of my own childhood memories in the Rockies—a world that had nothing at all to do with a city lawyer's life.

So now my children live in the city—and Lee and I live in the mountains with cows.

I CAME FROM an oil patch family, and I had something to prove—at least to myself, if not the rest of the world. I was born in Midland, Texas, and my family moved every few years up and down the Rocky Mountains from the Texas Gulf Coast to Wyoming. One of my grandfathers was born in a tent in Oklahoma, and could not read or write. My dad was the first in his family to earn a college degree—a petroleum engineer. My folks always encouraged me and my three younger brothers to do our best, and they were disappointed if we came home with a B on our report cards. After a semester at Southern Methodist University, where I was one of only two freshmen who didn't go through sorority rush, I bought a plane ticket (with all my summer earnings as a page at a bank in Tulsa) to the East Coast to convince some college to give me enough money to attend. I graduated from Smith College in Massachusetts, living in scholarship student housing, where we did all our own cooking and cleaning.

Lee's background was significantly different. Lee's dad put himself through law school by waiting tables at Chicago's Knickerbocker Hotel, but Lee grew up surrounded by art and exposed to opera; he went to a prestigious private school in

Chicago and then to Harvard and Harvard Law. When we met, Lee had clerked for Justice Tom Clark on the Supreme Court and was an assistant U.S. attorney, while I was a congressman's intern—a job that taught me I would have to have a graduate degree if I wanted to be anything other than a glorified secretary.

We got married within a week of my college graduation and moved to Chicago, so that Lee could practice law with his father and I could go to law school at Northwestern. I thought I wanted to go into politics (it was 1968, the year of Chicago's Democratic Convention), but I learned that I was far too blunt and didn't kiss other people's babies (or other parts of their anatomy) very well. I further discovered that I really liked law, especially litigation. I spent over five years in the U.S. attorney's office in Chicago, until Lee called me to say, "I need you, and I need you now." The next thing I knew, I was in Toronto telling Canadian government officials that they had a major problem with their uranium producers creating a cartel, and we were going to prosecute the producers in the United States. Just like that, I entered the world of huge federal cases, prosecuting everything from antitrust conspiracies and securities fraud to stopping New Hampshire's electrical deregulation plan, which would have bankrupted Central Vermont Public Service.

A big-time litigator is a very particular kind of mom. Living close to the office wasn't enough. We needed a surrogate mother (her name is Ida) who would be with the kids when I couldn't, especially when they were young, and would love them as her own. And Lee and I set our social life aside. What time we had was for our kids. When they were growing up, we attended all of their performances, almost every athletic game, and we made ourselves available to participate in any event where they wanted us. We had a rule: If they wanted to talk, about anything, all other chores or events were set aside and we sat down and talked. The front door of our apartment was never locked, and all their friends knew they were welcome for food, conversation, or a place to stay overnight. If we traveled, or went to a concert or to the opera, we took them with us. There was no boundary, no sense of "our life" and "their life." With work demanding as much of us as it did, the rest of our time was for family.

When it was time to let go, we were active participants in the kids' search for the right school—participants, but not dictators. We told each of them they could go to school anywhere they wanted, as long as they got a four-year degree and it was located someplace that we would enjoy visiting. It was a fascinating experience to travel to schools with them and talk about what they wanted out of a college and their life beyond college. We were amazed at how much more analytical and mature they were than we had been at that age. When the time came, we drove each of them to school (the eldest went to Williams, in Massachusetts, and the younger two went to Middlebury, in Vermont). We helped them get all their stuff into their room (I made their bed one last time, if they would let me), gave them a big hug, and wished them good luck.

Then we left, found the nearest pub, ordered a stiff scotch, had a good cry, and let go. That doesn't mean abandonment. While they were in school (and even today), we had many good talks about everything from roommates, loves, classes, career choices, to disappointments and thrills. Because they are performing artists, we tried to attend every school play and concert that they thought merited our trip. It gave us a much better opportunity to visit with the kids than the typical "Parents Weekends." We are thrilled that even today the kids (now thirty-four, twenty-nine, and twenty-four) want us to attend their performances, and that they love to come home several times a year for a visit.

But the focus of "home" has changed. Once the kids were out of school and on their own, we moved the family homestead from the city to the country.

The idea had hatched in my brain almost thirty years earlier, when our eldest child was only five years old. My mother had called to ask me when I was coming to see her. I told her that while I loved her and Dad, I didn't love Tulsa. What I really wanted was to go back to the Rockies, to meet them there; that was where my happiest childhood memories resided. So Crispin and I took a train to southern Colorado and spent a week in a log cabin with my folks. By the time Lee met up with us in nearby Vail (a lawyer about to start a trial can't spend a week in a log cabin with no means of communication), I had made a decision. I announced that I wanted a ranch—not a resort home, but a working ranch. We are not adept at being people of leisure. If we were going to work this hard for most of our lives, we wanted a place where we could retire, but not in the usual sense. We needed to have an occupation.

We had been looking for several years, with little success, when a client told us he had found, in Montana, the most beautiful ranch he had ever seen. At the time, we were both on trial and had no time (or money) to look at ranches. The next year the same ranch was back on the market, and after a great deal of deliberation (because its cost was our net worth), we bought it—the Master Key Ranch, named after the case Lee had been working on, which gave us the financial ability to buy our dream.

For years, we spent as much time at the ranch as our schedules would allow—typically a month or more in the summer (after the kids' summer camp), two weeks at Christmas, and an occasional hunting trip in the fall. Several times we thought about moving to Montana, but the kids were thriving at their schools, and our law practice was based in Chicago. But Lee and I always hoped we would someday call Montana home.

Once the kids were grown and gone, and after a particularly grueling case, I told the firm I had had enough. The wear and tear had finally gotten to me; I had proven what I needed to prove, and I simply didn't care whether I took another deposition or won another big case. Whatever time I had left in this world, I wanted to spend in Montana with Lee, the pups, the cows, the horses, and my visiting children. Last Christmas, we moved to Montana along with Ida, who has been part of our family for too long to consider anything else. The apartment in Chicago? I doubt that either of us will spend any significant time there, but we offer it to relatives and friends who are going to be in Chicago and need a place to stay.

It wasn't just the empty nest. Sure, the kids were all grown, and their lives were centered on the West Coast. But more significantly, it was time for a change. I had a desire to try something new for what remained of our lives—and to do it before we were too old to participate actively in the ranch work.

My energy level is no different from the years when I practiced law, but I'm so happy to be back to nature and the basics of life. Currently we're running about 550 pairs (cows and calves), and that doesn't mean sitting on the deck, drink in hand, while somebody else looks after them. We plow fields, plant them, irrigate them, and hay them. We birth calves, tag them, and brand them. We herd cattle, on horseback or with ATVs, and we monitor them daily to make sure they have sufficient water and grass and are in good health. We keep computerized records on every cow, bull, and calf in the herd

This is what our kids come home to now, when they make a visit—this, and the realities of ranch community life, a big change from the hustle and relatively impersonal world of the big city. The days of walking everywhere are over: A bottle of milk or loaf of bread is an hour's drive down a dirt road to the nearest town, which is also where we have to go to get the mail, including newspapers. On the other hand, all the neighbors help one another branding, shipping the calves, or doing any other project that takes more hands than those who live on the ranch. It's hard work, but it's also a social event—the host family always feeds everyone after the work is done, and everyone lingers after the meal to chat. Crispin, Clark, and Cassidy don't just drop by; they pitch in.

And for all the hard work, we are privileged to live in such a beautiful place. Getting up at 6 A.M. to turn on a generator to pump well water to a stock tank may sound mundane—not what many parents look forward to after all those years of getting up early to grab breakfast and get out the door to school and work—but the view of the rising sun lighting the mountains is breathtaking. And the ranch has become less remote, at least informationally, which is what counts when your children are far away. Our first telephone was a party line, but now we have satellite Internet and television, which gives us much more access to the outside world.

On the other hand, if someone drives up our two-mile driveway, they are either coming to see us, or they are really lost. Living here makes any visit from the kids a celebration, because it's not the sort of thing they can do spontaneously. We know they're coming, and sometimes we know there's a purpose to the trip—the introduction of a new beau or girlfriend, the desire to get far away from the pressures of their young lives, the need for emotional refueling. We expect them for holidays, and we continue the traditions we started when they were little, like tromping through the snow to decide which tree to cut and decorate for Christmas, or going to the Livingston Rodeo on July Fourth.

The ranch gives me the chance to recapture two sets of memories—when I was a little girl, and when my children were little. Home for them now is the ranch, rather than the apartment in Chicago. As for me, I'm ready to teach the grandchildren to ride horses and herd cattle. Isn't that the obvious next step?

The Godfather

Harry Shearer

In my early twenties, I befriended a childless couple
slightly older than me. Aside from their other admirable
qualities—intelligence, a self-effacing modesty in a town
full of rampant egos—what impressed me about them was
their certainty, their commitment, to the choice of childlessness. That word, of course, colors and misstates what I think
they had chosen. They hadn't elected to be without something
or someone, a minus state, an incomplete family, a—to use the
archaic term—barren marriage; they had chosen to live as two
adults, pursuing adult occupations and pastimes, leaving child-
ish things behind for good. As long as I was in close contact
with them—distance has taken its toll—I never knew them to
look back at that decision with anything other than quiet satis-
faction that it was the right choice for them.

For me, the choice to be an adult without children has always been conditional, temporal, hedged about with qualifiers and contingencies. I guess I envy those friends their certainty. Or do I? I know I don't envy the certainty of more politically anchored friends, whose very commitment seems to blind them to the stupidity or venality of those who share their label but with whom they may not even agree on crucial issues, like, just for a cheap example, war. I don't envy the certainty of folks I see who are convinced that their religion is the only true way to happiness, salvation, or surviving some cataclysm or other, and whose more fervent brethren may be inclined to kill to enforce that certainty. I clearly remember things I did feel certain about falling into the great vat of ambiguity as I experienced more, maybe even learned more.

When I've thought about the issue, one of the first, and most consistent, notions nudging me in the direction of reproducing is connected with the goofy-sounding concept: End of the Line. Goofy but true. I'm the only child of parents whose families were dispensed with by some good soldiers of a certain Reich. Genetically speaking, I'm literally the end of the line. When you think of the function of having kids in the most basic terms, I'm falling down on the job of passing on this DNA collection. Viewed most grimly, I sometimes fear that I'm handing a late little victory to Mr. Hitler.

Closely linked, part of the same double helix of thought, is this idea: Given my wife's and my inherited cupboard of talents—she's a masterful singer, pianist, and songwriter, and I'm Derek Smalls, for God's sake—imagine what a little musical gift we're refusing to bestow upon the world. (On the other hand, should the DNA lottery go the other way, the spawn could inherit my wife's dyslexia and my temper: bad times in reading class. ("Mr. Shearer, could you come in for a visit, please? We're having a bit of a problem.")

And yet it's that very confluence of careers, mine and hers, that has given me most of my doubt about the child-rearing project. A two-career show business couple, both members fixedly focused on the struggle to survive and prevail in the velvet jungle, seems like the kind of family unit, in all fairness to us, from which a sullen and drugged-out teenaged actor or singer emerges, a figure more familiar in the DWI suite of the Malibu sheriff's office than on the dean's list or the Carnegie Hall stage.

There is also, of course, the little matter of the home planet. Not to be too cosmic about it, but it's been a good while since the earth's primary need was for more humans. Even if that need were urgent, Nature seems to have provided an answer, in the form of rampantly reproductive Catholics, Orthodox Jews, and Mormons, just to single out three of the more ambitious contributors to the people supply chain. If you're not prepared to crank out that kind of *Cheaper by the Dozen* brood, you're not really being fruitful and multiplying.

None of this means that in my private fantasies—don't get excited—I haven't visualized the splendid dad I'd be, or the empathic mom my wife would make, or how superbly we'd handle the complications and challenges that seem to crop up for friends whose parenting takes place in the slightly more daunting environment known as reality. Nor has it kept me from holding firm opinions on issues we'll never face—public or private school, what do you say or do about marijuana?—or on what looks to me, especially as I observe families I know in Fiji and Australia, like the modern American fetish, nourished by the twin streams of guilt and fear, to over-schedule, over-enrich, over-control our children.

What do I know? Well, I was a kid once. And that fact leads me to another reason why our home most likely (see? Still no ironclad assurance) will not have to be childproofed: I have perhaps the lowest level of nostalgia for my own childhood of any adult I know. As soon as I was old enough to create accessible memories, I seem to have seen the stuff of childhood—the icky candy I never liked, the dopey fantasies, like a certain fairy and a certain bunny, the lame things (like "school spirit") that we were supposed to care about—as feeble attempts to distract us from the basic reality that adults had all the good stuff. I was obsessed with the parts of the grown-up world, news media and show business, that confirmed this suspicion in all its many dimensions. My solidarity with my age cohort was further shredded when the magic door opened, as if in response to my wish, and I entered the world of grown-ups, as a child actor.

A couple of years later, when my school decided to skip me a couple of grades forward, the process was complete. I bring all this up because it seems to me that often the most avid parents are the people who yearn most strongly to reexperience the joy and mystery of their own childhoods. Mine I couldn't wait to exit. And that's not even counting the cruelty that children exhibit even more freely than Hollywood producers do, despite America's long project to reimagine childhood as a garden of innocence and innocents, so much like America itself.

On the other hand—some refreshing ambivalence for you

for a change—there's that most primal fear: WHAT HAP-PENS WHEN I GET OLD AND SICK AND FORGET-FUL AND INCONTINENT? WHO THE HELL'S GOING TO TAKE CARE OF ME? Nobody's immune to that one. Yet, in a society in which we've long since stopped having kids as a way of enriching the family's labor pool, that what-happens motivation seems like one of the most pathetic and selfish of reasons to bring new life online. If you want to be totally crass about it, you can hire great caretakers for a fraction of what it costs to put a kid through private school. Grade school.

So, yes, I'm the kind of asshole who, when he sees a newly minted bundle of cuteness next to me in the Starbucks line, thinks, "It's only a little more than a decade until 'I hate you, you fucking hypocrite!' comes roaring out of that cute little mouth." I'm the guy who sits on the fourteen-hour flight from Australia, listening to one of the leaders of our future scream his tiny head off, wondering what happened to the fine old tradition of putting a drop or two of brandy on the youngster's tongue? And I'm the person who feels lucky that, unbowed by the pressures of supporting an additional human or two at a time when my career was, to put it mildly, tanking, I have no porn films, stupid TV series, or hideously irritating commercials in my résumé. Yet.

All this being said, I do have two wonderful godchildren, one on each coast, who fill me with affection and pride, as well as unlimited admiration for the job their parents have done in raising them. Godfathering was never a tradition in my family, that I know of, but two couples asked me, and it sounded like, to quote Oliver North, a "neat idea."

In one case, it was more serious from the start: The family lived ten blocks from me, and I saw my goddaughter pretty much weekly. The first real call to duty came when Ella was about six years old, and her parents, knowing my inordinate affection for the game of basketball, assigned me to be her coach. So, as documented in photographs, there we were on an outdoor court, me teaching her the grosser points of the arts of dribbling and shooting. I'm sad to report this did not, so far at least, imbue her with a lifelong affection for the game, but neither did it traumatize her to the point where she's phobic about leather spheroids.

In the other case, life played its nasty little joke; my godson's dad died when his son was only five, and although nothing was ever said, I felt the responsibility increase substantially. Simon's mom brought him out to L.A. when he was about eight, and we showed him something of a Hollywood week: a visit to a *Simpsons* script read-through, a tour of a western movie ranch, some surfing. We've had some chats I'd describe as more avuncular than paternal, but the Big Stuff is yet to come. I hope.

Both kids are soon leaving their nests—Ella to college, Simon to boarding school. I'll see less of them—though, because of my peripatetic life, I may actually see more of them than their parents will in the next few years. Their growth has necessarily been more obvious to me, observing the spurts rather than the slow day-to-day curve. I've been careful not to assume that either kid wants an additional parent, and I've never been unclear that I'm too old to be their friend. Each of them seems to have figured out the role he or she has wanted me to play in their lives, and I've tried to pick up the cues. And so, as those kids stand smart and strong on the doorstep of their adulthoods, our nest, never yet having been full, won't be really empty.

Juggling Lite

Ellen Goodman

First, may I say a few words about the passage of time?
I just turned sixty-five, entering senior citizenship,
when I have to resist clichés that pop up like age spots
on the surface of my conversation: "The last time I saw you,
you were only this high." "Can it really be fifteen years?"
"Where did the time go?"

The older I grow, the more the past seems compressed. I
find myself astonished that a neighbor's toddler finished high
school while I was moseying along through the routines of
midlife.

There must be some mathematical formula to explain this
universal experience. Five is to fifteen as twenty is to sixty—
one third of a life. So if five years seems like forever to a
fifteen-year-old, it seems far too swift to a sixty-five-year-old.

I start with time because it startles me that my daughter and

I have lived under separate roofs for longer than we lived under the same roof. It is now exactly twenty years since the fall day when my daughter Katie and I packed up the car and joined that long caravan of families moving the contents of a million bedrooms into a million dorm rooms.

My daughter wasn't fleeing the nest. We were companions and accomplices in that leave-taking. We were in that separation together—and yet with different emotions.

THOUGH I SPEND my professional days writing about social change, I've never been much for personal change. I've lived nearly my whole life in the same zip code. Indeed, the zip code changed around me while I stayed in place. When I was growing up, my whole family lived in one town. I never had to go home for the holidays. I was already home.

My daughter, like many children of divorce, grew up packing her bags for holidays and August, traveling to Florida and her father, back to Boston and her mother. I, on the other hand, spent the night before each of her departures stuck in some variation of the same anxiety dream. Over and over again, I lost her in transit, on the escalator, at the airport, on the highway. Any self-respecting analyst would have dismissed me as the owner of an impossibly boring interior life.

Before Katie left for college, she spent months commuting between childhood and adulthood, traveling between safety and emancipation. There were no doors slammed in our house, no voices raised, no outward rebellion. But in this long, exhausting process, she was the pedal and I was the brake. She wanted to do exactly as she pleased—with my blessing. She wanted her independence—with my approval.

That independence came slower than she chose, faster than I chose. When my husband, Katie's self-described "wicked step-father," listened to our strained conversations, he could pluck out the same, recurring exchange: "Next year you won't know what I'm doing." "Next year, I'll be on my own."

Finally, next year arrived. We took our place in the national swap fest of parents and children, a rite of passage in our culture. Standing together on a city street in Philadelphia, her green eyes and freckles half-hidden under the black hat she wore as a security blanket throughout her freshman year, this tall, exuberant young woman looked at me and said: "This is exactly what I want to be doing now."

I hugged her and turned the car north again, *The Big Chill* tape offering a background of rock-and-roll bravado to my mix of pride and loss. This is exactly what she wanted. So it was exactly what I wanted for her. But what did I want for me?

When I got home, I sat down and wrote about that day as if I had finally, actually lost her on the escalator of life, in the train station of adulthood. And lost something of myself in the process: "What do you do with all the antennae of motherhood when they become obsolete? What do you do with the loose wires that dangle after eighteen years of intimate connection to your own child? What use is there for the expertise of motherhood that took so long to acquire?"

I wrote too, "I will go home to a new demographic column:

households without children. Are these families? I will enter the longest and least-heralded phase, that of parent and adult child."

As I read these words today, on this twenty-year anniversary, my daughter is a mother and I am a grandmother. I think of all I've learned since, as a wistful forty-five-year-old, I said good-bye to my child.

Are these families? Yes, these are still families.

WHAT DO YOU do with the antennae of motherhood when they become obsolete? Those antennae do not become obsolete, even if they have been traded in for cell phones and e-mail and frequent flier tickets from Bozeman to Boston, Boston to Bozeman. Even if the software of this particular motherhood require continual updating.

The long and least-heralded phase? Yes, it is still unheralded. It still is relatively uncharted territory, a phase with its own rewards and complexities. The lingering assumption behind the "empty nest" label is emptiness, the notion that family and caregiving end when our sons and daughters walk over the threshold of childhood. The label implies that we live this phase of our lives alone, for better and worse.

But the least of the least-heralded part may be the attention paid to ongoing relationships between parents and adult children. Here is what I have learned in my not-so-empty nest phase: Those relationships are by no means the same, but they are by no means lost.

In America the narrative of growing up tilts dramatically toward independence. The gold standard of American adulthood is a person standing on his or her own two feet. The through line of the story is individualism. It is the most pervasive myth that colors our lives.

Raised to be on our own, every generation of young adults seems shocked when they are plunged into parenthood. I remember to this day being overwhelmed by full immersion into motherhood. I still remember the shock of being responsible to the utter dependence of my infant daughter. The most planned parenthood, the most-longed-for motherhood, propels us into the protection racket. We hover over our children, terrified by their vulnerability, filling the house with intercoms, webcams, V-chips, and milk cartons with missing children posted on the side.

If our culture values individualism to a fault, it also holds parents responsible for more and more of their children's lives—what they watch on television, what they eat, what they believe, their successes and failures. The intense involvement in college searches and SATs and admissions essays that is the source of so many middle-class suburban satires is ratcheted up expressly because it is our last official duty. And yet, paradoxically, parents are also supposed to pass on the message of independence.

We are then shocked to find ourselves out of parenthood. Is there any other job that defines success as becoming unnecessary? Imagine recruiting someone for a job by promising that if they do everything right, they'll be obsolete. But the cultural line on parenting is that if you do it right, the children will leave. Leave. You. Alone. If you do it wrong, they will suffer from a syndrome common enough to have spawned a movie: Failure to Launch.

It seems to me from my vantage point two decades out that we are still not raised to understand the reality: Most of us grow, making and remaking our lives in connection, in interdependence. Even adult parents and their adult children can continue that cycle.

WHEN I LEFT my daughter on that street corner, I already had a head full of empty nest fantasies from friends. What will I do when Katie is gone? Run around the house naked. Weep until Thanksgiving. Paint her room, pack up the stuffed animals and the Depeche Mode posters, and turn it into a guest room. Sell the house and go live in a condo or on a golf course. Pay tuition and reinvent my life.

My first act of emancipation was not so dramatic. What I actually did was to stop setting the alarm clock to school hours, only to discover that I no longer needed an alarm. One of the ironies of middle age was that my biorhythms woke me up at an hour that had exhausted me eighteen years earlier.

What I did next was turn in the car that my daughter had used for demolition derby in the first years after she got her license and buy a menopausal red Toyota Celica. Only to spend the next four years struggling in and out of the low-slung car before I gave up the ghost of youth to save the back of midlife.

What I did next—what we did next—was to reinvent our mother-daughter relationship again and again. We'd already gone from mother and toddler to mother and teenager—a transition that required the flexibility of a Bikram yoga instructor. Gradually, though, we were transformed from mother and college student to mother and mother, woman and woman. I changed from guide to confidante, from safety net to reality check.

When I think back on Katie's college years, they remind me of a commuting relationship. When kids go to college, we learn to play the accordion. Children come in and out of the house. They are in our peripheral vision and then in our face and then gone. I suppose the trick of these years is the trick of any relationship: managing closeness and distance.

Yes, that first Thanksgiving came sooner than I imagined. Katie came home, sure we would affirm how much her life had changed, and blissfully unaware that our lives might have changed, too. I couldn't give her a curfew and couldn't help listening for the car in the driveway. She assumed independence and needed money for the movies.

College administrators talk about helicopter parents who hover over their children, these days monitoring them via e-mail and cell phone, never quite letting go. We talk less about those children who may see that helicopter as an umbrella.

For a time, it seems to me, our children phone home as if home were 911. I have a friend who remembers to this day when her daughter placed her emergency call, announcing in her panic that she might be pregnant. For three sleepless nights, my friend agonized. When she finally called to check, this sophomore breezily updated her mother, "Oh, it's fine, I got my period."

When my daughter called in her problems, I felt an instant

recurrent need to "fix it," whatever "it" was. It took me a decade to understand that I didn't always have the answer and didn't always have to answer. My daughter, for her part, often wanted a conversation, not a rescue squad.

OF COURSE, IN that long-ago piece, I also wrote about being a working mother. "I thought that mothers who also had work that engaged their time and energy might avoid the cliché of an empty-nest syndrome. . . . Now I doubt it." I wrote about the end of the juggling act: "Tomorrow for the first time in eighteen years that part of my brain that is always calculating time—school time, work time, dinner time—can let go of its stop watch."

Well, guilt, that fellow traveler of the working mother, that Jiminy Cricket sitting on my shoulder when I threw together a last-minute Halloween ghost while my neighbor put the finishing touches on her homemade Cowardly Lion, went into neutral. But it's never entirely gone away. In my forties, fifties, and now sixties, I have a more muted version of the same parental-performance anxiety.

To this day when the phone rings—Can I come home this weekend? Can you come here?—I can feel the old pull to drop everything, to be there. Just last fall, in my determination to get home from a speech in California before my daughter, son-in-law, and grandson arrived for a visit, I ended up sleeping on the floor of the Denver airport.

I guess I've revised my juggling act. Think of it as Juggling

Lite. In my thirties, women were talking about "having it all." We were accused of being greedy for life simply because we wanted both work and family. Now in my sixties, I feel the same desire to have work and family. To make my own life and to share it with those I love.

If there is one thing women of my generation don't want, it's to be a cartoon mother, a supplicant in our children's lives, needy to be needed. A friend at work once laughed ironically because after weaning herself from years of waiting for men to call, she was sitting at her desk waiting for her son to call. Spare us the cosmic and comic whine: They don't write, they don't call.

At the same time, the older I get, the more I am aware that the true biological clock is ticking. The recognition of how finite time is doesn't make it any easier to decide how to use that time. When my daughter, Katie, and her husband, Soren, moved to Montana, I moped over the map until my friend Pat, veteran mother of four, living at the four corners of the country, said briskly, "You get in the plane and you go." And so I do.

But if the clock is ticking, I want to spend more time at my laptop and more time with my grandchildren, more time at creative work and more time with my feet up on the porch of the railing in Maine watching the birds. This juggling-lite act fits my status as parent emerita. Or for that matter, as a working grandmother.

Of course, what I could not have imagined twenty years ago, when my thoughts were so colored by the fear of loss, was the time when the "empty nest" life would be filled with grandchildren. If there were any more proof needed that caregiving does not end, that family continues, it is grandchildren. My husband and I have had the great fortune of falling in love with my daughter's boy, Logan, and my stepdaughter's girl, Cloe.

When the call came asking me to write about "the empty nest" again, I couldn't help laughing: "What empty nest?" Katie and three-year-old Logan had just moved in for three months while Katie's comedy troupe, Broad Comedy, performed at a Boston theater.

They were sharing the rooms I had finally renovated from one childhood to the next. Katie's old dollhouse sat on a new bureau. Puzzles and Play-Doh spilled out of large containers. Again, work was condensed; again, days were framed by the nature and nurturing of this boy. Again, those "antennae" were put to use. When my husband and I stayed alone with Logan, we slept at attention, waiting for a call or just a sigh relayed by the monitor whose volume was set on "loud." On Thursday, "Grandma Day," my grandson and I went on "coffee dates" and playground runs. Evenings often ended with another story about "Ishkabibble" culled from my fantasy, or another story about "mommy," culled from the past when that mommy was my baby, a fact that he found hard to believe.

We ended those months with love, down-to-the-bone tiredness, and deep respect for the grandparents raising children on their own.

Now I am writing from my studio at our Maine home. My granddaughter Cloe came in here yesterday to announce that Ella the Elephant's trunk was broken and needed fixing. We wrapped it carefully. With supreme confidence, she also tells me that my studio needs more pictures on the walls. "You need pictures of me. Because when you see them they'll make you happy."

Our house here—dare I say nest—empties out and fills up regularly. The refrigerator has a case of bulimia, overstuffed with food for the children and grandchildren, then emptied down to basics for the two of us. Sometimes we are alone, and wallow in it. Sometimes we are scrambling over the rocks after grandchildren. In this "unheralded phase" of life, I not only have the surprising and warming experience of seeing our two daughters as mothers, I also have the experience of mothering mothers, both their ambitions and their children.

Before this "anniversary" piece, I happened upon Barbara Dafoe Whitehead's portrait of parenthood written for the National Marriage Project, which she codirects. She portrays parenthood as "a conspicuous source of anxiety and distress," a hard stage of life made harder because it is sandwiched between two child-free, footloose, fancy-free, and even self-centered stages. On one end she describes the elongated, child-free youth. On the other end, she describes an elongated and child-free empty nest.

Well, I am a certified member of the first generation that has had and can expect such a long life after full-time parenting. Whitehead gets the life cycle right, but not the rest. For most of us, the later years do not fit the self-indulgent cultural portrait that she draws out of AARP ads that promote Fixodent with the image of kissing seniors. We are not floating unattached from one adults-only community to the next. For every parent with a bumper sticker on her RV—I'M SPENDING MY CHILDREN'S INHERITANCE—there must be a dozen juggling lite.

So these days, I wonder sometimes how our homes got defined as "empty," as if nobody—or Mr. Nobody, as my granddaughter would say—lived there anymore. Aren't we somebody? And if the empty nest is meant to describe a family that's fledged to parts unknown, or parents who have retired from the caregiving business, it doesn't happen that way. Family does not come to an end when childhood does. There is not only a chance, but a need to rewrite the parent-child script for the next act.

My husband and I never did sell our house. We looked at the classic downtown Boston condo and took the train back home. Last Thanksgiving, our dining room expanded with in-laws and a rasher of small people, grandchildren, cousins, great nieces. It turns out that our family is growing, not shrinking. Today when something goes awry and I can't figure out what to do, I turn to the "kids" as much as to my friends.

And sometimes, when I remember those two women, mother and daughter, on a Philadelphia street corner, I cannot resist the mathematical wonder of my age: Where did the time go?

The Old Blue House and the New Blue House

Susan Shreve

We were on the first trip I had taken with my four children and new husband when we got a call from Carlos, the house painter. He said that the historical society objected to the color of blue we were painting our house to mark it as *our house* and not the formal gray shingle it had been when we bought it.

My younger son received the call while he and the other children were playing cards, and he forgot to let us know—so the line remained open, and Carlos waited for forty-five minutes before Caleb remembered that he was waiting on the line. By the time my new husband, Tim, got the message that the person on the phone was the house painter, he explained that he couldn't afford to change the color of the paint, since he was already paying for forty-five minutes of long-distance waiting.

The house, as we discovered when we returned, was very, very blue.

It was also large, with a huge backyard and a big front porch, and it would have cost a fortune in Washington, D.C., if it were not for the fact that it is located at the third most dangerous residential intersection in the United States. That particular statistic was discovered when the elementary school up the street did extensive research on the number of ambulance-born accidents required to get a stoplight. Our corner was way over the mark for ambulances, but we never got a stoplight.

Somehow the combination of the big, beautiful, slightly run-down house sharing a corner with emergency vehicles captured our twenty wonderful years on Newark Street. My children spent their teenage years there, and most of them returned and stayed for weeks or months or years. Many of their friends lived with us between this and that going on in their lives, and even strangers moved in with their suitcases. We became accustomed to the kind of call that begins, "You don't know me, but I am a friend of Joany Hall's who is close to Marty Bernstein, and I will be coming to Washington. . . ." It was just that kind of elastic house. Never too full.

Never too full, I should say, for me. I grew up one of two children in a house not far from this one, and my family, which I certainly love, was simply not big enough to satisfy my need for company. I always wanted many children—six is what I had in mind—and dogs and cats and maybe farm animals happy with domesticity. I told my children that the quota for pets was high, and they could take their pick. We had too many cats and kittens and at least two dogs, sometimes three, as well as one short-term visiting goat. Anyone was welcome to come, to stay, to bring their friends, their children. No party was too large. In the years when my children were still at home—and the last one left only in the last two years—family dinners or parties or just ordinary company in and out the front door were messy, freewheeling, uncomplicated occasions. Everyone pitched in. There were meals under preparation in the kitchen and drinking in the backyard and conversation in the living room, suitcases in the upstairs empty rooms, long-term visitors on the third floor.

As the house began to empty, however, I came to realize that I had developed an expanded view of my capacity for guests, that my children and their friends had created an illusion of unlimited dishwashers and cooks and servers and conversationalists to sustain this small hotel, filling it with youth and the promise of their future.

Tim and I could not make this happen alone.

There was an absolute moment in which I recognized we had skidded out of bounds. I actually loved the parties given by teenagers and so did Tim, and my children gave many of them, especially my younger two. We chaperoned and mingled and danced on the old pine wood floors, the furniture pushed back, the music blasting.

But teenagers are a wily crowd, and we knew a great deal less than we thought we did. One evening—it must have been around three in the morning—everybody sleeping, we heard a loud knock at the front door. Tim went downstairs and I leaned over the banister to see three shaggy young men I'd never seen before.

"Is Shreve's Bar still open?" one of them asked.

"No," Tim said—no slouch when it comes to confrontation—and slammed the front door. But before it was closed, I heard another one of the young men say, "We heard it was an all-night bar."

"We're putting the house on the market," Tim said, climbing into bed. "Tomorrow morning after I have a conversation with your son."

"Maybe," I said, turning out the light.

"Not yet," I said when the morning light spilled through the window beside my bed, the National Cathedral carillon, soaring over the trees beyond the window, ringing through the house for us.

And we didn't put the house on the market. We waited, thinking maybe we'd leave, maybe we'd stay, but either way, we'd wait until the house was empty to see if it felt too large without a crowd.

THE CHILDREN HAD gone off to their various lives, and they wanted us to move.

Their departures had been circular, operating on the engineering principle of a boomerang, but finally the trajectory was as linear as mine had been in the generation that required us to leave home for good at eighteen. Porter left first for graduate school, where he met Bich, and they are now both writers teaching at Purdue—but he didn't leave permanently without returning home to live for a while on the third floor. Elizabeth left for college and New York City, returning briefly to the blue house, but hers was the only accelerated departure among my children, the only one my mother would have recognized as normal. Caleb returned from college to work in advance for the Clinton administration; since his job was constant travel, our house was home base. And Kate, the youngest, left last, with time in between for college and graduate school.

"You and Tim have got to move," she said, packing up to move to San Francisco. "I feel responsible to your old life, when we were kids." As long as we lived in the blue house, she felt the tug of home.

I understood this. It's all too easy, when you're just beginning a new life as the children were, to sink back into the quicksand of your childhood. I remember my own complexities and regressions, the accompanying sadness when I returned to my childhood home as an adult. In fact, the house didn't feel the way it had when my children had lived there with us and three aging dogs, two of which had belonged to two of them, and one aged cat, who had belonged to another of them, and often the plumber or the roofer or the electrician patching and patching. And then my younger son, who has an interest in the working parts of houses, pointed out that the kitchen ceiling was about to cave, that the stairway to the second floor had pulled away from the wall and was dipping precariously, that the electrical system was hazardous, that the place was just too big.

So we put the house on the market, recognizing that its deathtrap position on the corner of Thirty-fourth and Newark Street was going to make it hard to sell even without the falling staircase or cracks in the foundation. We called the real estate people, and they came and gave a price and put the ad in the paper. One afternoon, someone from the real estate office put a FOR SALE sign in the front yard.

The house is well known because it sits high up from the road, and because of its color, and because Thirty-fourth Street is a major route downtown from the suburbs of Maryland. We had become identified to strangers in the supermarket or the gas station, people we met at parties or events, as the family who lived in the Blue House on Newark and Thirty-fourth. And there was also a certain badge of courage about living there, since most people who traveled that route had come upon the ambulances and firetrucks and police, the smashed car thrown up on our sidewalk, against our stone wall.

I watched with a sense of violation as the real estate agent hammered the FOR SALE sign into the ground. Then I went to the kitchen to make tea so I wasn't drawn to look at the sign, to apologize to our devoted home for the betrayal of its grand and generous accommodation. Before the water for tea had even started to boil, the first of many telephone calls came in.

"Susan?" the voice was young and male. "I just drove past the house and saw that it's up for sale." I was moved by the intimacy of his reference to "the house," although I didn't recognize his voice; he must have simply assumed I would know who it was.

"It is for sale," I said.

"Well you can't sell it," he said. "I called a couple of people, Caleb's friends, other guys who've spent a lot of time there, some friends of Kate's." His voice was full of emotion. "And we'll really be upset."

There were other calls that day, more from friends of the children, but friends of ours called, as well. Of course we were flattered. Even Tim, who had some reservations about living in a house that doubled as a hotel, was honored to hear about these calls of devotion.

"It's kind of our responsibility to keep it," I said.

"Responsibility?" Tim argued. "I don't think so."

"But it *means* something to people," I said.

Tim didn't buy into my emotional argument, but he really didn't want to sell the house either.

"It means something to us," he said. "We got married here."

And so we had the sign taken down.

THEN THE PETS started to die, first McGoo at fourteen, then Sula, the slightly brain-damaged Siamese cat, at thirteen, then MacDuff at seventeen. Finally, last May, Stratis the dog, the baby, at twelve.

The children were gone. My younger daughter was in San Francisco, my older son and his wife in Indiana, my middle children had settled in Washington in their own places, and so had my older daughter and her husband, with their two baby boys.

I had this old-fashioned idea of a family house that lasts from one generation to the next, but that was no longer necessary or even possible. No one, not us, not the children, could afford this kind of life, nor was it desirable, except perhaps to me in moments of some kind of romantic nostalgia, a product of the 1960s, when all houses were our house.

The amazing old tumbledown Blue House, which had belonged to so many people in the twenty years we had owned it;
in which we'd been married and celebrated our children's wed-
dings and graduations and birthdays and other people's parties; which people who needed a big house for their own
celebration had used; where my son Porter had written his first
novel, and my friend Stephen had written his third; that
beloved house had begun to smell of age, of old dogs and
teenagers and stale beer, of years of gentle abuse.

We could still dim the lights, light all the candles, turn on
the music, fill the house with the warm smell of garlic and
wine. But a life lived in low illumination was a recognition of
the end of something, and not the beginning.

And we needed a new beginning.

THE HOUSE WE bought is a few blocks away from the Blue
House, which we sold in January to Tim's cousin. We bought
the new house in a competitive real estate market without an
inspection. It is a small farmhouse, much smaller than the old
blue house, with a large studio behind built by the sculptor
who had lived there for many years. Presently it is brown as-
bestos shingle and under construction, with many of the walls
taken down, new electric, new heat, central air-conditioning, all
in the process of installation. And we have added seven feet to
the house in the back. That's all we had room for in order to
keep the proportions of land to structure within the limits of
code. But in seven feet, I figure, you can fit a lot of people, and

sleeping bags can be lined up in the studio. We still won't have a television in the bedroom, so we'll have to fill the evening with conversation.

That is what I love the best: Talk. Talk over dinner and on the porch and in the bedroom, just the sweet and comforting sound of voices filling a room.

"Our home is wherever you are," my daughter Kate said to me sweetly.

We have come to the point of final decisions about our new house. Will the walls be all white, or wheat with white trim, nothing startling or too whimsical, no bright colors except maybe the bathrooms? Will the exterior shingle be painted something quiet, maybe pale yellow or beige or gray?

"Blue," I said the other day to my daughter Elizabeth's husband, Rusty, who has strong opinions on color and design and asked what we were painting the new house.

"Blue?" he asked. "You've already had blue."

I thought for a moment, because it's not as if I love the color blue—I'd be happier perhaps with pale yellow or mango or even beige with black shutters, to give an adult appearance to our lives.

"What do you think?" Rusty asked Tim, who is not in the habit of agreeing with me on house decisions.

"Blue," he said without hesitation.

"Why not branch out?" Rusty asked. "Slate, rust, dark olive. Something sophisticated for your new life."

"We are branching out more than I ever expected we would," I replied, "with a new blue house."

Karen Stabiner is the author of seven books, most recently *My Girl: Adventures with a Teen in Training*, a 2005 Books for a Better Life Award finalist, and *To Dance with the Devil: The New War on Breast Cancer*, a New York Times Notable Book. She is a regular contributor to the *Los Angeles Times* Opinion section, writing about contemporary culture, and her work has appeared in *Gourmet*, where it was nominated for a James Beard Award; *Vogue*; *O, The Oprah Magazine*, and other national publications. She lives in Santa Monica, California, with her husband, editor and writer Larry Dietz, and their daughter, Sarah, who leaves for college in the fall.

Anna Quindlen writes *Newsweek*'s "The Last Word" column. From 1977 to 1994 she worked at the *New York Times*, where she was the third woman to write a regular column for the Op-Ed page, and in 1992 she won a Pulitzer Prize for commentary. In 1995 she left the *Times* to write fiction; she is the author of five bestselling novels, most recently *Rise and Shine*, several essay collections, and two children's books. She and her husband, attorney Gerald Krovatin, have three children. They live in New York City.

Charles McGrath is a writer-at-large at the *New York Times*, and is the former editor of the *New York Times Book Review* and the former deputy editor of the *New Yorker*. He is married to Nancy, a businesswoman. His son, Ben, is a staff writer at the *New Yorker*, and his daughter, Sarah, is executive editor of Riverhead Books. He has one grand-daughter, two-year-old Elizabeth Kastenmeier.

Susan Crandell is the author of *Thinking about Tomorrow: Reinventing Yourself at Midlife*. A former editor-in-chief of *More* magazine, Susan is now a freelance travel writer. She and her husband, automotive editor and writer Stephan Wilkinson, live in Cornwall on Hudson, New York. They have one daughter, Brook, an editor at *Condé Nast Traveler*.

Annette Duffy has written for the *Village Voice*, the *New York Times*, the *Hollywood Reporter*, and the *San Francisco Chronicle*, among others. She now writes screenplays for such companies as Nickelodeon, Sony, and Disney, most recently a sequel to *The Dark Crystal* for the Jim Henson Company. She and her husband, David Odell, live in Pacific Palisades, California. Their son Thomas returned safely from the Middle East and is now living in New York City. Their son Benjamin is in Hawaii, writing a video game and surfing every day with his coworkers.

Vicky Mann teaches seventh-grade language arts and social studies at Islander Middle School on Mercer Island, east of Seattle, Washington. She and her husband, film composer Hummie Mann, have two daughters—Sarah, who is majoring in Spanish and dance at Chapman University, and Jessi, who heads for college next fall.

Hilary Mills is the author of *Mailer: A Biography*, and a former syndicated book columnist. Her magazine articles have appeared in *Vanity Fair* and other national publications. She is married to Robert Loomis, executive vice president and executive editor of Random House. Their son, Miles, graduated from Bates College in May 2006.

Harvey Molotch is a professor of Sociology and Metropolitan Studies at New York University, and the author, most recently, of *Where Stuff Comes From: How Toasters, Toilets, Cars, Computers and Many Other Things Come to Be as They Are*. He was formerly the Centennial Professor at the London School of Economics, and the chair of the Sociology Department at the University of California, Santa Barbara. He lives in New York City with his partner, Glenn Wharton, who is a special projects conservator at the Museum of Modern Art. Molotch has two children and two grandchildren.

Marian Sandmaier is the author of four books and a freelance writer and editor whose work has appeared in the *New York Times* and the *Washington Post*; in 2001 she won the American Society of Journalists and Authors' June Roth Memorial Award for Medical Journalism. She lives in Merion Station, Pennsylvania, with her husband, Dan Sipe, a professor of history at Moore College of Art and Design. Their daughter, Darrah, has just graduated from Wesleyan University.

Fabiola Santiago is a features writer at the *Miami Herald*, where she has worked since 1980, and was the founding city editor of the

Spanish-language *El Nuevo Herald.* She has also written essays, poetry, and short fiction. Santiago has three daughters: Tanya is a high school English teacher, Marissa is still in college, and Erica attends Florida International University and lives with her mother in Miami, Florida.

Fran Visco, a nineteen-year breast cancer survivor, has been the president of the National Breast Cancer Coalition since its inception fifteen years ago. She is also a member of the integration panel that oversees the Department of Defense breast-cancer research program, and she speaks around the world on issues of women's health and advocacy. She and her husband, attorney Arthur Brandolph, live in Philadelphia, Pennsylvania. Their son, David, attends Hofstra University.

Ellen Levine became editorial director for all Hearst magazines in July 2006, after having served as the first woman editor of *Good Housekeeping* magazine for almost twelve years. She is a member of the Magazine Editors' Hall of Fame, and in 2003 received a Leadership in Media Award for her antismoking work. Levine currently serves on the board of Lifetime Television. She has two sons and three grandchildren.

Jon Carroll has been a daily columnist for the *San Francisco Chronicle* since 1982. Before that he was an editor and/or writer for *Rolling Stone*, the *Village Voice*, *New York*, *Playboy*, and *New West*. He has two daughters, Rachel and Shana, and a granddaughter he spoils constantly. He lives in Oakland, California, with his wife, writer Tracy Johnston.

Martha Schuur is the dean of faculty and an eighth-grade history teacher at Marlborough School in Los Angeles, California, where she has taught for seven years. She and her husband, Robert, a manager for Southern California Edison, live in the home where they raised their three daughters—Casey, a communications major at Baylor University; Kelly, a double major in international relations and Spanish at Syracuse University; and Courtney, who is pursuing a BA in culinary arts at the Culinary Institute of America.

Andrea L. Chambers is director of the Master of Science in Publishing program at New York University, as well as a writer and editor. A former publishing executive, her experience includes senior editorial positions at *Time, People,* and *Seventeen* magazines and in the book industry at Penguin Putnam. Andrea lives in Manhattan with her physician husband, Bill. They have a daughter, Abigail, a college senior, and a neurotic bichon frise, Mina, known as the "First Daughter."

Grace Saltzstein is retired from the Political Science Department at the University of California, Riverside. Her husband, Alan, is a retired professor of political science and division chair at California State University at Fullerton. Daughters Rachel and Jennifer and stepdaughters Sylvia and Anneke are scattered geographically from one coast to the other; Grace and Alan divide their time between Yorba Linda, California, and Pagosa Springs, Colorado.

Douglas Foster is a magazine writer and editor who splits his time between Chicago, Illinois, and Johannesburg, South Africa. An associate professor at Northwestern University's Medill School of Journalism, he writes about politics and science for magazines, including *Smithsonian*, and for newspapers, including the *Los Angeles Times* and the *New York Times Magazine*. His son, Jacob, is a lawyer currently working as a clerk at the Constitutional Court and the Supreme Court of Appeals, in South Africa.

Letty Cottin Pogrebin is a founding editor of *Ms.* magazine, a past president of the Authors Guild, and the author of nine books, most recently *Three Daughters*, her first novel. She edited the anthology *Stories for Free Children* and was the editorial consultant on Marlo Thomas's *Free to Be, You and Me*, for which she won an Emmy Award. She is a columnist for *Moment* magazine, and her work has appeared in the *New York Times*, the *Washington Post*, the *Boston Globe*, the *Nation*, and numerous other publications. She lives in New York City with her husband, Bert, an attorney, to whom she has been married for forty-three years. They have twin daughters, writers Robin and Abigail; a son, David, a restaurateur; and six grandchildren.

Brenda C. Roberts is managing editor, Public Relations and Strategic Communications, at California State University, Northridge. She is the author of the children's books *Sticks and Stones*, *Bobbie Bones*, and *Jazzy Miz Mozetta*, and the short fiction "Like it is," "tender root," and "The Washtub." She and her husband, Virgil, an attorney, live in Los Angeles, California. They have two daughters—Gisele, an alumna of the University of Michigan, and Hayley, who recently graduated from Northwestern University.

Martha Tod Dudman is the author of three books: *Dawn*, *Expecting to Fly*, and *Augusta, Gone*, which won a 2002 Books for a Better Life Award and was adapted as a movie for Lifetime Television. She lives in Maine, where she has worked as president and general manager of radio stations in Ellsworth and Bangor, and as a professional fund-raising consultant. She is a director with Bar Harbor Bank & Trust. Her daughter, Georgia, is a student at California State University and a marketing specialist for Metromint, and her son, Richard, is a lobster fisherman and constable of Little Cranberry Island.

Lee Smith is the author of nine novels, mostly recently *On Agate Hill*, as well as three short story collections. She has received the North Carolina Award for Literature, a Lyndhurst Grant, and the Academy Award in Fiction from the American Academy of Arts & Letters. Smith recently retired from teaching literature and writing at North Carolina State University. In 1985 she married critic and essayist Hal Crowther, and they live in Hillsborough, North Carolina. Smith's stepdaughter, Amity, and her husband are expecting their first child; Smith's son, Page Seay, and his wife are expecting their second.

Jan Constantine is general counsel of the Authors Guild, a non-profit organization representing over 8,700 published authors, and formerly was legal counsel for News Corporation. She also has a cabaret act with her singing partner, Susan Elicks. She lives in New York City with her husband, Lloyd, an antitrust attorney. They have three children—Isaac, a writer; Sarah, who works in San Francisco with homeless teens; and Elizabeth, a college sophomore at the University of Wisconsin.

Roger Wilkins has been an assistant attorney general of the United States in the Johnson administration, an editorial writer for the *Washington Post*, and an editorial writer and columnist for the *New York*

Times. He was the first black journalist to chair the Pulitzer Prize Board. For the last twenty years he has taught history at George Mason University. He is married to Patricia A. King, a professor at the Georgetown University Law Center. His daughter Amy is an advocate for better education for poor children; his son, David, is a freelance movie and television production supervisor. His daughter Elizabeth recently joined the political department of Local 32 bj of the Service Employees International Union in New York City.

Rochelle Reed is the features editor of the *Tribune* on the central California coast, after having spent six years as a full-time mother in Sun Valley, Idaho. Prior to moving to Idaho, she was the Style editor of the *Los Angeles Times Magazine* and a freelancer for many national publications. Her son, Evan, is currently serving in Iraq and will be deployed to Afghanistan in 2008. Her daughter, Laine, is finishing her undergraduate degree.

Jamie Wolf is a journalist, photographer, and gardener whose work has appeared in the *Washington Monthly, Harper's, American Film,* the *Los Angeles Times Magazine,* and other publications. Her photography has been published in *DoubleTake.* She lives in Beverly Hills, California, with her husband, David Wolf, a screenwriter. Their daughter, Kate, is in the MFA program in creative writing at the California Institute of the Arts.

Roxana Robinson is the author of seven books, most recently *A Perfect Stranger and Other Stories,* and her fiction and nonfiction have appeared in many national publications, including the *New Yorker,* the *Atlantic Monthly,* and *Harper's.* She has received fellowships from the MacDowell Colony, the National Endowment for the Arts, and the

Guggenheim Foundation, and she currently teaches at the Wesleyan Writers' Conference and at the New School in New York City, where she lives with her husband. They have one daughter.

Kit Rachlis is the editor in chief of *Los Angeles* magazine. He has been the executive editor of the *Village Voice*, the editor in chief of *LA Weekly*, and a senior projects editor at the *Los Angeles Times*. His daughter, Austen, is in the graduate film program at Columbia University. He and the Emmy Award–winning actress Maia Danziger live in the Studio City neighborhood of Los Angeles.

Glynna Freeman has left behind a career as an antitrust litigator and a life in Chicago, Illinois, to devote herself full-time to raising cattle outside of Livingston, Montana, where she and her husband, Lee, live and work on the Master Key Ranch. They have three children— Crispin, a writer and actor who does voice-over work for Japanese anime; Clark, a director and actor, and cofounder of Sight Unseen Theatre; and Cassidy, an actor.

Harry Shearer is a writer, actor, and political satirist whose most recent book is the novel *Not Enough Indians*. He was a co-creator of and appeared in the film *This Is Spinal Tap*, and he also appeared in *A Mighty Wind* and *For Your Consideration*. His nationally syndicated radio program, *Le Show*, is broadcast weekly on NPR affiliates. He lives in Santa Monica, California, with his wife, singer-songwriter Judith Owen.

Ellen Goodman is a Pulitzer Prize–winning syndicated columnist for the *Boston Globe* and the Washington Post Writers Group, whose column runs in nearly four hundred newspapers. She is the author of eight books, including her latest collection, *Paper Trail,* and with Patricia O'Brien coauthored a *New York Times* bestselling book on women and friendship called *I Know Just What You Mean.* Goodman lives with her husband, Bob Levey, in Boston, Massachusetts. She has a daughter, Katie; a stepdaughter, Jenny; and two grandchildren, Logan and Cloe.

Susan Shreve has written twelve novels, most recently *A Student of Living Things,* and a memoir entitled *Warm Springs: Traces of a Childhood at FDR's Polio Haven.* She is a professor in the Masters of Fine Arts program at George Mason University. Shreve lives in Washington, D.C., with her husband, a literary agent. Their son, Porter, teaches at Purdue University, their daughter, Elizabeth, has her own business, her son, Caleb, is involved in philanthropic work, and her daughter, Kate, works at a stem cell research institute. Shreve has two grandchildren.

ACKNOWLEDGMENTS

To the contributors, my deep appreciation and respect. If I survive my own daughter's imminent departure with any grace, it will be in great part because of the stories I've heard about love through time.

Ellen Archer at Hyperion and Lynn Nesbit at Janklow & Nesbit made the match between this book and me, and I thank them for the opportunity to work with writers I admire, writers I didn't know but have come to admire, and people I like.

At Hyperion and its new imprint, Voice, I thank my editor, Leslie Wells, Pam Dorman, Michelle Ishay, Katie Wainwright, Sarah Schaffer, Jane Comins, Phil Rose, Miriam Wenger, and Danielle Smick. At Janklow & Nesbit, I'm grateful to Richard Morris, Eric Simonoff, Bennett Ashley, Michael Steger, Tina Simms, and Elexis Loubriel.

David Strick and Elizabeth Sloan made photography fun.

Three colleagues have become long-distance friends, from one book to the next—William Whitworth, who has perfect pitch; Sam

Freedman, who generously helped to expand the contributor list; and Peggy Orenstein, a valued pen pal.

Thanks to Phyllis Amaral, Jo Ann Consolo, and Lori Rifkin for thirteen years of watching our girls grow up together; to Barbara Wagner, for six years at a school that turns out great girls, not just great students; to Paula Dashiell and in memory of Dorene Tawa, for the years before that; and to two generations of women in Sullivan Canyon.

To dear friends from long before the nest was full: the transcendent Carolyn See, Ginger Curwen, Marcie Rothman, Patty Williams, Dora Warren, and Judith Owen, who caught up quickly.

My husband, Larry Dietz, has filled the nest with the kind of dogged optimism that only a lifelong Cubs fan can generate, and I like to think that it paid off at home more than it ever did at Wrigley Field. As for the object of our mutual delight and obsession, Sarah has a big heart, a passionate mind, and a wicked wit, and I will love her forever, wherever she is.

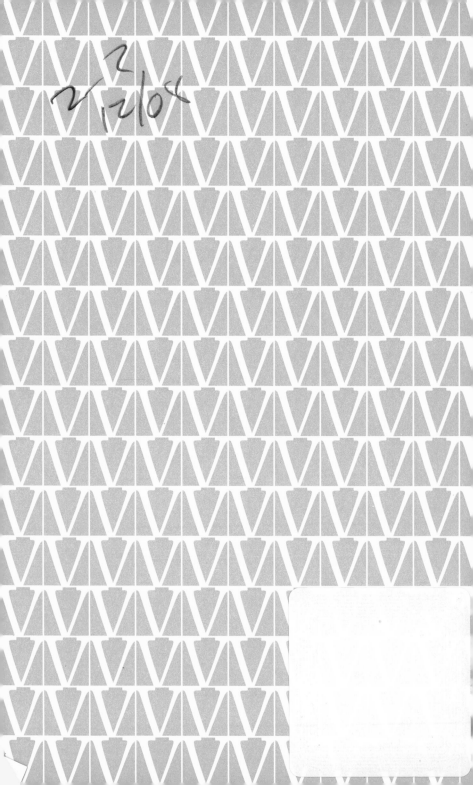